GUNS AND BARBED WIRE:

A Child Survives the Holocaust

Thomas Geve

GUNS
AND
BARBED WIRE:

A Child Survives the Holocaust

ACADEMY

CHICAGO

Published in 1987 by
Academy Chicago Publishers
425 North Michigan Avenue
Chicago, Illinois 60611

Originally published as *Youth in Chains*.

Geve, Thomas, 1929-
    Guns and barbed wire.

        Rev. ed. of: Youth in chains. 1958.
        1. Auschwitz (Poland : Concentration camp)
2. Holocaust, Jewish (1939-1945)–Personal narratives.
3. Geve, Thomas, 1929-   . I. Geve, Thomas,
1929-   . Youth in chains. II. Title.
D805.P7G47 1987   940.54'72'43094386   87-19421
ISBN 0-89733-261-X

In memory
of
Eva-Ruth
Sally
Jonathan
"Little Kurt"
"Long Kurt"
Blonde Gert
Saucy Gert
Ello, a lad from Slovakia
Mendel, a lad from Bialystok
Jendroe, a lad from Bohemia
Maurice, a lad from Salonika
Leo, a Dutchman
Poldi, a Swiss
Mr. Pollack, a Czech
Block doctor 7a, a Belgian
Sigi, room elder 7a, a German
Block elder 7a, a German
Camp hairdresser, a German

Acknowledgements

The publishers wish to acknowledge the gift of the Everett Family which made possible in part the inclusion of the photographs in this book.

The illustrations and the cover drawing are reproduced by permission of:

Yad Vashem
The Holocaust Martyrs' and Heroes'
Remembrance Authority
The Art Museum
Jerusalem

Preface

In 1946, when a flood of literature came out about events in wartime Europe, I looked at a stack of drawings of mine which portrayed the life of youth in German concentration camps. Now I wanted to put them to words. I tried to, but merely produced a badly written report. Then I was sixteen. I had spent only five years in school and these, too, were restless times of persecution and war.

Now I have tried again, for no one else has come forward to tell of those who grew up in concentration camps. The memoirs before you are not those of somebody famous but of someone who was only one among thousands. I did not intend to write a bestseller. I have merely recorded the truth.

THOMAS GEVE
May, 1958.

Note
to the American Edition

Thomas Geve was born in the Autumn of 1929 on the shores of the Baltic Sea. He lived in Beuthen in Upper Silesia and in Berlin, until his imprisonment in June, 1943. Just after liberation in April, 1945 he drew 79 primitive miniature pictures about the daily life in Auschwitz, Gross-Rosen and Buchenwald. They are the origins of *Guns and Barbed Wire*. Mr Geve now lives on the shores of the Mediterranean and works as a technical advisor. He is finishing a second book which will be the sequel to *Guns and Barbed Wire*.

Contents

PART I: THE LOST WORLD
Chapter I   *1929–1939*   1
Chapter II   *1939–1943*   10

PART II: THE HIDDEN WORLD
Chapter I   *Becoming a Prisoner*   34
Chapter II   *Youth in Chains*   55
Chapter III *Work Makes Free*   79
Chapter IV   *Old Hand*   102
Chapter V   *Moving On*   127
Chapter VI   *Finale*   149

PART III: A NEW WORLD
Chapter I   *A New World*   194

APPENDICES
Appendix I   "The Song of the Peat-Bog Soldiers"   216
Appendix II   *Looking Back, 1:3,000, Auschwitz, the Camp*   217
Appendix III *Looking Back, 1:20,000, The Working Territory*   218
Appendix IV   *Looking Back, 1:6,000,000, Map*   219
              Epilogue   220

PART ONE
THE LOST WORLD

CHAPTER I

1929-1939

It was a hot, stifling summer's day in the Berlin of 1939. Shoppers, travellers and sightseers crowded the Potsdamer Square. Delicatessen shops displayed the world's luxuries, neatly wrapped and labelled. A florist's water-cooled showcases offered the choicest roses. People admired the latest noiseless, streamlined tram cars and inspected the new subway station—a triumph of modern engineering.

Warehouses attracted buyers with escalators and fluorescent lighting. Queues formed up outside the Government experimental television studio.

At the big glass and steel topped railway terminus a semaphore arm was raised. The green light was given and yet another train puffed westwards. It was taking one of the last transports of men, who, threatened with renewed imprisonment, had no place in this new civilization. Jews, freethinkers, Democrats and Socialists—their destination was England, the historic refuge of the persecuted. Again the friendly isle had agreed to uphold the tradition of hospitality. But it was already crowded. Others were knocking at her door too: Austrians, Czechs, Italians and Spaniards. Father was among the lucky few that were admitted. Mother and myself were to follow soon on another kind of entry visa. A crate with our belongings had already been dispatched.

A boy of nine, tall for his age, dressed neatly, his hair soaked in brilliantine and meticulously combed, was standing in front of the florist's window. He was bored with waiting, and passed his time watching the rivulets of water trickling down the inside of the pane. Through the mist he could recognize roses, tulips and even orchids. What good care was being taken of them—just as if they were little boys!

An attractive, medium-built, dark-haired young woman wearing her Sunday best emerged from the stream of passers-by and stopped in front of the florist's. She was crying. The boy was abruptly jerked away from his dream paradise of dew-dropped flowers. Why must people be nervous and cry? Was it not a fine day?

The little boy was me, the woman my mother. The two who had been part of the indifferent throng at the Potsdamer Square were alone now. We had returned to Grandparent's place, our temporary home at 19 Winterfeld Street.

"I'll be busy making arrangements for joining Dad," sighed Mother, "and grandparents have worries of their own. So you'll have to be a good boy, without there being someone to spank you, from now on."

That day I thought for the first time about what people called the future. I grappled with my thoughts and tried to imagine the things that were to come. It had all happened so abruptly and unexpectedly— far too quick for me to grasp it.

I was born on the Baltic, near the Oder, in the autumn of 1929. Mother, too, was born there while Father hailed from Beuthen, in Upper Silesia.

As a toddler, strange faces seemed to have frightened me. My pastime was that of most babies—crying. The nightly wail of the siren that called the voluntary fire brigade also made a terrifying impression on me. It sounded like the howling of an invisible monster lurking in the dark, eager to snatch me at the first opportune moment.

Later, things became more cheerful. Auntie Ruth, my mother's sister, took me on rowing trips across the Oder, to our garden plot. Sitting in a boat in the middle of the wide stream greatly impressed me— even more so than being privileged to pick and devour the choicest tomatoes. There were also excursions to sea resorts together with lengthy, boring recitations on table manners. My favorite occupation, however, was snail hunting—the catching and collecting of colorful, slimy little rolls that climbed up the park walls.

When Hitler came to power, this leisurely time disappeared. Although I was only three then, I felt that I was being left more and more in the care of relatives. My father, a physician and surgeon, lost his practice and we had to return to his home town. Mother's family moved to Berlin.

Beuthen, a mining town of some 100,000 inhabitants, had a strong Polish minority. The border crossed suburbs, parks and even mining tunnels. Some of its streets had both a German and a Polish tramway running through them. They spoke Polish in what was Germany, and German in what was Poland, and when I returned from walks to the suburbs I was never quite certain to which of the two I had actually been taken.

The town's main square was even more confusing. It did not dawn on me why it should change names so often. To the simple folks it was the "Boulevard," despite the foreign way of pronouncing it. More pedantic people called it "Kaiser Franz Joseph Square." Then the new set of town fathers decided that it was to become "Adolf Hitler Square."

It was on that square that pure and loyal Germans swore allegiance to the new God. Had I been told to, I would cheerfully have joined them. I rather liked the new cult. It meant flags, shiny police horses, colorful uniforms, torchlights and music. All free, without pestering Dad to be taken to Punch and Judy shows, or being treated to an hour at Auntie's radio set—a mysterious box whose intriguing interior was, anyhow, kept secret from me. But I was criticized for my unbecoming enthusiasm. Its place was to be taken by the pocket money, of which I was to have more now. To avoid any further embarrassment to the family I was also ordered to toe the anti-Nazi line, whatever that meant to a four-year-old. I obeyed. The other youngsters on the square were told of their superior origin, their task and destiny. My role was to be that of the underdog.

After that my life became a more secluded one. In the morning I was escorted to the nearby Jewish Kindergarten. The afternoons were filled with solitary play or with piano lessons under the tutelage of father's sister, a music teacher.

I was supposed to have inherited much of her ability, but my rebellious temperament ruled out all possibility of becoming slave to a curved black "Bechstein" giant. My latent talents, therefore, were limited to gobbling up the big fragrant apples that had served to demonstrate splitting up notes into fractions. The most eagerly awaited trophy, of course, was the big one that had to be cut into 32. With it, then, vanished my interest in the musical world.

In 1936 I was launched out to school, the Jewish one. Father, too had once felt its cane, its punishment cellar and strict Prussian discipline. He, too, had retaliated by scribbling and etching on its benches. His teachers, already above retirement age, still taught and still could not afford more than sandwiches of white cheese which made them the subject of general ridicule. Aware of my family tradition, I tried to be a pleasant pupil—but that did not mean that I was more eager than was absolutely necessary.

We used both old and Nazi textbooks. Hitler's birthday was a holiday. On this day—in accordance with some quaint paragraph in the new educational laws— we gathered to hear recitations in glory of the fatherland. The more progressive of our teachers, however, hinted that we were to have no share in that glory.

There was to be no equality. Our only weapon seemed pride. We, too, wanted to vie with the new youth movements. Our school outings turned into occasions for showing off disciplined marching, impressive singing and sports competitions. But, one by one, these demonstrations were forbidden. To reply to stones that were being thrown at us, into our school yard, became a crime. We had become despised Jew boys. The only playground that remained safe was the park at the suburban Jewish cemetery.

On the initiative of my father I joined a Zionist sports club, "Bar Kochba," named after the leader of a Jewish revolt against Rome. Training was strictly indoors, but the self-confidence it gave us was not so confined. Our newly-acquired courage followed us everywhere.

Once, towards dusk, when a friend and I were making our way to the club and passed the wintry synagogue square, we were greeted by a hail of snowballs. Then came abusive, insulting shouts, and behind the columns of the temple arcade we caught glimpses of black Hitler-youth uniforms. Their wearers seemed to be our age. Pride momentarily gained the better of our obligation to be docile underlings, and we gave chase. Our perplexed opponents had not reckoned with the sudden fury that overtook us. Grabbing one of them, I threw him on the snow and hit away at him, but when he started yelling I had to retreat. His friends were nowhere to be seen, nor was anyone else. Darkness had set in to shroud our little adventure in secrecy. This, then, was my first and last chance to hit back openly.

Soon I grew more inquisitive about the world I lived in. We boys sneaked away to visit near-by coal mines, factories and railway installations. The glaring white blast furnaces, the endless turning wheels of the pit heads, the enormous slag dumps, the ore-filled trolleys gliding along sagging overhead steel cables, the small, squeaking industrial railways, and the big black locomotives that came in from afar and relieved their exhaustion by blowing off clouds of smelly steam—everything was teeming with activity. It was waiting to be analyzed by our young minds, inspiring us with a desire to understand life. The world was still to be discovered by us.

While we watched and learned, the Hitler-youth drilled, marched, and sang praises in glory of the Fuehrer. But not all of them possessed the required mentality for this training. Seeing their future predestined by authoritarian rules, some retired into a state of melancholy. Others, with less delicate minds, worried about flat feet, corns and blisters, for these were much more realistic obstacles in the path of aspirants to the title of Superman.

Now and then Mother took me on Sunday excursions to Poland. Kids there felt themselves less serious. Fishing a good catch or ruling a flock of geese amply satisfied their needs for sensation. While their bare feet trod the dusty country paths they would dream of becoming the richest farmer of the village. That would be enough. No tutor explaining the need for recovering lost colonies in the Pacific Ocean for them. Possibly, they had never even had an ordinary school teacher.

A few times a year Beuthen saw its streets circled by processions. On Ascension Day and Easter it was the Catholics, masters of pomp and ceremony. Robed clerics, swinging incense, heralded richly decorated floats. The bishop, carried along under a gold embroidered canopy, was the main attraction, greatly inspiring his chanting subjects.

Gay national costumes, exhibits of industrial and agricultural achievements, fairs and bandstands, decorated the town on May Day, Hitler's substitute for the First of May. On other occasions, black jackboots clanked in the streets to the tune of martial music. The Brown Shirts had even contrived a new kind of procession: nightly torchlight parades.

All processions were lengthy, for the sake of effect. Some ended with disbelievers, Jews or the like, being beaten up. Ordered to stay home, I watched the big shows from behind drawn curtains. Again Mother explained that the goings-on were not for our benefit. I was to avoid the streets and to concentrate on indoor games. Indeed, my Meccano set and miniature railway were worth my showing off to friends.

From then on I became more familiar with my school mates, inviting the more interesting ones home. Soon, however, the family objected to my choice of friends.

"Why must you bring these ill-mannered unkempt boys home?" I was reproached. "Aren't there enough respectable acquaintances of ours, doctors, lawyers, businessmen, with whose children you could play?"

My idea of having a good time demanded the ingredients of new ideas, alertness, mutual respect and freedom of action.

Playmates chosen for me from well-to-do families never succeeded in being good friends. Their knowledge of "the street" was poor, their temperament was affected by their parents' mood, and for every trifle they had to get permission from their maids.

The festival of the Torah was being celebrated at our synagogue. To the tune of the organ we children, dressed in our best suits, with colorful flags in our hands, lined up for a procession of our own. Then we slowly followed the scrolls as they were being carried through the passages between the crowded benches. At the second round through the temple, the traditional sweets and chocolates were bestowed on us. Being one of the older kids, I proceeded to survey the givers. Many gave generously to all, some only to the offspring of influential families, others with an eye to charity. Afterwards we compared our treasures. My pockets were fairly loaded. Other children, whose disappointment was written all over their faces, were listening to those few who vied with each other for the biggest catch. Why this difference in results? As we had all made four rounds—no more and no less—it was most puzzling. Maybe people gave according to one's age or looks.

I consulted my father about it. His somewhat hesitant reply brought yet another unpleasant perception to my young mind, and altogether spoiled the fun. Father had never liked this custom either. Its scheme was simple: if your family had any influence or standing, people would single you out for taking home their "visiting cards" in the form of sweets. Dad, too, was quite aware who was distributing which brand of chocolate bars or lollipops. It was a pity: if you came from a surrounding of have-nots, even a synagogue ceremony would make you aware of the fact.

*   *   *

The street underneath my window was humming with noise. I woke up. Weary of this constant reminder that it was time to get dressed for school, I got up and tugged at the belt of the roller shutter. But to my surprise it was only dawn. I peered at the opposite pavement. One of these high-powered black Daimler cars that boys are so fond of was parked in front of the shoe-shop. The street was littered with shiny, black, brown and white boots, sandals and high heeled women's shoes, and glass splinters. A team of uniformed Brown Shirts was busy loading the remaining stock into the car—an obvious robbery.

No other onlooker being in sight, I rushed off to arouse my parents, feeling rather like a successful detective. Visibly less glad about my discovery, Father phoned the neighbors. There seemed to be a general confusion, only one thing being certain: there was to be no school that day. In search for a more authoritative answer I consulted my wall calendar. It was the ninth of November, 1938.

More reports came in. The synagogue was burning. Fire brigades refused help "being busy guarding the adjacent buildings." All over town, heaps of books were put to the flames. Shops had been looted wholesale. Christians and Jews alike avoided the streets. Many people were being arrested.

Dreading the feared knock on the door, we all assembled in one room, fully dressed and ready for any emergency. Finally the knock came. It had to be answered. We faced an elderly Brown Shirt. His finger glided ominously down a lengthy, typewritten list. As it stopped, he snarled out the name of an aged Jew, a tenant who had since moved elsewhere. Luckily, the caller was not interested in taking along a substitute.

The synagogue had burned out completely; our school was closed down for good. Parents who could afford it sent their children away to the quieter countryside. My place of recuperation was a Jewish children's home at Obernick, near Breslau. Among its gardens and woods we had a wonderful chance of exploring nature; for me it was paradise.

Most of the Jews who could do so emigrated. My father, a veteran and well-known Zionist, planned to get us to England from where we would reach Palestine, the land of Israel. But slow progress was made; the world was not kind to refugees. People talked a lot about Biro-Bidjan, but few ever took it seriously. Polish Jews were deported by force, driven over the nearby frontier. The Poles were no more eager to have them than were the Germans. "This can't

happen to us," agreed the German-bred Jews, "we are Germans."
It seemed that they had never reversed this opinion.

Rumors—inevitable by-products of totalitarian censorship—
were popular and kept circulating like some oral, clandestine newspaper. We knew an "Aryan" (according to Hitler's definition of
pure Germanic stock) who was a member of the Nazi labor army,
O.T.* Unemployment had forced him to join this underpaid corps,
to work on local road and canal construction projects. Considering
himself to be in the know, he urged us to leave Germany as soon as
possible. His predictions for the future seemed more than reason-
ably grim, possibly even uttered with a certain amount of malice. If
he had mentioned the giant concentration camp that was already on
the secret building program of his brigade we would only have been
convinced of his insincerity.

The summer of 1939 saw us leaving for a working class district
in West Berlin to share Mother's family's apartment.

At that time Father left for England.

*Organisation Todt, Todt being a prominent Nazi.

CHAPTER II

1939–1943

Mother was busy with arrangements for emigration, so I was left in the care of her sister, a teacher of art and English. Aunt Ruth had all the qualities of a true friend. Abounding with new ideas and progressive thinking, she was the idol of her pupils.

Before long she took me along to her school at Ryke Street in North Berlin. My classmates were real city kids, conversant with all the local slang, swank and brag. At first I was looked down upon as a country yokel. But soon they came to like my soberness and finally I, too, became a fully-fledged Berliner.

The first frightening impact of city life gave way to an understanding of its make-up.

Seeking metropolitan warmth, one apartment house hugged the other to form a street. Less imposing buildings had to crowd around the backyards (of which there were as many as four to each facade) and, to obtain the right amount of *"Gemuetlichkeit,"* five stories were the rule.

The sun, not being in need of living space, limited its visits to these street-encompassed citadels to a minimum. So, when its cherished warm rays did penetrate the yards, versatile Berliners prepared many tasks for them: drying the laundry, alleviating Granddad's rheumatism, improving baby's complexion, lulling pussy into a sunny cat's paradise, and providing the warm impetus for the bedbugs to drop themselves onto the soft, white cushions on the window below.

A city day's hours were marked off by traditional visitors who, like their celestial counterparts, had a fixed time of appearance. The baker, milkman and newspaper boy began the day. Later on (making a strong impression on us youngsters), would come the hawkers of brushes, matches, shoe polish and flowers, the ragpicker and the organ grinder.

The dirty brick walls were host to many, a reverberating noise. Blaring radios, the beating of dusty carpets, crying kids and squeaking staircases, twittering canaries and raucous shouts of quarrelling couples—none could be escaped.

No matter under what Kaiser, Berlin's life would be dictated by herself. One could not expect an inmate of a working-class tenement house to concern himself deeply with racial questions. He could not really care whether the bugs that, in search of new feeding grounds, invaded his abode had previously sucked Aryan blood or that of supposedly lesser beings.

Then war broke out. Those who had made nationalism their business were exultant. They had prepared Germany for it.

War propaganda had not been defeated in 1918. On the contrary, it had received a new impetus by the very fact that peace had become tangible. The changeover, then, was a mere technicality. Rationing had started in 1938; now a few more items became scarce. Mock air raids and trial black-outs had already made themselves such a nuisance that the real thing—expected to be a less frequent but more victorious affair—was greeted even with some relief. Mass shootings of political prisoners had been carried out on quiet moors. Germany's sons could now be afforded a more spectacular end. As soldiers, recommended for Valhalla, their sacrifice would be glorified in public. Even bespectacled slit eyes in far off Japan would gleam their approval—not forgetting, of course, the applause of the macaroni-fed specimens of Aryan glory. They all agreed. Their various invasions had to be legalized, weapons modernized; glory for all superior men.

Mother Krause, the typical Berlin housewife, was not so certain of it. "It's an ill wind that blows no one any good," she sighed. "My old instinct tells me."

The occasional howlings of the air raid siren brought her down to the moist, improvised cellar, there to enjoy the company of the seventy-odd neighbors, their blankets, emergency rations, heavy suitcases, dogs and canaries. Even we were present. Mother Krause had known my grandparents for many a year now; she would not offend them. "My old instinct," she would mumble, "does not like Jews, but these don't seem too bad."

The time had come for me to enter a higher school. Great Hamburger Street, a mixed school, was chosen for me. Again there were snobs who tried to impress me with their city-mindedness. War had affected our being classed as a poor family, unable to pay the fees, and I had to rely on scholarships. The school, too, had troubles. It was transferred to Kaiserstreet, later to Lindenstreet. The authorities did not want to be bothered with the Jews' place of learning, still less with their feelings. The former Lindenstreet Synagogue next door, filled with grain, had attendants—well-fed rats—who also visited school.

A classmate of mine, a half-Jew, had a sister at an Aryan school nearby. Some freakish court decision willed it that he was declared a Jew, his sister a Christian. Meeting in the street, they had to ignore each other until an unobserved corner could be found, in case people found out about them. I often helped them in this by acting as scout.

Our class favorite was a frail blonde orphan boy from Halberstadt. His lot as one of the few remaining Jews in that town had left indelible marks on him, and because of this he received our deepest sympathy.

With the exciting war on, school seemed dull, even senseless. Accordingly I took more and more to exploring the streets. School being about an hour's journey away, my absence at home was easily blamed on traffic hold-ups—a by-product of air raids—or on extra lessons. Few questions were asked, the family allowing me ample freedom.

Tramping the streets, even blacked-out Berlin became familiar to me. My disguise included a Hitler youth uniform, without its insignia. Visiting exhibitions of captured war materials was a must for technically-minded youngsters. I, too, took up the study of airplanes, inspecting pilot seats and propellers—quite undisturbed by notices warning non-Aryans to keep out. Neither did I miss morale-boosting fairs, where Churchill's dummy head could be shot off. The current hits were clock-work puppets, dollies and soldier boys that danced to the tune "Lily Marlene" or "Wir fahren gegen Engelland."

For the more particular there were fleshy life-size dolls sauntering down Friedrichstreet in fur coats and the latest from Paris. Their bag of tricks could be enjoyed for five marks. The spirits of the less venturesome were taken care of by special holiday rations of booty from Western Europe, open-air loudspeakers, flags and displays.

Once, emerging from the subway station at "Unter den Linden," I was caught up in a big parade. As backing out would have attracted attention, I had to play the enthusiastic admirer, at least for the first minutes. Peeping through the ranks of closely aligned guards, I had a good view. Slowly rolling down the broad thoroughfare, accompanied by the noisy jubilation of the crowd, came the traditional open black Daimlers. The leading one passed by less than ten yards ahead of me. Hands shot up to give the Nazi salute. It was for a dark-featured, stern man who gazed ahead emotionlessly: Adolf Hitler. Then followed stout Goering and the Wehrmacht staff, seeming equally unappreciative of the applause. Were they afraid that there were too many spectators as loyal as myself?

The traditional haunts of the army staff and H.Q. were in the area between Tiergarten, Potsdamer Square and the Shell House. A friend, whose mother was the mistress of a high officer there, supplied an excuse for my penetrating it. Considering me to be a well-bred and well-mannered companion, he picked me out as the only classmate that could be honored with invitations there, to manipulate valuable white and red ivory chessmen.

Field-gray cars took up the space between the numerous villas. Teleprinters ticked, typewriters rattled and Prussians clicked their heels. The twittering birds in the garden plots had to put up with mobile radio stations humming out the words of war. Pairs of jackbooted military police, with Roman-style polished metal plates on their breasts, stamped through the streets. They wouldn't bother with kids. Neither would the colonel, who watched us playing chess in his garden. Probably he was familiar with the luxurious apartment of my host's mother and would not mind anyhow.

Books, cinemas and shows were not supposed to be enjoyed by "non-Aryans." So it was useless asking pocket money for them. My consolation lay in the monthly subway tickets provided by the school. Without them none of my extensive undertakings would have been possible.

To help finance the war, little figures were sold and pinned on people's lapels. Every other month there were new ones: carved wooden dolls, replicas of airplanes, guns, shells and so on. They made quite attractive toys. To get them we followed the example set by the street kids of North Berlin. Whoever still wore these adornments on his lapel after collection week was asked politely to surrender them to us. This sport became so popular that passersby even thought themselves subjected to a new kind of salvage scheme.

Another hobby was collecting the attractively colored children's magazines. They were surprisingly free from Nazi propaganda, possibly for reasons of export. Given away at big confectionery stores, we got them by making a good impression on the sales girl, or, as a last resort, by buying a packet of pins.

My strangest delight was the making of lists. Bombed buildings greatly fascinated me. All their intimate interiors could be seen, each house with its own characteristic details. Not even dissected whales could have been so thrilling. Excepting the one Jonah was in, they would have remained mere sea monsters, unable to reveal anything individual. So all the places recently damaged by bombs had to be visited and analyzed. My craze was to jot down in a book the place, date and extent of the destruction.

When mother found out about it, her stern reproaches made quite an impression on me. No, I really could not disprove my being a spy.

Food had become "Ersatz."* Jews had special ration cards with little J's freckled all over them to prevent their buying vegetables, meat, milk, chocolate and any special holiday allocations there might be. The "prescribed" non-Aryan shopping hour—at "approved shops"—was from four to five in the afternoon. If one was rich the food problem was eased by the black market. If one was both well-to-do and Germanic, high-class restaurants could be counted upon to provide a fair diet. Being neither, one could only hope for help from better qualified friends.

The bigger stores, worried by lack of provisions, were advised to stage shows. Around Christmas-time elaborate toy-land exhibitions were held, exploiting all the loot and ideas of conquered Europe. Large shop windows were filled with reconstructions and shots of scenes from Nazi films. Current hits were "Jud Suess," the twisted, violently anti-Semitic story of a rich courtier, "Ohm Krueger," an anti-British account of the Boer War, and "Robert Koch," a biography glorifying German medicine.

At the Wittenberg Square KaDeWe department store a whole floor was devoted to the propagation of what seemed to be the climax of German inventiveness in the field of "Ersatz." Sales girls were busy mixing, boiling and solidifying a mysterious concoction that was then offered to be tasted. Attempting to satisfy my curiosity, I stared at the lettering on the stacks of yellow envelopes that lined the shelves. It read: "Artificial artificial-honey powder. Sugar to be added."

In 1942 the Nazis put up a big show of force. Jews were ordered "to wear the six-pointed yellow Star of David over their left breast, stitched to all apparel, to be freely visible whenever and wherever they may be encountered by a non-Jew." Aristocratic ladies assured us over cups of "Ersatz" coffee that "Germany's honor will never allow such an outrage to materialize." "We are a civilized nation and can't go back to the Middle Ages. People will protest in the streets!"

*Substitute

When the first stars did appear, some people ridiculed the idea, others the wearers. Then followed a period of indifference, only to be succeeded by a general annoyance at being constantly reminded of the yellow rag of shame. For whatever reasons people were offended by the star, we went without it whenever there was a likelihood of not being recognized by informers. Under the light of the violet neon lamps that lit Berlin's thoroughfares, the yellow stars looked blue. Better still were blacked-out side streets, and, as a last resort, there was the inevitable portfolio pressed underneath your left arm over your heart. An evening curfew for Jews had also been imposed, but, its enforcement seeming practically impossible, it was generally ignored by us.

Soon there were other labels too: "P" for Poles, and "OST" for Ukrainians. The decade-old signs forbidding entry to "Jews" alone had to be taken down. New, corrected ones appeared. All public places, from the lone bench to the spacious park, from the telephone booth to the cinema, now displayed notices warning "non-Aryans" to keep out. Some establishments, striving to be even more respectable, hit the mark by adorning themselves with the latest in neatness and exactness: "Entrance to dogs, Poles, Russians and Jews strictly forbidden!"

The closing of Jewish schools came strangely enough as rather a relief: no more fear of being beaten up on the way home for being a Jew boy. Every day there had been fewer students. They were not necessarily playing truant; they may have been arrested or gone into hiding.

Four kinds of work were open to us youngsters: nursing at the hospital, cooking for soup kitchens, sorting files at the community's offices or gardening at the cemetery. I decided to devote a year to the upkeep of Jewish graves at Weissensee. There was no pay, but the privilege of holding a special travelling permit and the fresh, healthy air compensated for this. The vast, walled city of the dead with the quietness of its marble mausoleums and tumbling old tombstones, interrupted only by the rustling trees, became our paradise. Organized into work gangs, we cleaned the weedy footpaths, looked after the flowers and planted ivy. Autumn would mean sweeping leaves, winter removing snow.

It was a most ideal place for playing "hide and seek" and "robbers and policemen." The riotous moments when we chased each other over the vast expanses of the cemetery were our gladdest.

Besides gardening, I was also initiated into the various pleasures of driving a tractor, playing cards and teasing girls. My initial cigarette was smoked and, for the first time, a girl—Eva-Ruth Lohde—fell in love with me.

Another thrilling experience consisted of visits to a nearby home for mentally disturbed and backward Jewish children. More often than not those trips were secretly organized by the older boys, who were eager to catch females. My own young curiosity, however, was limited to a robust country lad, a few years my senior, who enjoyed talking about politics. To my surprise I found out that he knew more about it than a normal youngster.

Mother, who had taken a course as a seamstress, was doing homework for a concern mending army uniforms. Now and then letters could be found sewn into the linings of blood-stained *Wehrmacht* trousers. Their messages, the unheeded warnings of Germany's sons, told of hopeless conditions at the Eastern front: Leningrad and Moscow were out of reach; only death awaited them in the snow-covered Russian fields. No wonder the authorities had ordered the fall of Stalingrad to be followed by a week of mourning.

Mother and I had to move to Speyrer Street near the Bayrische Square, a once predominantly Jewish quarter. It was a fashionable district, and the rent for our 1 ½ rooms was so high that making ends meet was difficult. Our neighbors, fellow Jews, often invited me to see their valuable stamp collections and paintings—sometimes even for tea. None of them, however, showed an understanding of our financial troubles. Father's last letter, arriving in directly from England through the Red Cross, had urged us to be brave. One really had to be.

Hitler's cruel laws penetrated everywhere, having only one aim: victory. Confiscation orders were extended to warm clothes, radio sets and pets of non-Aryans. Our aquarium and the parakeets having already been abandoned, the attention was turned to Grandfather's wireless, a cherished crystal set.

Grandpa, formerly a physician, had been blinded by shell shock while serving as officer for the old fatherland of the Kaiser's days. When in a jovial mood he would sing me the sentimental song of "Ich hatt' einen Kameraden." I, in return, had once read him the newspapers, but now his only pleasure was listening to the earphones of the fifteen-year-old catwhisker set. A letter was sent off to the War Veterans' Federation begging their intervention to let him keep it. The reply was extremely sympathetic but of no avail; there were no appeals against the orders of the New Reich.

Grandpa died in 1942, at the age of 71, unable to understand the new ways of his fatherland.

Real anti-Semites avoided all contacts with Jews. Though causing us much suffering they personally remained unknown to us. It was the many helpful Germans who impressed me. Their sympathy was governed not by appreciation of any admirable Jewish traits, but by loyal obedience to their old ideals. Courage, indeed, was needed to follow beliefs that even a decade ago had been as ruthlessly outlawed as they were now.

Mother and I, unable to buy any influence, contacted all acquaintances whose aid could be hoped for. Once, having to hide from a wave of arrests, we visited the home of a Protestant clergyman of West Berlin's Apostel Paulus Kirche. But since his newly acquired son-in-law was a fervent Nazi—which we had overlooked—the cleric's efforts dwindled to no more than keeping even our plea a personal secret. The vital refuge, then, was finally granted by a widowed seamstress, Clara Bernhard, a workmate of Mother's, in the form of a field-bed put up in the narrow kitchen of her apartment house in Belzigerstreet. Many a year ago, when fate had taken her Jewish husband, she had had no inkling that someday she would have to reaffirm her loyalty.

Left-wing friends of Aunt Ruth's student days had their own fear of arrest, but could be counted upon for radio evenings. I too was taken along, to learn of a world I had never known. These sessions were a special treat. To begin with, Radio London talked of the allied efforts and successful air raids. Then came the secret rite they had now practiced for nearly a decade: the crowding of ears to the muffled loudspeaker to catch "Hier spricht Moskau." With exhilaration written on their faces, they listened to long lists of recaptured Russian localities. Their radiant hope was contagious.

The traditionally red Wedding district in North Berlin chalked its bombed buildings with anti-Nazi slogans. But the only impression left on the ordinary passersby, like myself, would be the obliterating whitewash. Quite possibly much of the lettering had been done by disillusioned Hitler youths who saw no other way of expressing their grudges. North Berlin friends of mine had already contacted some of this new brand of rebel. Their slogans seemed universally appropriate: "Down with the teachers—they teach ruin!"

Among the highlights of defiance was the bomb planted in a much heralded anti-Soviet exhibition. Arrests following this incident were so widespread, however, that rumors suggested that it was just a new version of the 1933 Reichstag fire.

*   *   *

The end of 1942 saw the deportations of Jews being started on an intensified scale—to Lublin, it was said. Friends and neighbors became fewer and fewer, with ourselves in constant fear of the dreaded knock on the door. For a few days I was recruited to help out at Grenadier Street bakery, which had received sudden instructions to provide loaves for the big transports being hastily sent off to the East.

Working there I got to know the slums of Alexander Square. Gypsy and Jewish tenants seemed to live in harmony despite the drunken brawls that characterized the district. Any whitewashed shopwindow pane in Grenadier Street was likely to be the front of an overcrowded Gypsy habitation, housing a family of six or more. During the day, dirty, lousy Gypsy kids called the street their own; further they did not dare to wander. Only grownup sons had the honor of pacing more spacious grounds. Dressed in Wehrmacht uniforms, they had been called upon to defend the fatherland.

Soon we were living alone in the Speyrer Street flat. The other tenants' rooms were sealed by the Gestapo. All the valuable paintings and stamp collections belonging to our neighbors had fallen into Nazi hands. Negotiations by the elderly couple from the other floor, to barter their properties abroad for exemption from deportation, had failed. Instructions were given to empty apartments of foodstuffs before they were sealed off. A huge chunk of black market cheese had been abandoned on the backyard staircase. Its owner had clung to all that was his to the very last. Now he bequeathed it to the voracious rats and the covetous Gestapo.

Mother had been drafted into a factory assembling miniature coils for speedometers. Only night shifts were worked there, so I had to get used to spending the evenings all alone in an empty flat. Heavy and almost daily air raids worsened my lot still further. I had nowhere else to go. Jews were no longer allowed into shelters. Even when an incendiary bomb whizzed down our backyard, I stayed where I was.

It was the many less eventful moments, however, that characterized my confinement: reading, preparing my frugal supper and cleaning up. Often I toyed with the idea of breaking into the neighbors' flat. The sale of a single picture or rug from that sealed off apartment could have eased our lot considerably: less overtime for Mother, a square meal and, perhaps, some entertainment.

The last dawn of February saw the beginning of an operation for the total liquidation of Berlin's Jewish community. As all the other urban and rural communities had already been concentrated in the capital or deported, this represented the end of Germany's Jewry. With the large influx of Eastern "volunteer" labor, work in important war industries had ceased to exempt anyone from arrest. Every other Jew was already listed officially as having changed his place of residence for Lublin, Riga or Theresienstadt—supposed to be autonomous regions. Now the final netting-in operation meant cordoning off the streets and ticking off the last names on the elaborate Gestapo lists. Only a skeleton staff for the operation of the

Jewish hospital, the provisions center and the burial place remained to wind up their respective responsibilities.

Special SS reinforcements and lorries converged into Berlin for this biggest round-up yet. Planning and supervising it were notorious Austrian officers who had already rehearsed a similar action on Viennese Jewry. Their first and most explicit training, no doubt, was back in 1934 attacking Vienna's worker apartments.

Unknown to us, the tense situation was exploited by the Gestapo-instructed police to swoop down on Berlin's unsuspecting Gypsy populations.

German Gypsies could find no explanation whatsoever for this sudden stab in the back. To German Jews the threats of ten years ago had materialized.

Looking back now, the date fixed for the final expulsion of Germany's Jews and Gypsies strikes me as odd. It came exactly a decade after the infamous arrests of left-wingers. On March 1, 1933, when the Reichstag was burning, many a Jew must have looked upon those arrested in the same manner as they themselves were to be stared at ten years later, when their turn had come.

Officiously loud knocking jerked us to attention. There was no doubt about its ominous character. A quick resolution decided that escape by the back stairs was futile. We waited for the knocking to stop. But it went on, accompanied by vile abuse. While I noisily clanged the dustbin lids, to prove our pretense of having been down to empty the rubbish, Mother finally opened the door. The following minutes were dominated by mental agony.

For not having obeyed the order to close all the windows with the required thoroughness, I was pounced upon by the officer. From this, my first encounter with the SS, I emerged with my ears boxed more thoroughly than I had ever had before.

With our keys handed over, the rooms sealed, Mother and I stumbled towards the waiting lorry, each burdened with a cumbersome suitcase. *"Heraus! Schnell, schnell!"*

A long tiresome tour in quest of new victims awaited us. Elderly people hardly able to carry themselves, let alone any suitcases, were dragged along the pavement and pushed into the truck. Children in the street spat at them. Other passersby, overcome by a mixture of surprise and shame—occasionally mingled with malice—just stared.

Through a slit in the tarpaulin I peeped at the surroundings, reminders of the air raid the night before. Roadblocks isolated the destroyed Prager Square. Razed quarters were still smoldering. The bombing had finally reached a stage where it had to be taken seriously. All the same it could not even delay such unmilitary events as arrests. The Fascist Beast was still strong and intact. Only its eastern fangs were bleeding.

Towards dusk our lorry joined others queueing up in front of an improvised detention camp. One of six, our cage was at the Grosse Hamburger street. Ironically it included my former school, the home for the aged and the ancient cemetery, now demolished.

Here the arrested were sorted out according to some mysterious scheme, and prepared for transports to the East. The guards were indifferent Berlin policemen. The time was spent wandering about the cemetery grounds racking our brains for ways of escape. Climbing the wall seemed possible for me—but not for mother. To the problems of an outcast illegal existence afterwards there was no answer.

A remaining tomb, imprisoned by a little wire-cage of its own, attracted many a contemplating glance. It was the resting place of Moses Mendelssohn, the famous philosopher.

Elder folks to whom the last rays of their onetime hope were still shining drew inspirations from this reminder of past glory: perhaps after all the great man's teaching would prevail. My naive mind required no elaborate meditation. Had his ideas been of any practical use, I reasoned, his tomb would not be where it was now.

A committee had been set up to hear pleas for the reunion of families. Few reports ever went through to the commanding police officer and those, too, were usually rejected, but the imprisoned were aware that this was their last hope. Half-Jews and nationals from neutral countries even had chances of getting released. Attempts to cheat the notorious talents of the police and Gestapo, now combined, seemed futile.

A crowded cellar prison provided the necessary intimidation. Trying to fake evidence foreshadowed severe punishment: special cells had been prepared to mete out whatever the Gestapo had in store for us.

I looked at my cards: no "Aryan" in the family, no foreign government to intervene, no money for bribes. Suddenly I visualized a last desperate trump: I could bury the dead.

At first I had to convince Mother. Then I approached the only Jew on the appeals committee, a rabbi who had now and then officiated at burials.

"Yes," he exclaimed tiredly, "I have seen your face before. You are one of these flowerboys. Don't kid yourself that you are essential; you can't even dig a pit." Mustering all my determination and courage, I promised my willingness to do whatever I would be called upon to do. Imposed on, perhaps, by my healthy appearance he finally gave way: "I'll check up on the number of cemetery workers still left. There may be need for replacements. What about your family?" "Only Mother." A searching glance fixed itself on me. Stare met stare. "All right, if it's only two of you I'll try."

Uneasy hours followed. Imagination's hopeful light struggled with the more obvious darkness of our common fate. Depression was winning over hope.

Finally the commandant granted me a hearing. I clicked my heels in the best German fashion and tried to be both correct and older than my age. An adjutant recited my usefulness to the Third Reich, vouched for by the pudgy, bespectacled rabbi: "Cemetery worker essential for the upkeep of burials." "Yes, yes," grinned one of the officers present, "this type will have plenty of work."

A casual motion of the commandant's hand was my sign to do a neat about turn and to march away hurriedly.

Shouts of "Mr. Geve and wife to the office!" were left unanswered. Their repetition, however, indicated that it was us. We seized our suitcases, grabbed the release papers and hurriedly made for the gate before the Gestapo changed their mind. The policeman on guard compared our resemblance to photos on the identity cards, then remarked apologetically: "Some slip; we didn't realize you were brother and sister, you are, aren't you?—but we can't correct the paper now. It's signed already." The gray street, reminding of freedom, bid me not to delay. "Never mind," I replied, "we'll manage without corrections." The steel gate swung open and we took quick steps towards the next street corner.

To be free again was a great sensation, but it had to be maintained. A form stating that "Mr. Geve and family have herewith been released" did not by itself prevent us being rearrested. My job was to seek real exemption papers. Calling at the only remaining office of the Jewish Community at Oranienburg Street, I pleaded for my rights. As I was not on their paylists, they would not certify my being essential. After heated discussions, however, they finally agreed to register me as a navvy employed at the Weissensee cemetery. With it came all the privileges originally intended for the confidants who helped the police to make arrests. In return for a solemn promise to attend work regularly regardless of air raids or any private troubles, I was handed a special badge together with numerous stamped and signed certificates. To match the yellow of the Star of David on my breast I now donned a red armband lettered with: "Ordner (steward) Number so-and-so." Why the authorities had chosen red, a color either banned for belonging to left-wingers or glorified as a constituent of Hitler's flag, remained a mystery. All I cared about, however, was the trump-card that had outwitted the Gestapo.

Ignoring all regulations, we plodded through blacked-out Berlin to our distant home. Towards morning we arrived, and woke the porter. Certain of having seen the last of any Jews, he showed great surprise: "What? You free? And at this hour? Are they all coming back?"

After carefully checking if everything was legal, he grudgingly handed back our keys. It seemed clear that he would have preferred the rich tip-giving Jews' return. Tearing the Gestapo seals from our doors, we then lay down for a deeply deserved sound sleep.

"He who asks many a question, gets many an answer," says the proverb. Our new maxim would be being inconspicuous. In the coming morning, wakened by the five o'clock ring of the alarm clock, I discarded all badges, then boarded the tram to the far-off cemetery. Only some six workers there had been spared deportation. My duty to give all my strength to the job seemed obvious.

Later on some half-Jews joined us, among them a few other youngsters. Though by no means the smallest, I remained the youngest. Work was hard, but we could not let the others down by being absent. Digging graves six feet deep became routine. Now and then the steep earthen walls would collapse, half burying someone—and then, when we had to extract one another, it even added an odd element of fun.

Soon I became a worker like the others: with big wooden clogs, pick and shovel, a fixed minimum permissible output and a weekly pay packet. More often than not there was overtime to be done.

Suicides came in at a rate of up to ten a day. We had to be thankful for the law that forbade persons under the age of 21 to attend to the dead, limiting our occasional help to hearse pushing and taking the place of the mourners, who were now absent.

When the time was available we buried scrolls of the Torah. Religious rules not allowing holy writings to be burned, the synagogues from all over Germany had sent them to a central store at the Berlin cemetery. No one was left any more to care for these richly ornamented scrolls, however sacred they may have been. Hundreds of them were carried to a mass grave to be given a suitably impressive burial. It marked the end of an epoch.

Other visitations came in the form of bombs dropped by night-raiders, who had missed nearby Weissensee industrial objects, onto what seemed to us the most unprofitable target possible—the city of the dead.

A few girls, mostly half-Jews, returned to revive the small flower gardens, which by supplying the market eased the finances of the cemetery management. Working with them was a Polish prisoner-of-war who quickly became our friend. We fed him with whatever little we had and taught him German. He, a simple but sincere soul, returned our favors with accounts of his native land.

Keeping occupied during evening hours became quite a task. Present whereabouts of relatives and friends were unknown. Work acquaintances lived too far away. Mother was busy peddling our last linens for much-needed margarine.

Loneliness was dispelled by a self-assembled wireless set. Working without electricity, its parts, headphone, crystal, condenser and coils, had been acquired clandestinely and piecemeal. A wire stretched across the room represented the secret aerial, and when the first crackling noises were identified as speech I was extremely proud of my achievement.

Lying in bed with earphones pressed on, scanning the ether became my favorite enjoyment. Once I really became startled: I was tuned to an English-speaking station, probably a secret one too. Though I mustered my best school English I soon felt disappointed, for it was only Nazi phrases that I could make out. It must have been Berlin.

Slowly I now realized that Hitlerism was not the German monopoly I had been led to believe, but an exportable enthusiasm. To my bewilderment I found out that the Nazis had many sympathizers in the very countries they had warred with.

The illustrated Nazi journals I knew so well had English, French and Dutch editions, exact replicas of the original. New German compound words like *Ferntrauung, Kriegseinsatzdienst* and *Pionierschutzmannschaft,* were left untranslated. Foreigners would have to learn them—either under compulsion or out of sympathy.

Our ration cards needed renewing, a procedure most Jews avoided as it meant reminding the authorities of one's presence. Unable to exist on black market food alone, we made the dreaded way to the food office at Wartburg Square. Knowing that in the eyes of white-collar Nazis every rubber-stamped swastika meant law, we took along an ample selection of documents.

"We supposed that there are no more Jews in the district and accordingly no cards were taken out for them," squeaked the unfriendly voice of a minor female official. After much pleading, however, the management finally phoned the central head office to ask "whether non-Aryans whose presence seems to have the approval of the Third Reich should be issued new ration cards." More calls followed to check the plausibility of our claim. It was still early in the morning, with bureaucracy still yawning away yesterday's monotony. So for lack of obstructing orders they handed over the precious booklets of colored cards. It meant a few months' vital supply of bread, flour, potatoes, jam, sugar and margarine. Only towards noon did instructions to stop issuing Jewish cards and to arrest their claimants come through.

Trouble arose, too, about our 1½ small furnished rooms. "Why," said the landlord, "I am not to blame for the Gestapo having deported all the other residents and sealed the doors. It's you two who live there now, so you have to pay rent for the whole 5 room flat." Hardly able to offer him compensation even for our rooms, we had to move out. Chance, and perhaps luck, made Eva-Ruth, a fellow workmate (the same that had once become fond of me), offer us a room at her Konstanzer Street home. We took along two suitcases each and moved in.

The new district, near the fashionable Kurfuerstendamm, was full of well-nourished, elegant snobs. It was the rendezvous of well-to-do Germans and foreign Fascists. Polished luxury cars shuttled between ice cream parlors, exclusive restaurants, connoisseurs' tobacconists, beauty salons and vendors of rare flowers. Berlin's West End, in the summer of 1943, nearly made one forget that there was a war on.

*   *   *

Something moved about the rubbish heap. It seemed bigger than a dog. The girls from the cemetery's flower shop begged us to investigate. Equipped with sticks, we advanced in warlike formation towards the tall brick wall, the spot where kitchen refuse had been deposited.

A ragged olive-green uniform bent itself up from the smelly, rotting heap. It contained a human being. His unshaven head was topped by a forage cap, his bare feet housed in wooden clogs. A moldy turnip adorned his uneasy hand. In response to abusive shouts he hastily turned to where he had come from.

Suddenly one of us became startled: "Look at his back, there's a big black SU printed on it. Whatever does that mean?" "Yes, it means Soviet Union," we were told by some bright boy, known for being able to distinguish all the latest makes of cars and airplanes, "it's the place where the subhumans come from." This specimen's looks and actions certainly befitted the description, but Russia being an ally of the British against Hitler, we decided to call the rummager back for a friendly investigation. With the aid of a hurriedly summoned workmate who knew smatterings of Polish we somewhat hesitatingly accepted the intruder's explanations: He was Russky soldier—soldier Kaput—he work hard, eat little—he escape— escaped Russians shot—German bad—Jew friend—he not eaten two days—he hungry.

Yes, now we could quite imagine this robust figure, his uniform shining in its old glory marching on parade somewhere in far off Russia about to enter the battlefield against our common foe. He surely deserved our sympathy, even if we had not made up our mind about the more accurate definition of subhuman. Anyhow, he ate raw turnips. We hastily fetched him some more and wished him good luck. Then he had to leave as unceremoniously as he had come. After this, we tried to find out more about people like him.

* * *

It was Eva-Ruth, the girl I worked and lived with, who first aroused my interest in sex. A buxom, red-blonde lass of fourteen, she had taken a liking to me. "Don't come in now," she would cry, "I am only dressed in my kimono. There are only me and you in the flat, so don't be nasty." When after a few minutes she would still clamorously announce her being only scantily clothed, I would naively continue to wait outside. Too young to understand her hints, my sole rewards were rebukes for being clumsy. We toyed with each other, lay on the same sofa, but could not make ourselves understood. The more I adored her body, the more did I hate her mind.

She was coquettish, but too outspoken. Her arrogance and prejudices were repellent. Liking workmates of non-German birth was below her dignity. Occasionally, when I was the object of her heated quarrels, even I would be denounced as "dirty Eastern Jew."

Her education, like that of many a German Jew, had been one of "Deutschland ueber Alles"—Germany above all; acclimatization to the accepted social pattern was all that mattered. An educated person's superior attitude may have been fitting in more secure and comfortable surroundings, but now it was hopelessly out of place. The orderly German way of life was crumbling: there was no point in clinging to its memories.

One Sunday afternoon in June a guest arrived at our place for tea. A friendly character, the type that would have made a good salesman, he wanted to have an intimate chat with Eva-Ruth's mother. Slowly but cleverly he unravelled his story. Himself a Jew, he had been recruited by the Gestapo to seek out candidates for deportation. He did not hint at the means which had been used to make him undertake this unpleasant task. The few remaining Jews had become more elusive and anyhow did not merit any large scale action. So a new scheme had been decided upon: arrests by persuasion, enacted by an inconspicuous fellow Jew over a cup of tea.

Having come down with influenza, I had not been to the cemetery for a few days. Now I heard through him of a round-up having been staged there, with only a few workmates managing to escape by the back gate. Eva-Ruth's arrest order already lay on the table. My name was not to be found on the visitor's pencil marked list, but he applied all his professional cleverness to impress upon us that it soon would be. A final netting in of the few remaining Jews and half-Jews, whether in hiding or not, had already been decided upon. "To come voluntarily would be better than facing nerve-racking days, waiting for the inevitable knock on the door," he said. Not convinced, we decided to let events take their turn.

Mother and I spent two more days in the deserted flat pondering about the future. With no indications of the war's end being near, a reliable hiding place was not to be found. Our resources could hardly finance a month's illegal living. On the other hand I was used to hard work. "Eastern working camps" could not be all that impossible; a good worker may even make a fair living. Finally there was the unquenchable hope that I might effect yet another release.

Then, once again, we set out across town weighted with the inevitable four suitcases. At the same street corner in North Berlin where we had three months ago taken them off, we now refixed our yellow Stars of David. Entering the assembly camp were yet two more volunteers.

This time different types of inmates crowded the Grosse Hamburger Street detention cage, the last of its kind. Crowded a dozen to the room, with food as scarce as a prison can make it, an atmosphere of defiant hope nevertheless prevailed.

A group of young Zionists had arrived from a German farm-turned-prison. Every evening they organized discussion groups, sang sentimental Palestinian tunes and even danced the Horah. Where their enthusiasm sprang from was beyond me; so was the technique of their queer dancing steps. Another dancing circle centered round a pudgy, half-Jewish, blonde accordion player, an expert on cooking and step-dancing. This was the flirting group whose clients included many of our police-guards.

Attractive girls having affairs with the officers were in utmost disgrace. Still, nobody could have blamed them for liking the Christian half of their parentage as much as the other. A successful friendship could even effect their release. Fondling among the inmates themselves was more pronounced. Eva-Ruth, too, had finally found her mate there, someone less naive than myself, and to the general disgust, had gone to live in his room. Jealous and feeling lost, I then sought any companion who did not mind being imposed upon by an ignorant youngster like me.

The motley but high-spirited prison crowd was made up of half-Jews, caught "illegals," foreigners, community workers and old people. The few odd Polish Jews who had escaped from so-called "concentration camps" attracted everyone's sympathy. Those Easterners told their stories with such repetitious zest that only few doubted their being exaggerated. Outstanding among them was a depressed, nervous, pitiable young man who claimed to have fled from "Auschwitz," one of the supposed Silesian working camps. His lack of self-control alone precluded any confidence in his accounts. His wild accusations against western civilization, for which he offered no proofs, only caused general annoyance. It was not a question of mere hot-headed charges; it was, in fact, blasphemy. Sorting out for the impending transports started. Old people and owners of war medals would be sent to Theresienstadt,* the rest to the East. Lectures on how to behave on the way were followed by the distribution of identification numbers and journey rations. Next morning we mounted the lorries taking us to the Stettiner Bahnhof goods station.

Behind the engine was a passenger car for the police guards, followed by some dozen closed goods wagons. The opposite embankment was lined with sentries, tensely fingering machine pistols. On top of the last coach a long-barrelled machine gun threatened us.

Mother and I, doing our best to keep together, were hustled into a wagon laid out with straw. Its four small barricaded ventilation apertures and the lone sanitation bucket were to be shared by twenty other candidates for the East.

My eager eyes had just about managed to catch sight of an inscription left over from our carriage's prewar days in France. When we had settled down I summoned my companions' linguistic talents to translate it: the freight's supposed character had once been fixed as "40 men, 8 horses." Official evaluation of its present contents—the crucial point of our worries—remained a mystery.

Then the train pulled out. As a gesture to his native Berlin many an uncertain soul intoned a last song of farewell. Tall factory chimneys, signposts of the metropolitan's eastern suburbs, silhouetted against the falling dusk, receded along either side of the track. The teeming city seemed covered with a mantle of silence, her blacked-out self being unable to sense her few departing children. Maybe the others, the many who would never see her again, had perceived a last, sad nod of goodbye. To me she remained strange and cold. Perhaps she was ashamed of herself.

As we rolled away from Germany, with the regular rhythm of the wheels counting off rail by rail, we were leaving a world that was lost for us—the very world that had lost itself.

*Terezin, Czechoslovakia.

PART TWO
THE HIDDEN WORLD

CHAPTER I

Becoming a Prisoner

The train passed familiar sights—the coal mines of Upper Silesia. Whenever it was my turn to get some fresh air, I pulled myself up to the ventilation grille and hoped to catch glimpses of our home town Beuthen, but without success, for we seemed to have made a detour.

Much time was spent waiting at sidings, to free the mainline for reinforcements to the Eastern Front. This procedure, occurring mostly at night, when no one took any interest in it, quite upset any time table we may have imagined. Even the talkative had ceased suggesting where and when we would arrive. People became touchy and irritated.

At the few halts where we were allowed to empty the lavatory bucket and fetch water, heated quarrels broke out as to who must clean what and who may use whose pots. Courtesy and understanding had been blotted out by a surge of egoism, heralding a ruthless struggle for survival. A mere two days' journey of fear and discomfort had succeeded in breaking down the traditionally polite manners so typical of city folks.

The only place where all of us were permitted to have a little stroll was at a lonely, forest-surrounded country stop. To catch a breath of fresh air was good, but visiting the lavatory a must. The station's facilities were represented by a rectangular pit topped by a wooden beam. "Ustempo," said the signboard next to this curious contraption. Translated, it meant a place where, if skillful enough, one could relieve oneself. It meant too that we had reached Poland. Later the landscape disclosed stranger objects: wooden towers sixteen feet high, with ladders attached to them. In my opinion these could only serve for aircraft spotters. But why so many of them? Then big wooden sheds appeared, lined up in rows, with people in blue and white zebra-striped uniforms around them. Back home convicts, dressed the same, had occasionally been seen pushing refuse-carts. Here local prisoners seemed to pass their time working in fenced-off storage depots.

Apparently the Polish supply of criminals was a record one. I consulted my watch: five minutes, seven minutes, ten minutes; still there was no end of the barbed wire. Craning my neck through the aperture I searched for a prison building—without success.

The train stopped, then shunted onto a branch line. Silence was interrupted by a shrill whistle. Doors were pushed open. All around us we heard harsh shouts of "Out! Out!" Facing us were armed field-gray SS men.

It was the evening of June 27th, 1943, the place Brzezinka, near the town of Oswiecim.* Our familiar police guards had been relieved long ago, for this was a secluded world not fit to be watched by outsiders. "Out, you bastards!" "Faster, *Schweinehunde!*" "Run, you sow hounds!" yelled our new masters, the supermen of the super race. A whole SS company was drawn up along the station. Both ends were guarded by machine guns. Bloodhounds, threateningly tugging their leashes, barked out a warning welcome.

The landscape offered no consolation: for miles no tree was to be seen, only the empty field. Mist rising in the distance, to herald the dusk, hid whatever was lurking there.

"Quicker, quicker!" Now and then a whip swished down. "Everything to be left behind!"—"Able-bodied men to the right, women that can work to the left, the rest stay in the middle of the platform." I hurriedly hugged Mother good-bye and made for the right. Blowing myself up, to look impressive, and walking as erect as

---

*German names: Birkenau and Auschwitz.

possible, I passed the scrutiny of the supervising SS officer, then lost myself among the crowd of men.

Dusk had fallen. Lorries arrived to take the old and ill. Mothers and children still waited. We men arranged ourselves in rows of five, were surrounded by guards and marched off.

After about half an hour our column of 117 males, still stupe-fied by the ominous reception, reached a guarded turnpike. Dirty puddles, ringed by muddy, barren soil, suggested that nature took no interest in the place. Again we were counted and recounted, till the sentries let us pass.

Soon we reached a building of red brick which, if a bit smaller, might normally have been a farmhouse. For its sinister surround-ings, however, there was no comparison. Radiating from it were elec-trically charged barbed-wire fences eight feet high and paralleled with smaller ones. Regularly spaced black signposts, showing a white skull with cross-bones, read "danger." The central feature was the tower with two-storied wings abutting on either side. Running through its wide gate was a railway track, while topping the pyramid-like roof was a mushroom-shaped siren whose wailing could have been the only fitting accompaniment for those passing there. Beyond, illuminated by a sea of lights, an endless pattern of wooden barracks, arranged in rows, revealed itself.

Yet another count-up and we, too, were heading for this monstrous city of prisoners. Charged wires on either side of the road hummed in the new arrivals. No trees, no shrubs, nothing green was to be seen. It was another world, unique in its depress-ing gloom. A sign at an opening in the ever-lengthening fence caught my continuously searching eyes. In an attempt to seek more knowledge of our whereabouts, I painstakingly deciphered it: *V-e-r-n-i-c-h-t-u-n-g-s-l-a-g-e-r,* destruction camp. Maybe they had lots of secret documents to dispose of—or could it be vermin?

Then we turned towards one of the many camps, a group of huts among hundreds.

A halt was made at a dull, gray, uncanny-looking edifice, with one story below ground level, another above. A tall chimney stuck out from it. We queued up to enter.

Finally my turn came. Supervision had partly passed into the hands of healthy-looking prisoners who to me represented murderers and thieves. They ignored being talked to, their only reaction being a shaking of the head. I entered a room filled with numerous piles of textiles.

"Undress!"—"Clothing to the right—underwear to the left—valuables and documents into the basket—shoes to be taken along; nothing else."—"All other trifles also into the basket: money, photos, rings and so on." Naked, I hesitantly surrendered my watch. My identity card was dropped on to a stack of others: another name had ceased to exist.

Next came the hair. Shaving followed cutting to ensure that no tuft was left on any part of the body. I myself, as yet, had hair on my head alone. It joined the others, dark, blonde and red, already heaped on the floor.

A final check-up was made on me, revealing a couple of cottage-cheese sandwiches. Shrivelled up and stale, they had been saved all the way from Berlin. In no mood to eat them, I had tried to hide them and carry them through together with my shoes.

More depressed than ever before, I entered the "Sauna" (a Finnish-style steambath). There my companions of the last few hours sat row by row, on the batten-covered floor that rose up in steps towards a few small ventilation apertures. Naked, shorn, I failed to recognize any of them. Crowded together as in some weird, enigmatic theater, we were anticipating an unworldly performance. Nobody noticed me, no one voiced his view. Everyone seemed absorbed with his own worries.

Left to myself, disturbing fears took hold of me. What if all the rumors of mass killings were true? Didn't one of them mention gas? Still not having resigned myself to fate, I scanned the metal-lined doors. They had heavy bolts. Only the high little windows seemed penetrable. Locked up, we waited.

Some time later the door swung open. A group of our blue-white uniformed wardens entered. After some consultations in Polish with his aides, one of them stepped forward to address us: "You are now concentration camp inmates. The easy life has finished. Old habits will have to be changed. If not, we'll change them. Complete obedience to your prisoner superiors, and of course to the SS, is a must. Don't illusion yourselves with ideas of ever getting out of here. Plenty of hard work will take the place of thought. This camp is called Birkenau and demands strictest discipline. You'll now be disinfected.''

Then we were chased through a pit of detergent into a cold shower bath. Shivering, I tried to avoid it, but our new bosses were impressively thorough in their vigilance. Accompanied by renewed shouts of "Quick! Hurry!" underwear, jackets, trousers and caps were thrown at us. Hastily I dragged my share of heavily patched clothing over my wet skin. There was no time to consider the grotesque proportions of my oversized rags nor to tie any strings or laces: we were already being driven out into the sleeping camp. The introductory ordeal had started.

"Run!" "Run quicker, you lazy pigs." At every step I struggled with the obstinate mud for the mastery of my precious but untied shoes. Even the hatefully big trousers had joined the conspiracy by slipping downward towards its allies, the cold, splashing puddles. I fought back, ankles thrashing, hands tugging at my clothes and sweat pouring from my whole body.

Victorious, but exhausted, I arrived at the reception barrack. At its entrance a figure in prison garb emerged from the dark. "Any valuables? Rings, gold?" he accosted us confidentially. "Don't hide them, the SS will get them after all. Better leave them with me, in the trust of a fellow inmate. Now come on, don't hesitate. You must have something cherished that needs entrusting into friendly hands!" Some responded to his pleadings. I only wondered whether he would have considered picking up my dried up cottage cheese sandwiches from the "Sauna."

The registration hall was lined with tables laden with cardindexes. Prisoners and SS men were seated behind them. We were told to arrange ourselves alphabetically in rows of five—a laborious procedure for people not versed in drilling methods. A whip and an ample selection of Nazi tricks soon took over to quicken up matters.

"Now where are the fat Berlin merchants?" jeered the SS bully. Two rather pudgy individuals, who seemed to fit his concept of rich traders, were ordered to run around the barrack. "Are there rabbis too?" No one answered. Any beards that may have revealed them had been shorn off. Feeling himself cheated, he fished for new victims: "I hear there are bastards among you whose fathers raped Aryan girls. Let's see these blond ones with crooked noses!" Most of us had light hair, so this brainwave too had to be given up. Exasperated, he resorted to threats: "This is your last chance to rid yourselves of hidden valuables. We'll find them anyhow. Drop them on the floor. If after leaving this barrack anything is found on you, you'll be shot!" This, the money-raking part of an SS official's duty was, it seemed, the most vociferously proclaimed and thoroughly enforced of all.

We passed on to the desks. A young Russian prisoner took hold of my left arm and started tattooing it with a double-pointed pen dipped in blue ink. He did it gently, perhaps even with care, but it hurt like the continuous prick of countless pins. When he had finished he scrutinized me and saw that I was young. To my surprise he then muttered: "Good luck to you."

I looked at his work, a neatly executed, six-figured number— somewhat too big for my liking. It added up to thirteen. Was it to be lucky?

An insignificant name had become an insignificant number. Another male "protective custody prisoner"* was filling in the inevitable forms. More than 100,000 others had done so before me, in duplicate: one copy for the camp, the other for the Gestapo.

"You idiot, here you are no longer an 'Israel'!" the prisoner clerk shouted at me as I was about to write the additional forename which, by a decree of 1938, was compulsory for all male Jews. I continued to fill in: 13 years—Beuthen—Berlin—gardener's apprentice—emigrated—deported—none—measles, scarlet fever, mumps—none—none—none. Rounding it up was the signing of a

---

*Schutzhaeftling

statement, declaring myself to be stateless and property-less. That this farce could be one of the numerous documents trying to keep up the prestige of the Third German Empire, was beyond me.

There was a sort of interval, a hot tea-like drink being poured into metal bowls and distributed. Again there were shouts, this time for physicians and other specialists. About a dozen stepped forward.

My defiant mind reawoke, eager to try yet another get-away from the Gestapo. If not now, then never. The plan was a desperate one, but its first stage seemed tangible. I headed for the SS officer, clicked my heels and tried to be as smart as my pitiful appearance would allow me to. "I kindly beg you to consider my transfer. I am not fourteen yet and feel out of place here." A sardonic grin appeared under his skull-and-crossbone adorned, peaked cap: "And where would you like to go to?" "To the children's camp," I replied, proud that my trick was working. "We have no children's compounds," he retorted, somewhat annoyed. I persisted: "At least have me placed with other youngsters, please." Obviously irritated, he seemed to admonish me: "One day you'll be pleased I didn't. Now you are here and that's that. Off you go!"

Registration finished, we were led through the pitch-dark night to the sleeping barracks. One of the innumerable huts opened up its standardized interior. Partition walls rationed off the space into boxes of 6 feet by 6 feet, 30 inches high. Three above each other, every one of these bunks, or "buxes," laid out with straw-filled sacks, was the home of six prisoners. Along the center of the barrack projected a square, brick-built heating duct, a stove at one end, a chimney at the other.

We were left in charge of the "block-elder"*—a veteran prisoner entrusted with keeping the barrack inmates under control— who with the help of his several "room-elders" busily ordered the newcomers to their quarters. Hardly having grasped the sardines' artful way of lying on one's side, straight with your head enclosed by both neighbors' feet (a must for bunk sleepers), we were called to attention by a shrill whistle. Our new boss, the *blokovi*, wanted to

---

* Also *Blockaeltester* or *Blokovi*

deliver his speech, which he must have known backwards by now. "This is Block 7a, men's camp Birkenau—Nobody is allowed to leave the block—You may only leave your bunks to relieve yourselves but only one at a time. An improvised lavatory is in the middle of the barrack—You must keep absolutely quiet. Orders of block-personnel, or other prisoners, are to be obeyed with precision. We are your appointed superiors and can order you to do whatever we like. Obedience must be complete. If you wake up tomorrow morning to find your shoes missing, don't dare to complain. Woe him who will bother me with trifles: he may never leave this block alive. When you see an SS man you have to stand at attention, your cap at the seam of your trousers. Should he enter a block or approach a group of prisoners, you must rap out "*Achtung,* Attention." On hearing it, you jump to attention without delay. When he leaves, you call "*Weitermachen,* Continue," and go on with your work. If you choose not to greet an SS man, you will feel the consequences by yourselves. I have warned you. Lights out now, and quiet!"

I was dog-tired, but the combined effects of an eventful day and a bowl of tea soon necessitated my wriggling out of the crowded bunk to start searching for the lavatory. People groaned and scratched themselves in their sleep. The boarded lining of the roof was alive with mice. My goal, the two vats, were filled to the brim.

Penetrating whistling abruptly ended our sparse two hours' sleep. My Sunday best shoes were nowhere to be seen. I grabbed whatever had been put in their place, a big black worker's boot and a brown shoe fringed with leather ornaments—much too small for me. Someone shouted "thieves." Muffled blows were heard.

Again we lined up in fives, this time much quicker. Shouted commands and distant steps penetrated from the dark camp. We seemed to be in for a sinister surprise. Standing in the last row I fell asleep against a bunk-post. A cuff from the room-elder accompanied by "be lucky I'm no SS man," made me stand at attention again.

Again something disturbed my dozing, but this time its origin was less pronounced. I shook myself awake and tried to listen attentively. Grotesquely out of place and certainly unexpected, it was all the same true: music, an orchestra playing marches.

Several hours later, with our position still unchanged, an SS delegation arrived, including high-ranking officers. They pointed out the stronger looking men and had them separated for work at the Monowitz camp. "Where is that half-Jew who was in the army?" called an officer, whose corded epaulets denoted a high rank. A blond young man stepped forward. He was familiar to me. His education was as German as German could be, but his many passionate appeals for release had been of no avail. "You'll remain in this camp," he was told, "and be allocated easier work."

Then the guards came, bringing along two bloodhounds. We the six remaining five-men rows of prisoners turned left and were marched off. Through the early morning mist Birkenau revealed itself in its own sad, warning way. Even the worst pessimist could not have imagined conditions more shocking.

Women prisoners, hampered by the boggy ground and threatened by shouting supervisors, pushed away at big supply wagons. Behind them trotted a few bald, haggard children who now and then lifted their ragged garments to scratch themselves.

A squad with black and red circles stitched on their garb was feverishly breaking up stones for paving a new road. Watched over, as they were, by SS men carrying whips, they did not dare look up.

We left behind the jungle of barbed wire and checkposts and trudged through an indifferent, deserted countryside. An impartially hot mid-day sun meant equal sweating for all. Led and leaders alike, we had to realize our insignificance against nature: we slowed down. Curiosity, too, knew no human-made distinctions. Now and then a guard would come closer to ask questions. "Where are you from?—Why are you here?!—Yes, now you are going to work! From now on you will realize what toil means; you'll be surprised!" "Don't ask questions, you'll see for yourselves." "How long do you think you'll stand it here? You should have enquired about the place before coming here. Why did you come?" "But now get a move on! Quicker, first row!"

An hour later we again passed barbed wire. The blue-white garbs had reappeared. Prisoners lifted stones, carried bricks, dragged tree trunks and shovelled coal. Parallel to the road waited loaded railway wagons. To either side of it were immense pyramids of bricks, coal and timber. Around them hustled hundreds of prisoners re-enacting ancient Egyptian slave scenes. Shrill voices shouted orders and curses.

We, too, attracted attention: calls in a Babel of languages greeted us. Only a few could be made out. "See, there come the *Vollgefressenen*, they want to help push the wagons!" "They won't stick it for long, the fat-bellies!"

After another twenty minutes we reached the camp gate of Auschwitz. Its inscription, in ornamental metalwork, read: "Work makes free." Checked in, we were led to the disinfection barrack and crowded into the steam-filled laundry hall.

There we had the first opportunity of talking freely to fellow prisoners. From them, 24 hours after our arrival, we learned the bitter truth: there were no children camps, no camp for the old, none for the ill. There was only the forest of death behind the Birkenau camp. Its depths were filled with gas and destruction. We felt as if the ground had receded from under our feet. Our vague, but desperate trust in civilization lay shattered.

I did not think that any individual or even set of individuals could be responsible for the enormity of the crime. Neither busy Hitler in far-off Berlin, nor the guard that had been sweating along the dusty road, seemed the right target for my wrath. A terrifying realization overwhelmed me. The refined city manners, the studying of Greek and Roman achievements, the strivings of democracy, the neutral nations' eagerness to help the oppressed, the many impressive churches I had seen, the beauty of art and progress I was to have understood, the trust in my parents' judgment—it all seemed to have been a disgusting farce.

There was no time just now to ponder over our, perhaps inevitable, fate. Old-time inmates, eager to get news from the outside world, were showering us with questions. Our replies soon proved to be assets: every description of world events was traded for valuable explanations of camp life. Soon the jig-saw puzzle, that had been vexing every new prisoner, was assembling itself in our minds. Bit by bit we grasped the mechanism of a concentration camp.

Eighty percent of the inmates were non-Jews. Of the 18,000 prisoners in our new camp, only a handful were Jews of German origin. Poles, Ukrainians and Russians constituted the majority, Frenchmen, Czechs, Slovaks, Germans, Gypsies and Jews the minority. Most Jews came from Poland, Greece, France and the Low Countries.

The national proportions were nearly the same as those at the surrounding camps, but varied from time to time. Previously other groups had been predominant. Since 1941 there had been large contingents of Red Army prisoners, Dutch and German Jews. By now, however, they had "ceased to exist."

To facilitate identification, each prisoner wore a colored cloth triangle followed by his number stitched to his garb over the heart and over the right upper leg. Every category had its separate sign. A green triangle, apex down, meant that its wearer was a professional criminal, apex up, a first-time offender. The official meaning of a black triangle was "work shy." It was worn by Russians, Ukrainians and Gypsies. Red triangles, signifying political opponents, were reserved for Germans, Poles, Czechs, and Frenchmen.

Convicted homosexuals, few as they were, wore pink ones. Members of pacifist religious sects were designated violet, but they, too, had "ceased to exist."

An elaborate card-index at the political department of the SS camp administration, listing the official reason for arrest, determined who was to wear what. Jews had a red triangle or, now and then, a green one superimposed on a yellow one so as to form the Star of David. Triangles of non-Jews were imprinted with the initial of the wearer's nationality.

A young Polish-Belgian Jew, who had attentively listened to our story, seemed amused by it. "So he played that shoe swapping trick on you too, that old scoundrel," he grinned. "That damned Birkenau block-elder, a notorious Polish criminal, is a Jew like ourselves. He deserves to be gored like a pig. One of these days we'll have to do away with him. You are lucky to have got out of that hell there; you couldn't have stood it for long. Here conditions are more tolerable: we do our best to eliminate characters of this type."

Emerging from between the boiling steaming laundry kettles and joining the throng came another listener. With his short frame he pushed his way towards us. On his smartly tailored garb we recognized a green triangle, followed by a number in the thousands.

"So these are the latest arrivals," he surveyed us with blue, penetrating but ageing eyes. "Germany, Germany," he mumbled, "it was my home, too.

"We are all caught in the same spider's web now. Honest citizens or adventurers, our fate is the same. Don't be misled by my green triangle; my term in prison has long been served. I am here for the same reason as you: extermination! There is no escape from here. Ten miles around us, everything is controlled by the SS. You have only seen one camp so far. There are seven more like it at Birkenau. Men, women, Jews, Gypsies and Germans, they are all kept separately. One of the compounds is for death candidates. Birkenau can hold 100,000 prisoners; the rest are sent to the crematoria. I don't want to horrify you with further details.

"Our camp Auschwitz is supposed to be the 'model camp.' It is the show-piece for visiting Red Cross delegations, and you can be glad to be among its 18,000 privileged. Monowitz, where some of you were sent, is an exhausting tread mill. Its 11,000 prisoners work like slaves building a synthetic rubber factory. Even with the reasonable living conditions and food you have there, the work wears you out in weeks."

Our patron seemed to take pleasure in showing his exact knowledge of the surroundings. He listed them with German thoroughness: "Birkenau, Auschwitz and Monowitz are the three main camps. Sprinkled all around them are subsidiaries whose role is to suck the last drop of energy out of the prisoner, while he is still alive. Like Janina, Jawoschno, Jawischowitz, Myslowitz, Sosnowitz, Schwientochlowitz, Fuerstengrube, Guentersgrube and Eintrachtshuette, most of them are mines. There are factories at Gleiwitz, Bobrek, Althammer and Blechhammer, quarries at Gollischau and Trzebinia, and agricultural establishments at Babitz, Budy, Harmensee and Raisko. Some, with about 200 prisoners each, are no more than cages. Others, with the same lack of facilities, house up to 5,000. The total number of slaves in this SS empire called Auschwitz may already be 150,000 and, despite all, it is growing day by day.

"No," he shook his sharp featured head with its protruding triangular nose, "there is no way out. Even if you escaped from camp, could you get through the rings of checkposts that surround all eastern Upper Silesia? Would your German tongue win the Polish population's confidence? I, cunning fox and privileged old-time prisoner that I am, have had to abandon the idea of escape, even though my friendship with the SS officers made it a possibility. You, the newest and lowest type of prisoners, should never even dream of it. During the last two years only four of the handful that escaped appear to have got away. Have no illusions about the future: the only hope is outside, allied intervention. That, however, we have been waiting for since 1938."

As the speaker walked away I admired his elegant uniform. The widened ends of the neatly ironed trouser legs were flapping over a fashionable pair of shiny patent leather shoes. Perhaps he could afford to be a pessimist.

Still squatting among the steaming laundry vats, we also got to know each other. Heavy-hearted, we talked of our pasts and our families.

There were four youngsters among us who had not yet reached eighteen: Sally, Jonathan, Gert and myself. We solemnly agreed upon a "quadrilateral pact," promising to share our sorrows and joys, our hunger and our food. Sally Klapper who, together with his mother, had emigrated from Poland, had been a Berlin acquaintance of mine. A little older than myself, I had always admired him for his choice of buxom girl friends. Gert Beigel, like myself, had at one time worked at the Weissensee cemetery. He and his elder brother, being born Berliners, had managed to go into hiding, but were betrayed and caught.

There was a sudden stirring among our visitors. They either dispersed or went on with their work. Heading for us came a gaunt prisoner, his wizened, stern face adorned by glasses, his breast by a green triangle. The yellow band around his left arm read: *"Lager Friseur,"* camp hairdresser. He surveyed us in a superior manner, then turned to us youngsters. "I am in charge of new arrivals here," he told us impressively. "Together with my 17 assistants, called Blockfriseure, I am responsible for keeping the camp—and you—clean. Don't be misled by our armbands, the cutting of hair is none of our business. There are enough of your sort to do the menial work. With us lies the responsibility for sanitary arrangements, disinfections and the working of the barrack you are in now.... Instead of being in command, we try to help you. If you kids ever have troubles, do come to see me.

"Now you know-alls," he grinned with his almost toothless mouth, "how are politics outside?" He wanted to know how and when we expected to regain our freedom. Everyone's answer, fifty in all, seemed to interest him and was appreciated by a satisfied "Hmm." Some of us seemed to be good strategists: "Oh, we hope to be back in Berlin by Christmas. The Allies are already in Italy!"

The doors opened and the rush for the shower room started. Our reception was warmer—in all senses of the word—than the previous one at Birkenau. Gladly we took off our patched clothes, painted over with broad, red streaks. Even soap was issued. A little kindness worked wonders and, warm sprays turned on, we momentarily felt as free and careless as any normal bather does.

Afterwards we were again sprayed with an irritating disinfectant, then given striped garb together with wooden clogs. The blue-white uniform was of thin, cardboard-like material but clean and new.

Soon we clattered off to the upper story of the brickbuilt barrack opposite. "Block 2a," it said at the entrance.

First we had to show our skill by sewing on our new number badges. Then we were lined up, together with about a hundred Russian prisoners. Again the inevitable "block-elder" came to deliver a talk. He spoke in his native tongue, Polish, which, to his obvious annoyance, none of us showed signs of understanding. When he had finished, a volunteer translated the instructions into Russian. There must have been someone present who also could have said it in

German but, as this was the language of the SS, no one wanted to speak it.

To our surprise we found out that in our block, where we were to spend our four weeks or so of quarantine, everything was said, ordered and proclaimed in Polish. Russian was also heard occasionally. In Germany talking a foreign tongue in public was a punishable offense. Here, too, everyone not completely ignorant of German was supposed to talk it. Yet it was seldom heard. We had such difficulty in understanding our prisoner superiors that some of the die-hard Germans among us even voiced their intent of complaining to the SS. They were overruled, however, and we embarked upon learning the Slav tongues, mainly Polish, the language of the country around us.

Our fellow block inmates, Ukrainians with here and there a Pole, were a stubborn, dull lot. Strongly-built country people, their open enmity had to be avoided by all means—including passively accepting their cheating us of the rare, second helping of midday soup. Despite our servile attitude, however, or possibly because of it, we were usually looked upon as two evils in one, Germans and Jews.

We felt rather forlorn, as prisoners from other blocks were not allowed to see us. The main events of the day were marking off the date with our fingernails onto the wooden posts of our bunks, gobbling up our sparse rations and wishing for more. Soon we had heard enough about each other. Accounts of tasty dishes ceased to make us forget our hunger. Intimate details of our favorite girl friend's female attractions became annoying. Bored and impatient, we waited for what was to come.

One day, his shaven round head accentuating the Mongolian features of his pock-marked face, a squat little Russian arrived at our corner. A square piece of cardboard under his arm, he had come from the room opposite to look for chess players. He had found the right place and soon became a regular visitor of ours.

By and by, as we gained his confidence, the little chess player became our friend. His smattering of German had been acquired at school and from his German grandfather. With the Ukrainians around us, who had been "volunteered" to work in Germany, he had little in common. He had been a fighter, an ally, the way we had imagined them to be. As a 19 year old airman he had flown one of those short-bodied Soviet planes that I had seen at the exhibition back in Berlin. The dogfight in which he was shot down was explained to us in a pilot's impressive way, hands representing planes, deep gurgles imitating engine noises and the low head room between the bunks being the open sky. Yes, this little chap had fought and been captured. We, if at all, would have to do our share of fighting after the capture.

"Don't think your room mates are representative of the Red Army," he whispered. "With them we would have lost the war long ago. Don't worry, the Soviet Union is a large country. Our lovely modern planes can easily handle the 'Luftwaffe.' It is only a matter of time. I'll come along every day now to tell you the latest rumors, but don't ever talk about me to anyone. There are many informers about, especially among my own crowd, the Ukrainians. You may have heard what the Germans do to 'communist propagandists.' I prefer to be just a chess player."

As a batch of prisoners left the block, making it less crowded, we were allowed to spend some hours a day in the yard between Blocks 13 and 14. There we sat in the sun, talked and made acquaintances.

Poles had been allowed to receive food parcels which they never let their eyes leave, in constant and justified fear of being robbed. The continuous presence of these treasures, being judiciously inspected by their owners and then devoured bit by bit, slice by slice, greatly annoyed us hungry have-nots. Food also represented power, and the prisoners who cordoned off the yard were far from incorruptible. Water would be bartered for chunks of Polish sausage, bread for bacon, and tobacco for margarine. We starvelings turned away our envious eyes and concentrated on traditional prison hobbies.

The knife-making craze, though forbidden, was in full swing. A few precious rusty nails I had found took turns in being flattened out between two stones. They proved useful for spreading margarine but never succeeded in becoming saleable assets. Another pastime was the fleas. They emerged black and shiny from our felt-lined clogs to start their jumps across the dusty, stone-littered yard. There revengeful prisoners lay in wait for them, a successful chase being rewarded by hearing your well-fed opponent explode between your fingernails.

What we could see of the camp seemed weird and incomprehensible. To the right, 60 yards away behind the fence, was the crematorium—a small unimportant branch of the ones of Birkenau, it was said. From the left, the camp band could be heard playing smart marches for the returning work groups. Outside the barbed wire SS men busily hurried from office to office.

Exuding from the ominous chimney on the right, and lingering above us, was thin gray smoke. A sinister "guess-what-I-see' game had developed around it. People with crooked minds tried to analyze its shape and smell. "Look there, doesn't it look like old Willie?" "No, no, you ass, it's a virgin; can't you see the small breasts sticking out?" "Go away, that's his nose!" I, however kept my eyes to the ground, looking for more nails.

The daily blessings of civilization consisted of a quarter loaf (350 grams) of black bread and one liter of foul-tasting soup brewed from weeds and thistles. Forty grams of margarine, which Germany produced from coal tar residues, were issued on Wednesdays and Thursdays, 50 on Saturdays. On Monday, Tuesday and Thursday there would be 50 grams of sausage, and one spoonful of jam on Tuesday and Friday. Sunday's "treat" was 50 grams of cheese, half a liter of goulash soup and a handful of potatoes in their skins. That, together with the morning and evening ladleful of acorn tea, was all that the working machines of the German Empire lived on.

Few prisoners kept food for later on. Rations were swallowed up as soon as they were received. As bread was issued in the evening, we went hungry till noon. If, due to some mistake in the distribution, there was any food left over, most of it would go to the block personnel.

The ordinary prisoner's lot would be to worry about when to join the queue, to achieve the right timing for holding out his enamelled metal bowl. Individual manners of ladling out soup became a study. Different soups, too, had their characteristics, fats making for the top, potatoes for the bottom of the vat. Skillful calculations would get results worthy to boast about: thick, rich vegetable soup, chunks of potatoes or meat, and sweet tea. Indeed, it was a subject to dream about.

We had been kept ignorant of the camp and of the outside world, when, one day in July, something unexpected happened. During the usual roll call I was told to step forward. My name, number, and place of birth were checked, and, to the surprise of the whole room, I was led away. Overcome with fear and uncertainty, I searched for reasons why, of all the many prisoners, it had to be me, the one who tried by all means to be inconspicuous. Had they found out about Father? Had anything happened to Mother? Did they think I was too young?

At the block office I was addressed by a cleanly dressed, rather short and stout prisoner speaking fluent German. His hair, contrary to camp regulations, had been allowed to grow and radiated like prickles from a hedgehog.

"I am one of the prisoners working at the registration office of the SS, in fact I am in charge of it, a very responsible position," he said with quiet self-confidence. "Having seen your index card I should like to know more about you. Tell me about your family. What happened to them after 1933?"

As I vaguely told him our story, he interrupted, asking for further details. Then he wanted to know more about Father. I tried to be tight-lipped. "Never mind," he bawled triumphantly, "you need not tell me. I know he left you in the lurch!"

"I have not forgotten you," he surprised me, "I knew you the day you were born. I used to live opposite your house, near Stettin. Don't you remember Keding, the one who brought the groceries? That is me. They got me in for alleged juggling with party funds; but now they regret it and are going to release me. That's why I grow my hair and got that confidential job. While I am still here, I will do my best to help you; but I have to do it secretly. There are many friends

of mine, old fellow prisoners who also need my assistance. They will
be envious and may even spread evil rumors. So don't tell anyone
about me. You'll find out that keeping silent will be for your own
good. Tomorrow, same time, be at the middle window, southern
side. When you see me, open it, but keep quiet. So long, and good
luck. I've to return to work now.''

I kept my promise, and next day I sneaked away to the appointed window. As he entered the yard below, I looked out. A little
parcel was thrown in. It contained bread and sausage.

The food was divided amongst us four friends—the first mani-
festation of our mutual sharing agreement. Suddenly, solely on
account of my new acquaintance, we youngsters had become everyone's favorites. After only three weeks of concentration camp even
former intellectuals saw fit to degrade themselves by implying that
we should help them too. Was youth going to follow their example?

The end of our time in quarantine was heralded by working
groups being assembled and sent off to other camps.

At Monowitz the giant I.G. Farben plant that was to produce
Buna, synthetic rubber, demanded an ever greater supply of cheap
construction laborers. Motorized Fascist armies cried out for tires.
Industrialists requested more workers; Birkenau's crematoria had
reaped in the exhausted bodies of those whose toil had ceased to
bring the expected profit. Their place had to be taken by new victims
fresh from quarantine.

To fill in the quota, even those of us who at the previous selection had been considered too weak were now sent along to this notorious sweatshop. Only seven of our transport remained in Auschwitz, among them we four youngsters.

Inexperienced as we were, we nevertheless had to make up our
mind about the impressions we wanted to make upon our superiors.
We gathered to decide upon a common attitude. Sally and Jonathan
wanted to apply for permission to join the bricklaying school, a most
peculiar camp institution. This, they had heard, was a kind of asylum for the young, where one could spend a few weeks in safety,
learning the trade. Gert and I, being familiar with gardening, and
imagining ourselves to be "tough guys," thought of undertaking
work straight away, hard as it might be.

After much pondering, however, we decided that we could not desert each other. Keeping together, pooling our weaknesses and strengths, we would endeavor to enter the school, dangerous as it might be to manifest one's unreadiness for work.

At the beginning of August we finally left the quarantine and had our first look at the camp. Its core comprised a few two-storied buildings of red brick, that had once been erected for the Polish army. Now there were three rows of them, 28 blocks, connected by asphalt paving. Cheerful flowers greeted one from weedless beds bordering the streets, and looked down from gaily painted boxes on the window sills. A well-kept lawn separated the camp from the surrounding wire fence. One could not help being favorably impressed by this model concentration camp—a show piece for any delegation, German or neutral, who should venture this far away from their sphere of interest.

The blocks were filled with small wooden bunks, every prisoner being privileged to have one of his own together with a meager sack of straw and three gray blankets. With bunks being arranged three tiers high, a block's capacity was 200 men in the basement, 400 on the four-roomed ground floor, 600 on the two-roomed first floor and 300 in the attic, 1500 in all. Seven blocks were reserved for the sick and three for administrative purposes. There were three storage barracks and a kitchen compound.

Fenced in by two rows of electrified, barbed wire, three meters high and shut off from the outside by a concrete wall, we had seen all now that was obvious about this new version of a prison.

It was only during the two daily roll calls that we saw SS men. Camp affairs were run by the prisoners themselves. Inside the fence the hierarchy, wearing appropriate armbands, consisted of the camp elder, the camp hairdresser, the camp interpreter, the camp secretary and the labor distributor. Overseers and block-elders made up the small fry. At work there were head-capos, capos, sub-capos and foremen, "capo" being Italian for commander.

The camp elder, a German, was an old-time criminal whom the SS had picked out from among the capos of one of the older concentration camps. His experienced superiors had found the right one to terrorize us. A favorite caprice of his was to get hold of some innocent, unaware bystander and to beat him up savagely for no reason at all.

Most of the supervising posts were filled by German criminals who, like him, also had their bouts of aggressiveness. Russians, Jews and Gypsies were not eligible for anything higher than a sub-capo.

Only at Birkenau, the hell on earth, no national distinctions were made, and there criminal specimens of any race would be allowed to show the weird cruelties they were capable of.

For us it was only now that we were to feel the full impact of the prisoner's lot. Only after surviving much suffering would the complete picture of the hidden, brutal set-up reveal itself.

CHAPTER II

Youth in Chains

A dozen shy youngsters, flushed with expectation, climbed the stairs of Block 7. Heading them, taking two steps at one go, were Gert and I, who, endowed with the charms of a fluent grammatical German, tinged with pleasant city manners, had been chosen to be the spokesmen. Then, step by step, came Sally and Jonathan. Following slowly, and at some distance, were the timid Poles and Russians.

Uneasy and aware that making a good impression was our only weapon, we entered the attic. Groups of young prisoners, some standing, others sitting, were ringed around heaps of blunt-cornered, moist red bricks and vats of mortar. They laid out brick bonds, built walls and took them down again, carefully scraping off the mortar and returning it to the vats. One instructor explained the secrets of arches, another demonstrated the skills of plastering. This was the brick-laying school.

The block personnel and some teachers, greeting us in a surprisingly kind manner, took down our particulars. Whatever their nationality, they, like ourselves, seemed eager to show their best. The block elder, the one to decide, was not in yet. "It's all up to him," we were advised, "so you had better look neat and disciplined." "He is very peculiar and full of whims. If he dislikes someone, he can be ghastly, and to those who offend him, he unleashes a fury of cruel brutality from which there is no escape." "His cold determination is like a double-edged sword. It protects his flock of youngsters from the inquisitive snifflings of hostile SS men with the same fearlessness that it mows down opponents. Be careful!"

When his arrival was announced, we quickly lined up in one row and stood at attention, caps pressed to the seam of the trousers.

Strolling in, like a sailor on leave, came a medium-sized prisoner wearing a faded but well pressed striped blue-white uniform, trouser legs widened at the bottom. His face, showing angular, severe features, might have been that of a simple German workman. The triangle on his breast was red, the personal number, next to it, in the thousands. It was obvious that he was a political opponent who had spent many a year in West German concentration camps before being sent here two winters ago. Now he was in charge of this unique asylum of youth, the brick-laying school. Some forty years old, he was father and dictator to 400 youngsters, coming from anywhere between Siberia and France.

He looked at us like a general surveying his troops. Then he approached a little Ukrainian, closely inspected his shaven head, scraped at it with his fingernail and exclaimed "dirty lout." The next object was myself, standing at the head of the row with ears rather prominent and high up. I had them pulled and peered into. Frightened at whatever he might find there to annoy him, I was nevertheless flattered by the way he had to look up to me. "Next time I'm going to pick you out for growing carrots on," he growled. Our prestige seemed at its lowest now.

Again he faced the row legs apart, his arms at the waist. "You can stand at ease now, you May bugs," he bawled finally, "you are now members of the brick-laying school." Then, flapping the wide ends of his trouser legs, he walked up and down fixing his glance on each of us in turn.

"Don't think you can live here as you did at Block 2a," he warned, stopping in front of the Polish boys with their food parcels under their arms. "This is Block 7a, where I determine the rules. Forget about the camp around you, and stay in your rooms. Even Block 7, the ground floor, is out of bounds to you. Don't ever let me catch you lingering about where you are not supposed to be!

"There are not going to be any thefts nor wrangles in my block. Woe to him who dares to offer bribes. Block 7a means order, cleanliness, discipline and comradeship. Those who will not adjust themselves may stay outside with their grown-up friends, and see how long they will be helped to live. But I shan't take an interest in you, when you come back, half-dead, begging to be let in again.

"Anyone daring to disobey my orders or those of the block-personnel will be sent to me. I'll make him feel the consequences," he continued, threateningly expanding his chest. "If the offense is serious, I shall have as little mercy on him as he had concern for the rest of you. I don't want to have the school closed down because of a few irresponsible ones. There will be controls to see that you are washed, make your beds properly and have no hidden food, that your heads are clean, your hair cut off adequately and that you don't sleep with your socks on. If you will co-operate, I'll do my best to 'organize' additional food and to keep you alive. When you have learned something you'll be sent to work as a group on your own, but still continue to belong to this block. I expect you to do me all honor then because our common future depends on it.

"Remember," he said in his provincial dialect, "there are to be no national cliques or quarrels about your pasts. In my block, there have been none so far, and I want to hear no complaints about you.

"Room elder, take charge of them!"

After the roll call we trod the freshly-cleaned, red concrete floor of our new home. We four were given bunks in the German compound of the room which, the boys there being Jews from Berlin, was called Little Berlin. Most of the block inmates, just coming back from the building site, were exhausted from a tiring day's work, but this rare occasion, the questioning of new-comers, warranted giving up some hours of precious sleep. Crowding together for a welcome, we were soon involved in lively conversation. Little Berlin now had a "Blonde Gert," a "Dark Gert," a "Saucy Gert," a "Little Kurt" and a "Long Kurt," nine members in all.

The other new-comers joined Little Kiev and its numerous Waskas and Wajnkas or Little Warsaw with its Janneks and Taddeks. Looking on were boys from France, Belgium, Czechoslovakia and

Austria. As a first sign of understanding we would have to learn the names of all of them, pronouncing them correctly. Later, we might even attempt to tackle each other's languages. Till then the odd names of the Gypsy boys seemed too short to be distinguished; the long, elaborate ones of Little Salonika too complicated to be remembered.

The main camp of Auschwitz had a comparatively large number of young prisoners. Out of every hundred inmates about two were between the ages of 13 and 18. In 1943 nearly all of them were either Russians, Gypsies from Czechoslovakia, Germany, Austria and Poland, Greek Jews or Poles.

It was surprising how much we youngsters differed from our grown up compatriots. We had not yet absorbed all the national prejudices and illusions that hate thrives on. There was no particular way of life that we had become accustomed to, for throughout the years of our teens there had been war. Now we were facing our fate as one unit: youth.

Differences among us never caused serious troubles, but they provided entertainment. Ukrainians, proud of their muscles, did acrobatics, inviting those who still had sufficient energy to challenge them. Wherever those skillful Eastern performers may have come from, they were just as capable of friendship as the boys I had grown up with.

Gypsies were harder to understand, but once you had proved that you respected them as your equals, they would even reveal the secrets of Romany to you, the language that kept them together. This was the greatest honor possible for an outsider, accorded only to the few true friends who succeeded in gaining their confidence. Other acquaintances of theirs were merely treated to sessions of clair-voyance.

Jews, proving themselves to be workers just as good and skillful as anyone else, adapted themselves to the new surroundings best of all. Proud to show their knowledge, quite a few of them had been nicknamed "professor."

We could not help being impressed by this hopeful atmosphere that youth had created for itself among the holocaust of its elders.

Perhaps the block elder was right in his cruel threats against those who might have disturbed it.

As the days passed, we accustomed ourselves to the daily routine. In the morning at 5 o'clock sharp, the ringing of the camp bell jerked us away from warm, blissful forgetfulness. Thousands of bunk frames all over the camp started shaking, littering the rooms with flakes of straw and driving off clouds of dust as if these were futile dreams. Rushing out, hastily dressed in their trousers, and heading for the crowded washrooms came human beings who lived on bread and water. They emptied their bowels and wet their skinny hands and shaven heads. Back in the room, they lined up for whatever it is that acorns give up when boiled in water. It seemed good, even to the many who had not hidden a crumpled slice of last afternoon's meager bread ration.

Then beds were made, carefully fondling the sacks of straw to induce them to look full and straight—the way the Third German Empire expected of all its subjects, especially the blonde ones. *"Das Tausendjaehrige Reich"* was so keen on this "bed-building" process that it frequently had it supervised by one of its agents, who was fully aware of the enormous difference in life expectancy between the equipment of the Fuehrer and the prisoner who used it.

By six the blocks were empty, their inmates assembled in working groups called commandos. Fifteen minutes later, passing the bandstand, they marched out of camp. The block personnel and the seven-dozen-strong brick-laying school remained behind.

At twelve the bell rang again to announce dinner time. Big heavy wooden vats with soup were being carried from the kitchen. The carefully-ladled-out liter was a mere stimulant, except once or twice a week, when as a second helping it acted as filler. Our mid-day hour's break, then, was spent walking about the camp in the hope of "organizing" more.

To organize meant to get something by any means from begging to looting. If you looked pitiable enough, some soft-hearted room elder—who had received too big a vat and whose own protegees were out of camp—might treat you to a bowl of soup. The others, the Ukrainian country boys at the head, invaded the kitchen dump, stinking and rotting as it was. When driven away we returned to push long, pointed rods through the railings in order to poke away at whatever treasures we may have been deprived of—moldy bread, rotten cabbage, and potato peelings. If by the ringing of the one o'clock bell you had fished something worthwhile, it meant being admired for your success and begged to share it.

Then we resumed counting the bricks we laid and the hours towards the next meal.

I often thought of that Russian prisoner-of-war back in easy-going Berlin.

At a quarter to six the dirty and exhausted working columns started to come back. The roll call, commencing at half past six, usually lasted from a quarter of an hour to an hour. Then, as we streamed back to the block, rations were issued.

Two hours were left for "private affairs." Most youngsters spent them in the search for potential benefactors, adult friends who were able to organize extra food. A few took advantage of the vacant washrooms or mended their clothing. Others queued up outside the dispensary or lulled themselves to the land of fantasies by listening to orchestra rehearsals. Some looked up friends to get themselves educated on subjects ranging from "organizing" to politics. For others still the strenuous working day had dispelled all the interest they may have had in the world they found themselves in. After gobbling up their rations they went straight to bed.

Members of "Little Berlin," having few friends and still fewer compatriots, stayed home. Dark Gert and Jonathan, silent lads, just sat on their beds contemplating. Long Kurt, his big frame making him perhaps the hungriest of us all, had set up a sock mending business. As his cherished needle bobbed in and out of the dilapidated socks of his clients, he kept up our spirits with tales from his native Koenigsberg. For those wanting to laugh—like little baby-faced Kurt whose childish naivete still did not seem to leave him—there was Saucy Gert, never tired of unravelling his stock of spicy jokes.

At eight-thirty, sometimes nine-thirty, the bell rang in the curfew. A few minutes later it announced: lights out.

Our instructors had been chosen for their knowledge of languages. All but one of them were Jews and had no previous knowledge of the building trade.

Outstanding was a Polish Jew from Belgium who, already lecturing in Polish, Russian, Czech, Yiddish, German and French, was now embarking on the study of Greek and Romany.

Then there was Mr. Pollak, an elderly surveyor from Slovakia, the school's one and only natural bald head (an accomplishment he seemed immensely proud of). It certainly served him well as a subject for jocular conversations with outside visitors who, as a kind of liaison officer, he was supposed to entertain. One of his clients was the stout contractor, the civilian responsible for our school who, it was said, had come all the way from Berlin. Whenever this jolly-looking guest arrived for his monthly tour of inspection, he quickly walked past us and then shut himself in with Mr. Pollak. These sessions, lasting well over an hour, ended with the civilian rushing off with as businesslike an air as possible. Minutes later Pollak emerged, his straightened finger rubbing his stubby nose, then adjusting his spectacles. Pacing as correctly as a schoolteacher was supposed to, he tried hard to conceal his grin. Then he gave it up, sat down and lit the cigar, his cherished reward. "Yes," we would hear him say to the other teachers, "it looks bad for Germany, but not much better for ourselves."

Leopold Weil "Poldi," a Swiss Jew who had been arrested in France, was our youngest instructor. His mother applied for his release and after much waiting, a date was fixed for his return to Switzerland. A few days before it, however, he was put in solitary confinement. He was accused of "spying for a foreign power" which, had he been freed, would have become true. They sent him to a punishment squad, never to be heard of again.

Our room elder, Sigi, was a frail little German Jew who, because of some criminal offense, had many years of concentration camps behind him. In one of them, before the war, while working in a machine shop he had lost one arm and severely mutilated the other.

With the 5 o'clock morning peals hardly faded, he would rush about the room to shout "waky, waky!" Jerking his stumped arm he managed to pull away blankets, and sometimes to pour water onto our sleepy faces. As we admired his agility, we only had our own laziness to blame for these early morning showers. By and by, we even came to like his pranks.

We, his compatriots, tried hard to get favors from him but without success. He never budged from his stand of a fair share for all.

The youngest of our superiors was "Ello," the deputy room elder. A robust lad, he enjoyed treating us to episodes from amorous exploits back home, rounding off each of his tales with "Oh, let me go, Ello, you are a pig" sung to his favorite tune, a Czech variant of "Roll Out the Barrel," called "Rosamunde."

At 19, he, a Slovak soldier, had been lined up at the railway-station, ready to be transferred to the Eastern front. Present, too, were Gestapo agents. They read out the names of the Jews, disarmed them and sent them straight to Auschwitz.

It struck me as odd that the number of Jews in the fascist armies of Eastern Europe, who fought side by side with Hitler, had been so much greater than the total surviving Jews in the camps of Auschwitz.

To lessen the rush on the hospital during the busy evening hours, when many of the ill had to be turned away, the authorities had consented to let our school have a "doctor" of its own. This we were grateful for, as visits to the camp dispensary meant risking one's life.

The "doctor," a male nurse too soft-hearted to be strict, who treated us as if we were little children, had set up shop in a corner of the attic. Daily, one by one, we sneaked away from the piles of moist bricks and queued up to see him. Most of us saw him every week, either because of real ailments or because we liked to hear him say exasperatedly: "Oh, go away, you little scoundrel, there's nothing wrong with you, you'll still live to be a hundred!"

His equipment consisted of a tray with many-colored ointments from which he would let you choose the one you liked best. "Little Jendroe," he would call good-humoredly to a Gypsy boy passing by, "do tell our Janek, who is very, very ill, what color you liked best for your skin disease."

We kept him busy because, hidden from the eyes of the SS, our various complaints remained a secret among ourselves. When he had time to spare, he, a Belgian Jew, spent it trying to "organize" medicines. Sometimes a hospital friend of his would give him vitamin tablets. Distributing them judiciously was one of our benefactor's gladdest moments. "Only for those who get no parcels from home," he would announce, impishly aware that, excepting the five Poles, we received no mail at all.

With no means to fight my hunger I tried to contact Mr. Keding, the family friend whose sudden appearance at the quarantine block had caused such a sensation. Evening after evening, vainly hoping to catch a glimpse of him, I loitered in front of Block 3 which, divided into comfortable little rooms, was the home of the prominent prisoners, capos and old-time "criminals" from Germany. No ordinary camp inmate, even if invited, could dare enter it.

Then one day I met him. He told me his story: "As you know I was a shopkeeper and you may wonder what brought me here. Well it was a kind of family affair. There was cash missing from my till and I suspected my wife. I made up my mind and told her of it. We got excited and quarrelled. She claimed that she had given the money to the N.S.V., the Nazi Welfare Fund, but in my temper it made no difference to me and I must have cursed both of them a bit too hard. Then my wife left me. She must have told people about the incident, because I was soon accused of 'violently' attacking the institutions of the party. That's why I am here."

"Now," he said, seeming not at all glad of it, "they are going to send me back again. My old party membership must have impressed them, especially now that things look grim for Germany."

He introduced me to an aggressive-looking German "criminal," a friend of his: "This buddy here will stand by you when I have gone. Remember his name and his block. When you need advice, go and see him."

Keding inquired whether I liked sugar. I certainly did and we arranged to meet again the next day.

Wondering why, in this world where there were not even stale bread crumbs to gnaw, he should take an interest in my sweet tooth, I could hardly wait to see him again. At once after the evening roll call I rushed off to Block 3. Keding was waiting for me with a bag of wet brown sugar.

"That's the only thing I could do for you," he apologized, "but it is quite a clever trick of mine. Once a week, as I come back from work, entering the gate as a one-man working group, I am allowed to take in a big jug of coffee for the German inmates of Block 3. At the SS kitchen they let me sweeten it myself. So, I fill the jug with sugar, then saturate it with coffee. At the block I drain off the brew and there you are."

Clutching the generous gift, I felt like a beggar receiving a ten-pound note but uneasy about guarding such a treasure.

"Farewell then," called my busy benefactor as he headed for his room, "you won't be seeing me anymore, I am going home next week. Good luck, kid."

Coming back to our block, I was at once surrounded by my roommates. Sugar was an unheard-of thing in a concentration camp. They all wanted to taste it. I could not refuse them, who were beggars like myself.

The rest of the bag was divided among us four friends, the members of the sharing pact. Gobbled up as fast as possible, it nevertheless lasted two days. But far outliving the sweetness on our tongues were complaints that "he had made himself popular with the others at our cost." "You had no right," I was reproached, "to be generous with our part of the bag."

It was long afterwards that someone told me another version of Keding's past.

Before 1933 our friend's hobby seemed to have been scouting. A leader, he now and then used to accommodate his little group of boy scouts at his home. He ceased these activities on being brought to court and accused of having had homosexual relations with his proteges. Then Hitler came. Keding donned a brown SA uniform and all was well again.

Why then, I asked myself, was he classified as a political prisoner? Faded as it was, maybe his triangle had not been red at all, but pink, pink the color of the convicted homosexuals! This, too, may have explained his desire not be seen in my company so soon before his release.

As the stream of prisoners kept coming and going, the true Keding story remained a mystery. The stout little shopkeeper had been forgotten.

New arrivals necessitated some of us being sent away to other camps. This time the destination was Birkenau, the supposed job there brick-laying. But it was only a five-minute ride from there to the forest which hid the camouflaged gas-chambers. We knew that only too well. So did our block elder, the one who would do the painful picking-out.

We were lined up. There were a hundred too many of us. At first the block elder, without even looking up, called out the list of the troublemakers: the Polish lad who did black market business, the Gypsy boys with weak bladders, the kids with contagious scalp diseases, the few extreme nationalists and—those who slept with their socks on. Then he walked along the row. Having no alternative he picked out those who, he thought, could take care of themselves without him.

That evening we stayed in our rooms. Our morale was severely shaken. All that was left of Little Berlin was Blonde Gert, Little and Long Kurt, my friend Saucy Gert and I. We were not even certain that we had been lucky. Only eight months ago, when all the surviving youngsters had been concentrated at the brick-laying school, the whole block, teachers and all, had been transferred to Birkenau never to be heard of again.

The youngest of the camp inmates was a baby-faced, Slavic-looking twelve year old Polish Jew. Together with four cousins of his, a little older than himself but just as small in appearance, he had come to Auschwitz in May 1943. At the station, as their newly arrived transport had faced the fatal selection, these five boys had been picked out to serve as camp messengers.

The three allocated to our camp lived at Block 16. Known as "runners," they spent their busy day rushing about to keep up the contact between the capos and the SS command.

We tried to be on good terms with these smartly dressed, midget-sized kids for, besides knowing all the latest news, they were the intimates of many an influential camp personage. Spoiling the friendly ties between us and the "runner" boys, however, were ever re-appearing accusations that their continued success in such envied positions was being bought by playing the whores. Rumors even had it that their underpants were laced and pink.

"Well," Blonde Gert lectured me, "why shouldn't they? Back at the Monowitz camp, I too had homosexual relations with my capo. It gave satisfaction to both of us and there was no point in refusing. What else could have saved me from hard work, hunger and illness?

"Look at Little Kurt, childish and naive as he is," Gert went on to tell me, "even he has been had. You just ask him and see how much he giggles about it, the silly ass."

Youngsters who through lack of self-control had surrendered themselves to the lusts of their sex-starved acquaintances were looked upon with disgrace and had to keep quiet about their experiences. Kurt, however, could not be blamed for actions he was too innocent to understand. His helpless self, pulling grimaces and reciting nursery rhymes, could only evoke pity.

Kurt was our problem child. Coming from a reputable family of Berlin intellectuals, he must have been spoiled at home and kept in ignorance of the world around him. Now he made such a nuisance of himself that, beginning to doubt his senses, we earnestly started to father him.

One of his crazes was to bother us boys, teachers, room elders and all, with a newly learned ditty about girls, which actually we ourselves had taught him. We even caught him at it, poor kid, in one of the neighboring blocks, where his ridiculously serious way of singing was being greeted by hilarious applause—and later charitably rewarded with a bowl of soup.

Another, less easily remedied whim of his was to spit at anyone who was teasing him. Comic a character as he was, it was only natural that one poked fun at him. He himself even admitted that he looked like an "arse with ears." When it came to picking his opponents, from whom he later on depended on us to rescue him, he also, unfortunately, acted like one—for his favorite choice was big, muscular Ukrainians.

The majority of the SS men doing guard duty had been recruited from fascist satellite countries. Although representatives of "Germanic glory," they were as ignorant of its language as the prisoners who had come from these places. Mere mercenaries, they may even have developed the same hatred for it.

One did not have to be a philosopher to seek the irony of our present-day civilization. It was right at our block, its victim a Gypsy boy. His very father was wearing the uniform of the suppressors. A Slovak, he had enlisted before Hitler's decision to exterminate the Gypsies—possibly the oldest race of Aryan origin. With the silvery skull-and-crossbones emblem of the SS pinned to his forage cap, he drove a truck, the same kind of truck that had taken his next of kin to the gas chambers. Sometimes he passed our camp but his son did not dare talk to him. Fearing denunciation, they would just wave at each other. Maybe they were even glad not to be reminded of each other.

It was a queer world we were living in, but I could not figure out who was causing it to be so. I picked on the obedient tools of the SS Empire but the image of the Gypsy boy's father, governed by orders and fears, driving on in his lone cabin made me change my mind. I thought of blaming our plight on Hitler, but then I had seen him myself only a few feet away. He was no more flesh and blood than my helpless self. I concentrated my hate on the aristocracy whose trade was war, whose profits came from the I.G. Farben plant at Monowitz and whose officer sons had come to supervise us, yet I was challenged by the world, which is not governed by impulse but by tradition.

I contemplated about God, the heavenly being I was not aware of. Could it be that he was more concerned about the human animal than he was about all the other creatures of the universe?

Our nearest subject of thought was the room we lived in. The daily routine had made it our home, a place we were no longer afraid of.

To eliminate the troubles from straw and dust, which each morning fell unto the freshly made lower bunks, we had evolved a bed-making schedule. The occupiers of the upper bunks (veteran prisoners and block personnel) should be the first to spread their blankets, within a certain time limit. Then came the middle and lower bunks.

Prominent inmates chose upper beds because, these having more head-room, they could be walked over when there was need to escape from them. It was people in the middle bunks who bore the brunt of the various room inspections. Floor level occupants again, were out of sight but the ones who suffered most from carelessly stepping feet and spilled liquids—hot or cold.

As if wanting to cheer us up, some rooms had been painted with camp slogans. Blazoned upon the whitewashed upper half of the wall and staring at the upper bunks of our room was the inevitable "There is only one road to freedom—its milestones are diligence, obedience. . . ." We ignored it either because we could not read it or because it annoyed us.

Trying to impress us were the same phrases that had lulled German youth into fateful subservience to the evil designs of their teachers. Now they were merely ridiculous. When the room was repainted, they disappeared.

The daily roll call when, standing to attention ten deep, we were counted by the gloved finger of an arrogant SS corporal, was a constant reminder of our insignificance. When the total of prisoners present and the number recorded in the books did not agree—a nearly weekly occurrence—our ordeal would drag on for hours. To see a whole camp of tired "subhumans" lined up at his mercy was a sure bait to any mastermind of sadism, and the Nazis quickly exploited their chance.

"Block-Leader 7a" was keen on "flower box drill" and had a favorite candidate for it, our school doctor. It meant holding up one of the jolly but heavy green boxes that lined the window sills and keeping the balance while the corporal, his revolver drawn, built a pyramid of flower pots on it.

Before long we developed a method of "screening off" potential victims with stronger, better-looking prisoners, less liable to be picked out, who made up the front, back and side rows. When the SS found it out, however, they gave up "walking around" and started to enter our rows, kicking and beating.

To look too much of a Russian or to have a Jewish nose meant to be a continual scapegoat. But to make the impression of not being the caricature you were supposed to be was little better.

"How dare you lousy Gypsy brat be blonde?" they would bark. "Your mother must have been quite a whore!"

A camp Sunday was a relatively quiet event.

The morning hours were occupied by numerous tasks for which there had been no time during the busy, tiresome week. Your one and only set of clothing always needed a brush-up. There were new, clean numbers to be sewed on and socks to be mended. Those who felt that a fortnightly change of underwear was not enough, laundered their pants. We queued up for the hairdressers and cleaned the block. Then, at noon, we greased our rough leather boots—usually two odd ones—and went down to the roll call.

Sunday roll calls meant inspections, and one block would have to be picked out for being the dirtiest. We of the brick-laying school, in our precarious position, certainly could not afford to be conspicuous.

The distribution of the soup was followed by a two hours' curfew during which the camp was supposed to take a midday nap. After that, with the exception of the few who slept through till the next morning, we woke up with an empty stomach urging us to spend the rest of the day "organizing," to get things by all means possible.

Our afternoons, then, meant roaming the camp in a vain depressing search for friends and food. Our plight was further aggravated by the fact that, while misery and hunger tend to be things invisible, wealth and plenty have ways of manifesting themselves. We did not see the feelings of our fellow sufferers, only the food parcels of the few privileged ones. Also catching our eyes as if mocking at our helplessness was the arrogance of the SS families beyond the fence taking their leisurely Sunday walk.

The only consolation was a good, long sleep.

One day a tall, friendly Pole came to see me, the first visitor I had since quarantine. "I know that your block elder doesn't like strangers here, but I had to see you personally," he said slowly in broken German. His self-confidence impressing me even before I knew his mission, we made for a quiet corner. There he produced a carefully-folded little slip of paper: "That is for you. Give me an answer by tomorrow, when I'll be back at the same time. I am in a hurry to get out of here. So goodbye, good luck!"

Unwrapping it fold by fold, I was finally faced by a smudgy sheet bearing a pencil-written message. I looked at the words that stood for the signature. There was no mistake about it; they said "your mother."

I was flushed with excitement. News of my luck spread quickly and soon I was surrounded by dozens of roommates who, claiming to be my best friends, wanted to hear details—but above all to see the word "mother." There was a double reason for rejoicing: someone had found a mother, the being dearest to all of us; and some noble friend had risked his life to smuggle in a message from the women's camp of Birkenau.

Next week, the note said, some women, among them mother, were to pass through our camp. Nearly all the roommates who did not go out to work were eager to come along with me to welcome her. More than the "mother," it was the "women" that attracted them.

They had long been craving to view females; but—a stunning disappointment—the block elder, fearing trouble from the SS guards, decided that only the room elder and I were to see her.

After a week of impatient waiting, then, we two, baskets under our arms for the supposed purpose of fetching the rations, walked down the main street, deserted as it was during the morning hours.

The column of women in striped dresses with drab kerchiefs on their heads was led along by armed gray uniformed SS women. We had expected to see glamorous females, but they turned out to be miserable prisoners like ourselves, veterans rather than women. Their sufferings were written all over them.

I hardly recognized mother. Still in her early thirties, she looked as harsh as her companions. I kissed her. Without stopping in her walk she expressed her hope that my work was not hard. Then she wanted to give me some bread. While I refused it, the guard came to chase me away.

Our encounter had lasted a bare fifteen seconds. . . .

The women's lot, I found out from the messenger friend, was no easy one. Factory and store yard workers, navvies, farm hands and seamstresses, their working day like ours was eleven hours. Only the young and attractive among them—for reasons that did not arise with male prisoners—were eligible for office jobs.

To have seen mother and to be in contact with her had a great effect on me. My determination to survive, no matter what the dangers, was now encouraged by three considerations. At the neighboring camp there was mother, waiting for letters that would quiet her fears. Beyond the sea fighting with the Allies was father, hoping that his efforts might help us. Out in the world there was the future, beckoning us youngsters to become men.

Following the news of my mother I decided to see the camp hairdresser at Block 1 and to tell him of it. Maybe the vague promise of help that he had given me on our arrival would materialize.

Impressed by his being such a personage as to have a room of his own, I knocked at his door. "How nice of you to have come," he greeted me. "But before we talk, do have something to eat—anyway that is what most people come to see me for."

As I looked down the little window that opened onto the shower-room, where a trio of Gypsy songsters with a guitar entertained a group of camp V.I.P.'s, he laid out food the like of which was scarce even in the capital of plenty, Berlin. Then, with the sentimental Romany melodies of the other set of canvassing have-nots resounding from below, I helped myself.

When I had polished the plate clean, I told him the news. He remained quite unimpressed by it. No, he could show no good will to me, or the other youngsters, except between the four walls that hid him from his rivals.

"But I always have some tidbits left for you youngsters. Come along sometimes in the evenings, you might even be good company," he consoled me.

"You know I am an old jailbird and have some experience of 'organizing.' That has been my life for over ten years now. Hitler or no Hitler, I won't get out of here—but you who could get out, won't survive it. It would have been better for you never to have seen such a place."

"Look out of this window," he said, pointing to the endless rows of electrified fence topped by red and white light bulbs. "Do you think they and the gas chambers and crematoria at Birkenau have been built so that we may survive them? They mean destruction. This then is the world that wants to show us criminals and you youngsters how to be civilized!"

My newly found benefactor was far from being a beacon of hope but, as he was hospitable and one of the five most influential camp inmates, I decided to cultivate his friendship. As a rule I went to see him twice a week.

The shrivelled up face of my companion might have been that of a simple, unpretentious book-keeper. He was bald and wore dentures. His blue eyes looked through a cherished pair of glasses. Something, however, reminded one of his illustrious past. On his chest and arms was a fading, bluish assortment of tattoos: hearts, daggers and initials.

He told me stories of his exploits as a safe-cracker, the days of glorious independence, of his family that had long since forgotten him and of the hardships at the moorland concentration camps on the Ems. As a veteran expert on prison life he seemed to have resigned himself to it.

"You know why I take such an interest in the naked arrivals just before they take their showers?" he asked me. "I don't do it out of sympathy. It is my job to interview the new prisoners. If they talk to me I quickly pass on to another group. It is those who keep silent that I am looking for. People afraid to open their mouths have something hidden in them. My task, then, is to find out what. Usually it is valuables which I am supposed to hand over to the SS.

"But," he continued, pulling open his drawer to reveal glittering jewels and golden coins, "I am no such fool as to let them have all of it. Trusted friends of mine exchange these treasures for whatever I am in need of, and I can tell you that even SS officers are not indifferent to them."

The camp hairdresser drew my attention to a square patch of flooring next to the wall, that was of a different shade. "You see this? Back in 1941, with a cupboard over it, this was the entrance to an escape tunnel dug by Russian prisoners of war. It seems incredible, but they got within a few yards of the last fence before being discovered. Now, of course, it's all blocked up and none of the poor devils are alive anymore."

Then, one day, having told his usual disheartening stories and again mentioning the many enemies that were looking for a chance to ruin him, he startled me.

"The time has come when I can no longer afford to help you without asking something in return. You know that not only do we miss our women, but we hardly remember their pleasures." He had locked the door and was starting to unbutton his trousers. I was bewildered. My only way to get out would have been to hit him, and that I did not dare. For lack of inspiration, I just sat there motionless, not giving the slightest sign of willingness. Again he beckoned me, pleading that he was getting cold.

Then he gave up. "I am sick of you sitting there as if someone wanted to kill you. You are no good and I am just wasting my time." As he unlocked the door, I wanted to rush off, never to see him again, but he stopped me. "Never mind, I'll find plenty of others. Still I won't abandon you altogether. Go to Block 1a now and then and take yourself the bowl of soup they reserve for me."

Saucy Gert and Long Kurt just laughed at me when I told of my adventure. "Yes, that damned old wretch is famous for his passions," they grinned, "and if someone tries denunciation, the old schemer sends him off to Birkenau. You can be lucky he didn't use threats. It's not a bad idea pretending to be naive and innocent. Many boys do this trick, but at the crucial moment it becomes rather dangerous. After fooling the old fox for all these weeks, however, you should be quite an expert now."

Old camp hands, they were probably right. Nearly all of us younger boys had been made offers and only a few of the prominent prisoners abstained from making them. Homosexuality was an open secret, despite the efforts to stamp it out.

A few months later we learned that the camp hairdresser, after being in trouble with an SS officer, had been sent away to a newly-erected subsidiary camp. Our block elder's cynic remarks about "adult friends" seemed justified now. "To fool around with people in the limelight becomes a dangerous sport. When they go under, they drag along their associates."

Block 7a, despite its strict and sometimes merciless rule, kept on being a refuge from the intrigues haunting the camp. It was a haven where the ups and downs of prison life faded against the brightness of a free, honest exchange of views—lost themselves among the overwhelming radiance of youthful hope.

Before long we experienced one of the dreaded selections, the picking out of prisoners no longer profitable to their masters for the mills of death at Birkenau.

After the evening roll call the whole camp was marched into the roadway leading to the bath-house, the Birkenweg. With electrified wires running parallel on one side and guards on the other, there was no escape from the lane. With our spirits at the lowest possible ebb, we waited for hours while the huge queue crawled on to enter the inspection rooms. The ominous silence was broken only by a lone clatter echoing from the main street, the hasty running steps of the lucky ones who had passed the ordeal.

Some of us prayed. A few thought of home. Others, having given up hopes for survival, seemed indifferent as to when fate chose to call them.

Trained on us from the watchtowers was the firepower of four machine-guns, well able to put an end to our speculations. Even the veteran German prisoners, confident of their privileged status, were afraid. Whatever our thoughts were, we kept silence.

It was now our turn. We entered the moist, cold bathroom, undressed, took the bundle of clothes and ran past the SS doctors as quickly as our young legs could carry us. Those who passed ran back to the safety of the block, hardly bothering even to dress again.

The block elder used all his influence to save us and then whispered into the ears of the officer: "The kids really worked a lot today, let them run through quickly so that they can go to bed." This time the gamble was successful and only a handful of us were retained.

Sleep came hard, however, that evening. We who had been given another month's lease of life thought of those driven away in lorries, the youngsters who would soon see the terrors of the gas-chambers. The world had forgotten them. There was nothing we could do about it.

The ever-recurring onslaughts of fear and our common hardships made us draw together still further. Acquaintances became companions, companions comrades.

Among my new friends was Mendel Tabatshnik, a bright Jewish boy from Bialystok whom I was extremely fond of. Not much older than myself, he had been in the camp since the winter of 1942, quite an achievement for a youth. An idealist, living on the past and for the future, his moral conduct was admirable. He never talked about camp problems and did not concern himself much with "organizing." His food seemed to be his dreams and recollections.

One of the most impressive moments of his life had been at Moscow where in 1940 he had participated in a mass display of gymnastics. "Imagine yourself to be on top of a human pyramid, with a vast crowd looking on, in the most famous square of the most talked about capital in the world," he would say, his eyes glistening with enthusiasm.

Then there was "Little Berger," an amusing young Gypsy from Austria. A bright lad endowed with intelligence and wit, he had used his time in camp to acquire the art of writing. We adored him for his realistic criticism of the staged primitiveness and egotism displayed by the other small Gypsy boys, the block favorites who were actually much older than they looked and behaved.

Little Berger was an open-hearted friend as long as talk revolved around camp affairs; but when one mentioned the outside world, he would retract into his protective shell. He definitely had an inferiority complex. "You needn't think that because I am only a Gypsy—" was a standard phrase of his. Maybe he was even right when he said "The Jews outside are all big shots, just as eager to hurt the Gypsies as anyone else is."

"Should he ever have a chance, he will make an eager, promising student," said our instructors. "But till then, our world would have to do a lot of changing."

"Jendroe," a Czech Gypsy of thirteen, was the smallest and, as a result, the most ostentatious and presumptuous among us. Backed by his several brothers, he knew well to exploit the sympathy we all accorded him—a skill that made him a personage. Clustering around him were the other Czech Gypsies, members of the same clan, ever anxious to guard their common mysticism from the prying eyes of modern minded rivals, lads like "Little Berger."

Another noisy block inmate, also trying to gather followers, was an Odessa boy who proclaimed himself to be a Jew-hater. His father, a participant in pogroms, had always urged him to be anti-Semitic and now that "the Jewish bosses had abandoned him to the Germans while they themselves retreated to Moscow" his prophecies seemed to have become true. "Even here in the camp," he howled, his frail, blonde forehead beaded with sweat, "it's the Jews who are going to kill me." His fears were not unfounded; we did beat him up occasionally.

Also honoring the school with his presence was a lone German, an ignorant country lad wearing a red triangle. How he managed to be a "political opponent" remained a secret. Even he, himself did not "remember" it. He may have been picked up as a suspected Gypsy while loitering about the countryside, and by the time he became aware of his fate, his captors of their mistake, it was probably too late for his release. His slow mind was now being troubled still further by the unkind fact that we all avoided him as much as possible. Like "Little Kurt" he was a candidate for madness.

At the women's camp of Birkenau lived the only Jewish child, a boy of four—very popular with guards and prisoners alike. Once he came to our camp to see his mother who at that time was at Block 10, the experimental hospital for women. Having come with the same transport and knowing him from the transition camp, I contrived to see him.

"What do you want?" the blonde Berliner hissed at me, contemptuously waving his tattooed little arm the way they had taught him, "Get away with you, *Schiess in Wind!*"

A prisoner's best friends were melodies. On Sunday mornings, when the camp band gave auditions at the SS compound beyond the fence, many of us crowded ourselves into the roadway between Block 1 and 12 to catch a glimpse of it. The band, dressed in their zebra striped presentation suits and equipped with an assortment of highly polished brass, was seated on a lawn surrounded by a hedge. Promenading about the landscape garden were the leisurely guests of honor, the officers and their girls, the wives and their babies. Looking on, surrounded by high voltage wires, shifting from one tired leg to the other, was the other crowd, neither invited nor worth considering. Tunes, impartial as they are, make for forgetting, and while our ears absorbed their magic, eyes on either side of the fence became indifferent.

In summer, when every other Sunday afternoon meant concert time, the members of the band were seated on a wooden platform near the camp-kitchen and formed a real orchestra. Its conductor was a Pole, formerly a well-known member of Radio Warsaw.

It seemed as though the melodies had been picked to be inspiring and we felt that there could have been no other place where their meaning would have been deeper.

When the evening clouds floated westwards as if in a hurry to leave us, taking along scraps of music, our thoughts mingled with them. The clouds were free. Music was ageless. Thoughts were limitless.

But we and millions like us were held by chains; chains we did not see and could not break; chains we had not known of; chains forged by a dying civilization to shackle its youth.

CHAPTER III

Work Makes Free

It was a dismal morning, with the foggy dew from the Sola River lingering over the camp, the first eastern sun rays faintly penetrating the darkness.

The camp bell rang in the daily fight within ourselves, heavenly sleep against worldly reality. I rubbed my eyes. At first I realized where I was; then I remembered that it was my fourteenth birthday. There had even been a lone letter reminding me of it, from mother. It was tucked away in my shirt pocket, urging me to be brave.

A child's birthday is a big affair, but as he becomes older, less and less presents are bestowed on him. That day I had none at all; I seemed to have become a man.

In the evening I went to see the courier who had brought the birthday letter, the same loyal irreplaceable Polish well-wisher who had delivered the first message. When I arrived at his block, fittingly numbered 14, it looked as though he expected me. Waiting for me was a bowl of soup and some bread, a real birthday treat.

To cheer me up, he told me more about mother. She worked as a mechanic at the "Union" metalwork factory and lived in Block 2 of the Birkenau women's camp.

Then my new friend, tall and in his thirties, took me for a walk. "Now that I know you better—and that you are older by a whole year—it is only right that you should learn more about myself and the ideas I hold," he said in a low voice, looking behind him to see that no one was following us. Slowly but clearly he then unravelled before me the story of his life—a struggle for his beliefs, which seemed more vital than ever before now.

"The old Poland was no pleasant place either for Jews to live in," he confided in me. "I have no particular liking for their kind, but as a socialist there can be no such distinctions between human beings for me, especially as it is a common desire now that unites us.

"We do not suffer in silence, as you youngsters have to. We keep up our connections with our friends outside, among them the prisoners at the other camps. Our spare time is not wasted, it is used to the full for the benefit of the new Poland, the homeland as we once hope to regain it and, whether in words or in deeds, there are many of us, striving to remedy the mistakes of the past. As different from each other as the two of us may be, I am, nevertheless, glad that you, too, can benefit from our efforts. All I can promise you, however, is to keep on letting you know about your mother, but that you can depend on!

"To help you out with food," my friend had said, "would not be fair to the other young acquaintances of mine, fellow Poles that I cannot let down." I liked his frankness and even convinced myself that his attitude was justified.

The other Poles I knew, rural and uneducated, rather unpleasant characters, had led me to generalizations similar to those that they themselves had arrived at about the Jews. Only now did I realize that not all of them were the aggressive egoists they seemed to be. Some, apparently, were even capable of helping foreigners—their supposed object of hate.

Poland's neighbors, the Ukrainians, had been doing slave labor in Germany prior to being imprisoned. That may explain why these rough people, shying from nothing as long as it meant a gain for them, had earned themselves the notoriety of being the camp hooligans. Friends of neither Russians nor Poles, they had embarked upon a ruthless fight for survival, a drive that made them capable of assaulting fellow prisoners for the sake of a slice of bread. In some way, however, odd to us, but logical to them, their robberies were justified. A Ukrainian's loot was always gobbled up at once, and usually shared among friends.

Every prisoner was a potential thief, every Ukrainian a potential robber. Open attacks on weak-looking inmates had grown to such an extent that we formed defensive squads, using the marauders' own methods. A typical bait was a haggard, frightened-looking prisoner, one of the chaps they used to call "Mussulman," trying to peddle his bread ration for tobacco. Then when one of the inevitable gangs would molest him the counter force, also largely made up of Ukrainians, would swoop down to hand out an equally ruthless revenge.

Thieves were harder to detect. At night, unseen, unnoticed dare-devils would wriggle their skillful hands deep into your straw sack in search of any precious slice of bread you may have saved up. In the richer blocks the incentives for sneakers were so strong that their roamings had to be countered by voluntary night watchers. When sleep was interrupted by lights being turned on to reveal one of the many elusive offenders scurrying to his bunk, he would be pounced upon with a ruthlessness only a concentration camp can teach. A thief, once caught, would be lucky to get up again after his punishment had been meted out.

Less dangerous, but a greater feat, was stealing from the camp kitchen. Called "organizing," it actually was a way of outwitting the SS, as no prisoner receiving his daily bowl of soup could possibly have attributed its lack of nourishment to the lone turnips the cook had been deprived of.

A few daring youngsters practiced soup-raiding. When a couple of prisoners, bending down under the heavy load of the vat, carried along their block's allocation of fresh, steaming soup, agile lads would swoop down on them to dip in their bowls. As, however, it usually ended up with the raiders, carefully balancing their watery quarry, being chased around the camp until making for the safety of some secluded lavatory, it was sport rather than theft.

When the ever-brewing troubles, contrived by orders from above or caused by the prisoners themselves, seemed likely to get serious, we had a block curfew. That meant early to bed and a grim, yet humorous, lecture by that ace of cynics, our block elder.

As usual, he warned that only rigid self-control could save us. "And to those who believe in celestial happiness," he sneered, booming his voice in the direction of Little Warsaw and Little Salonika, the Catholic and Jewish corners of the room, "and who imagine my admonitions to be trash repeated merely to hear myself talk, I can only say that I do not begrudge them their haven. If that is what they are after, they won't have to go far to look for it. The 'ascension squad' assembles every fortnight. I only hope that by the time you rise up the chimneys of Birkenau, you will still be clean enough for your angels to receive you."

"The rest of you," he roared, pacing up and down the gangway, "will better do what I tell you to. If I catch you sleepwalking May bugs again tonight, you'll have nothing to laugh about. Once I beat you I'll thrash you hard. No one, I repeat, is to hang about the washrooms after bedtime. Understand? No one!"

Then it was lights out. We knew that they were no empty words we had been listening to, but even as energetic a block elder as ours needed his rest. When, half an hour after the light in his room had been switched off, we thought he was asleep, it was time to enjoy our traditional night life. Heedless of warnings, there would always be some dozen absentees at a time. We ran down the cold stairs, rushed to the urinal and then refilled ourselves with the only thing not scarce—water.

Bleak weather heralded the coming of winter and, with much of our strength sapped away, we dreaded it. Nothing had changed to our advantage. The prophets had been wrong. Germany's army—thanks to those who showed no desire to put a quick end to Hitler—was still a powerful force. Nazism looked as triumphant as ever. All we could do to fight it was to suffer.

In the gamble for survival, the cards were heavily against us. On the side of the SS were four trumps, menaces we lived in constant dread of. They were the whip, the torture cell, disease and the gas chamber.

The daily candidates for punishment, three as a rule, were led off to the kitchen square shortly before the end of the roll call. There, one at a time, they were strapped to a scaffold to be whipped. Minor offenders got 25 lashes, others 50, 75 or even 100. Suspects whose cross-examination had not been revealing enough were sent to the punishment cellar at Block 11, where the implements of torture included dark and moist single cells designed to fit around the standing body of the inmate so as to prevent him from moving even an inch.

It would have been folly to expect the harsh camp life to show leniency towards the younger generation. Boys at the working sites caught having a nap were in for 25 strokes. Those on outside jobs who were accused of dealing with civilians had to taste the cells.

A strong body encouraged by a determined mind could outlive punishments. All one could count upon to ward off malaria, typhus and the gas chambers, however, was fate.

A new enemy had now made his entry: the Polish winter, cold and indifferent. "Last year," said the veterans, "it was hard; only a few of the westerners unaccustomed to it survived."

This time our chances seemed better. There were striped prison coats, shawls and gloves to help us. To the shielded youngsters at the school, the frost even brought entertainment. Skating fans, old and new, had all the slippery streets to compete upon. Tougher lads recalled their childhood with snowball fights.

It became quite a usual sight to see someone vigorously stamping his feet or grotesquely flapping his arms—a self-styled heat-generating expert, trying to convince a gathering of disciples that his method of keeping warm was the best. Waving limbs to fight off cold was not much use to us, however. We just had no time for it. By day we worked anyhow. Later, during roll calls, cold's biggest chance to gnaw at us, we had to stand at attention helpless and motionless. Afterwards we all rushed for the cozy block.

The winter evenings, in general, were spent in our rooms, waiting patiently near the lone iron stove for a vacant spot to toast a slice of bread, or skillfully trying to smoke big, precious cigars made of the straw from the bunks, splinters from the wooden scaffolding we had worked on, and paper torn from bags of cement. In the deserted wintry yard, meanwhile, our dark footprints, still lined up in rows of ten from the roll call, would slowly be covered up with fresh, fluffy white snowflakes.

Now and then our fortnightly bath was coupled with a disinfection, vainly trying to banish the tenacious fleas. It meant emerging stark naked from the hot showers and running through the ice-covered camp all the way back to the block. Having performed this feat quite a few times without coming to any apparent harm, I then became oddly aware that we and the fleas had become toughened together.

My time at school was up and I joined the working squad. Some 400 strong, with our capo, an experienced brick-layer, at our head, we assembled in the yard long before dawn. Then we marched out past the band stand. Penetrating the dark were the vigorous strains of "Colonel Bogey" and "Stars and Stripes," the tunes of our Allies. (Either the Nazis had declared Sousa, the band's favorite composer, to be German or they were being bluffed.)

After an hour we reached the snow-covered working site. Our job was the construction of the women's camp, twenty blocks, identical to the ones we lived in. Most of the foremen were civilians, Poles, Czechs and Germans. Already housed in a camp, they shunned us as much as possible, lest they too be imprisoned.

There were no guards except those surrounding the three mile outer camp zone we worked in. This area was ringed by watchtowers 200 yards apart. When the prisoners were at the camp and had been accounted for during the roll call, the chain of guards withdrew for the night. If someone had escaped, the wailing of the siren would tell the guards to stay on. With reinforcements arriving for the additional dugouts, the ring would then be strengthened till there was a gun to every 70 yards.

The work, mainly concreting, brick-laying and plastering, demanded the fulfillment of a daily quota and keeping a look-out for the supervisor. Cement bags were unloaded running at the double, concrete shovelled with a speed governed only by the mixing machine. Accidents were so frequent that they ceased to distract us. Under the ever-watchful eye of the commanding SS officers we had developed a habit of being in constant movement. Working or not, we always looked busy. A favorite trick of ours when, on rare occasions, we had finished our quota ahead of schedule, was sneaking away to rooms on the upper floors to relax. There had to be at least four of us to make a success of the show. One was posted to watch the staircase, while two others, each of their hands clutching a hammerlike object, imitated working noises.

To acquaint oneself with our workmates, their quirks, their strengths and their weaknesses, took time. My own initiation came with a taste of once-loved schoolboyish plotting. Together with some muscular Russians I was vigorously pushing a lorry full of sand. Going uphill, the load seemed to be getting heavier and heavier. We slowed down. "Push, kid," they shouted at me, "do you want the lorry to roll back again?" "If it does it will only be because of you, lazy bungler." "Want to exploit us, you son of a bitch?" I really got frightened and pushed with all my might, feet apart and wedged to the ground, shoulder pressed to the cold steel of the lorry. My efforts seemed useless, however. The wheels stopped, then started to roll backwards. Someone quickly put a log under them. The broad Slavic faces of my workmates were grinning. "You big pusher!" "You willing to help." "You push all alone, you brave!" "We— you—comrades."

They patted my shoulders. The new member of the team had stood the test.

During working hours, interrupted only by the short midday break when the soup arrived, sitting was a pleasure reserved for visitors to the lavatory. The hut covering the stinky pit, forever threatening to overflow, was the only place affording privacy. Never lacking busy admirers, it was rivalled in popularity only by the warmth of a treble-blanketed camp bunk.

Other favorite spots of ours, contrastingly modern and grotesquely in public, were the block lavatories. Traditional places for meeting one's campmates, they had two rows of basins like seats in a bar. Squatting on them, appreciative of the water flushing, trouser belts slung over our necks, we would make acquaintances and exchange news. Now and then we were joined by incorrigible smokers who, having found a bit of scarce paper, tried hard to make the best of it. Rolled around wood shavings it would burn. Sucking at it would make it a cigarette.

Returning from work, tired and frost-bitten, we made straight for the lavatories. Ten minutes later, with the bell ringing in the roll call, we were standing again—the prisoner's lot. Counting up usually finished at about seven. When the daily arrivals and departures had been so numerous as to necessitate calling out names, it took longer. When someone was missing, the process of finding out the details would drag on till well after midnight, with our exhausted selves up since twenty hours before. All we could do about this was to shift from leg to leg and to hope that next time there would be more sympathy from those we could expect it from—if there were such.

Our experienced camp veterans had been right in their grim prophecies that we newcomers would not stand it for long. The pitiful rations, although enough to prevent one dying from starvation, could not be counted upon to sustain an ill-clad, emaciated body against the gnawing cold of a Polish winter.

One evening after work the inevitable came. My head humming with fever, I dragged myself to the hospital compound. Waiting in front of Block 28 were throngs of ailing prisoners, grouped according to nationalities. I joined the queue that would be the last to be admitted, the one of Gypsies, Russians and Jews. If there was still time left to consider us, we would get the worst treatment of all. Aware that I was about to surrender myself to the mercy of people to whom life and death meant nothing, I tried to work out an alternative. But there was none.

After hours of standing and pondering we were let in. We undressed, again grouped ourselves according to nationality and then paraded before the SS doctor. His job was to jot down: "back to camp" "accepted" or "to Birkenau." Apparently there was still room at the hospital that day, for I was transferred to Block 19. When I fell asleep, I remembered only three things I was sure of: that there were bed-sheets, that I was supposed to have influenza and that the thermometer reading had been 104° F, 40° C.

When I recovered my senses, it was the beginning of a new year—1944. This was a challenge to resume the fight.

* * *

On being released from hospital, my fever somewhat abated, I happened to glance at the surgical department. I had never imagined that it was all that easy to treat boils and abscesses, the inevitable camp diseases. Afflicted legs or arms were simply strapped to a railing and the center of inflammation cut—the operation and the shrill yells of the patients vying with each other for barbarity.

When I returned to the "brick-laying school" I discovered that it had changed considerably. Most of my companions and friends had gone, making room for new faces. I was to stay on for a few days and then look for a job. Again I felt like a newcomer, the type of prisoner the others did not have to show sympathy for because they simply did not know whether he was worth it.

A few of the teachers said I looked very pale and advised me to seek out grown-up friends who could help me, a thing I would have done anyhow. To assist my recovery and to prevent my becoming one of those whose bodies could no longer support their spirits—the emaciated prisoners whom we called Mussulmen—extra food was more essential now than ever before. Accompanied by my friend Saucy Gert, I set out to find it. Evening after evening we toured the camp, searching for acquaintances. Like disappointed beggars we found out that our sole gain was experience; only advice, vague and futile, was given away.

Saucy Gert knew a fellow-Berliner, a Jewish mechanic who had a job that was called good, one where there were civilians to do business with. As we considered him to be "rich," we tried to seek his friendship. Our part in the affair was to wait for him, often for hours, at his block, 22a. Occasionally he showed his appreciation, bestowing on us the utmost he was willing to deprive himself of—a bowl of soup, half a liter for each.

Had our acquaintance been frank, he would have said: "Sorry, boys, I can't help you. I never knew your families, so you can't expect me to feel attached to you. Besides, one of you isn't even a Berliner. As it certainly wasn't I who caused your plight, you should not wonder if I fail to alleviate it. We all suffer alike. The surplus food of mine is earned by daring feats of smuggling. Whatever profits I make have to be used to ensure that they keep on being made."

He was a hypocrite, however, polite but ruthless all the same. He rather let us wait till we gave up bothering him. Maybe he really was the Zionist he professed to be. Possibly even he still cherished the religious beliefs he had been brought up on. He knew all the finesses of modern civilization, but all his qualifications seemed to work against us.

Our eager counsellors at the brick-laying school had said: "Go to your fellow-countrymen, the German Jews." We had approached them, all the pitiful two dozen odd of them. The only one who could have helped us had proved a failure.

For lack of a better mentor, I looked for the German criminal, the prison veteran that Mr. Keding had once introduced me to. When I finally found him he was glad I had come. "To go around begging is foolish," he lectured me. "You just have to use your elbows and be aggressive. The cleverer your opponents, the harder they deserve to be kicked."

Excusing himself for never having been much of a businessman and living only on the rations and occasional parcels from home, he regretted that in the line of food he could not help me. Then he showed surprise at my inadequate clothing. "You'll never be a tough guy with rags like these over your bones. They make you look like a 'Mussulman.' Here, take these," he continued, handing me two decent warm shirts, gifts from his family, "you'll be more respectable in them."

I thanked him, but did not forget to ask what to do at the next inspection when they would be confiscated. "Just tell the block elder they are from me," he replied. "He should know who I am."

Weeks later, when what I feared was about to happen, I decided to say goodbye to my shirts rather than attract the block elder's attention to my being familiar with criminals—whom none of the political prisoners like him had ever been keen about. Again I showed my allegiance to those who warned against being conspicuous. As a result I never had the courage to return to my well-wisher who was both the generous giver of the shirts, now lost, and the advocate of aggressively sticking out one's head.

Still in the search of food, I often lingered about Block 1a, trying to take out the soup the camp hairdresser had once promised me.

This brought me in contact with a Belgian Jew, a frail tailor of about thirty. "Come along to our bunks," he said, "and let's hear a bit more about you." I followed him gladly, the more so, when I saw that he and his friend, also from Belgium, occupied upper beds, a sign that they were "rich." Nor did their cupboard, a rare privilege, escape my notice.

"The camp hairdresser is not a good influence on youngsters like you," they said—as if I did not already know this. "It's good you don't go there anymore. You can come to us, we have good connections with civilians and access to clothes, an excellent article for bartering. We don't mind sharing our luck. All you'll have to do is to come and see us. We like you and want to be friends of yours."

After that warm welcome I was almost a daily guest of theirs, often being invited to share their evening meal, a luxury that only few prisoners knew. They taught me French and many a sentimental song about the Foreign Legion. Although ordinarily Belgian tailors would have little in common with the conscripted toughs of the Sahara, it now seemed that their common hardships had made brothers of them. Sung with fervent enthusiasm, the catchy tunes of the desert soldiers far away from their loves never failed to enchant me.

My share towards our entertaining gatherings were schoolboy anecdotes, jokes and the latest exploits of our block elder—the "sleepwalking May bug," as we had nicknamed him. We became good friends and I felt as though I had found a second home.

Then, one evening, a visitor came, a friend of theirs whose lack of humor was the first cause for my disliking him: a Jewish capo from the Birkenau camp. The newcomer, about to be transferred back, had a proposition to make: if I was willing to become his "girl-friend" he would take me along to be his confidant.

To my friends that seemed to be a wonderful deal. "You are lucky he takes an interest in you; he is rich and a personage. To be his protege will keep you immune from camp dangers." "Once you are in a position of prominence, helping your mother will be easy."

Rather impressed by all these promises, I had a talk with the visitor. He took me to one of the dark, floor level bunks. There, instead of answering my questions, he started to fiddle about with my trousers. A quick decision was called for. I jumped up and left the block.

After that I never returned to my friends. Meeting on the streets we looked away from each other, one party ashamed of vile intriguing, the other of having been about to fall for it.

"You're telling me," was Saucy Gert's comment to my latest adventure, "you are not the only one who finds out that these 'friends' are all the same once you get to know them. There is no one you can trust—except yourself."

Later I heard that my unsuccessful wooer, long ago returned to Birkenau, had escaped. I wished him luck!

Looking for a job, I was allocated to the building materials yard, the largest and most monotonous working squad of all. A thousand strong, it was made up largely of newcomers, unskilled laborers who were the least valuable kind of slaves. The work was hard. Railway wagons, loaded with bricks, cement and aggregates, had to be emptied according to schedule, a feat that could only be achieved by speed and overtime. When there was nothing to unload, we were kept busy building the materials at the yard into pyramids—or even more exasperating, just transferring them from one stack to another. Spending our days carrying block by block, plank by plank, we were oppressed by the realization that our lives had been lived merely to end up as human wheelbarrows, modern galley-slaves.

During my first days at the yard, when my face was still new to the foremen, I occasionally managed to sneak away. With boyish curiosity I then scouted about the district, the industrial area of the Auschwitz concentration camp. It was a real city, workshop after workshop, housing a busy bakery, the big D. A. W. joinery works and the Union ammunitions plant. Working day and night, the sweat shops never failed to reach their quota. With eight-hour regularity their products rolled away over the single track that, leading to the railway station, fed Germany's war machine.

From the same station, over the same track, there returned other goods, also to be sorted, classified and stacked by silent slaves—the masterless belongings of new transports that had been herded off to Birkenau.

After a few weeks of seemingly senseless work, dominated by constant shouts of "Keep moving," I was exhausted enough to feel that I could not go on anymore. My hands blistered, my feet sore, I made my way to the camp's labor exchange, the prisoner who assigned us (more or less permanently) to the sixty odd working squads. Aware that jobs called good were only to be obtained with bribes I, nevertheless, hoped to be transferred to a place of work less difficult than the present.

"There are many like you who want easier work," he replied to my pleas. "It's not my fault that you are young. Once I could have sent you to, let us say, the brick-laying school, but now since you are a prisoner of eight months' standing it's too late. There is nothing I can do for you."

The cold indifference with which my request, so easy to grant, had been rejected greatly depressed me. In my despair I sought the advice of the block elder. I argued that it was unfair to treat a youngster, just out of hospital, with the same harsh inconsideration as a newcomer. The father of Block 7a had no say in work arrangements, but he had determination and an unconquerable sense of justice. My trust in him—despite his being the arch-enemy of favoritism—had not been displaced. Somehow he pulled the necessary strings, and before long I was transferred to a squad of building laborers.

Arrangements at Block 7a were much the same as they had been when I visited the brick-laying school. The same type of lads speeding up and down the stairs to the leaking taps in the washroom. The same familiar inspections to see if ears and feet were clean. One still cheated the room elder by washing only the foot that one expected to show him.

But the faces of the occupants had changed. My old acquaintances had gone. There had been selections after selections. The dark moments when, curfew bound, we had to watch the lorries driving off to Birkenau, taking away friends and relatives, had become part of our existence.

Little Kurt had been sent away. Blonde Gert was in hospital. Saucy Gert, still my best friend and eager to be helpful, had been transferred to the farm laborer's block. I was the block's only remaining German Jew, the last of Little Berlin.

Having no one to share my griefs with, I felt lonely. When despair was greatest I looked at mother's letters, notes of hope that still kept arriving. Spring was coming—but for the first time in my life it failed to bring joy.

When in a depressed mood, I found relaxation in philosophizing, in trying to analyze our plight. My never-failing partner in this pondering over things not taught in schools, was Schorsch. A year older than myself, with a good educational background, he was the only friend who could appreciate my striving for knowledge, my desire to understand.

Blue-eyed, with a fish-like expression around his mouth and nose, Schorsch had the typical bearing of an intellectual in the making. Adopted by an Austrian family, he had been preparing for an engineering career. Then with the return of Hitler, a countryman of his, it was discovered that Schorsch's parents had been Gypsies.

"We Gypsies," reasoned my friend, "might be closer to being Aryan than those crossbred specimens who call themselves supermen. Perhaps that is why they want to kill us off. The Jews, who no one can deny are foreigners, have always been warned to get out and their present fate might have been predicted. In our case—there was no reason why the Nazis should turn against us. Our plight was as unexpected as could be.

"True," he admitted, "there did exist that loitering rabble that drove about in caravans. They were an unpleasant lot, despised even by ourselves, Austrian and German, the Romanies who had become town dwellers. But don't imagine that we all walked about in lousy rags. Gypsies have succeeded in becoming professors, doctors and world-famous musicians. I myself knew some of them. In Russia, they say, we even have a theater of our own.

"Another common mistake is to label us cowards. Once we part from that clannish caravan mentality, we give up fears and superstitions. What better proof do you want than the accomplishments of the Gypsy who got as far as being a Red Army General?

"So you see," Schorsch went on, "we are just a people like you Jews; there are good ones and bad ones. Although we have no Bible to prove it by, our history may even be older than yours. But you have always been luckier. You always had your Palestine. Had we Gypsies, like you, been told what was in store for us, we still wouldn't have had anywhere to go. Behind the Jews are money and influential friends. For us there was nothing but scorn."

Schorsch, along with the other Gypsies, still in their civilian clothing, had at first lived at a special camp at Birkenau. The inmates, encouraged by a fair diet, no work and agreeable living conditions, were hopeful. "As soon as the Wehrmacht clears the area of partisans," they were told, "you will be resettled in the Ukraine."

Then, one day, the order came to liquidate them, men, women and children. Helplessly trudging to the gas chambers, they encountered an officer looking for candidates for the brick-laying school. Schorsch was saved.

It was from Schorsch that I had the first eye-witness account of Birkenau's forest of death. Realizing our common suffering, I could not help taking an ever greater interest in my Gypsy acquaintances.

I had even seen some of the Gypsies' families, groups that had temporarily been at Block 8. Separated by barbed wire and paint-covered windows we had, nevertheless, watched them arrive. A conglomeration of attractive girls in colorful, national costumes, women in rags and jackbooted men in farmers' dress, they were a motley crowd, not easily forgotten. We could tell where they came from by the tailoring of their clothes. By their shabbiness we could even guess how long they had been in camp. Only their thoughts remained a mystery.

The bulk of the camp's Gypsies lived at Block 7a—ours—which had somehow become a traditional home of theirs. Attempts at mutual understanding, however, brought little success, for the Romanies sought salvation in keeping to themselves. Outstanding in their secludedness were clans that came from the mountains of Czechoslovakia and Poland, primitive superstitious people whose ignorance kept them in a constant state of fear. Using a sign language and a Romany dialect of their own, they puzzled even their fellow Gypsies, the kinfolks who had become modern.

When the block was overcrowded, we slept two in a bed. For a few nights I had a Gypsy for a mate, a shy and cowardly fellow. The only thing he was persistent about was his determination to sell me a small pair of scissors, a rare treasure; I wondered how he had got it. I told him that I could not possibly have any use for it, but he kept on trying to convince me that it would make an excellent tool for slicing bread.

"I never barter away my rations," I excused myself, "certainly not for fancy gadgets."

"I know I too have got a big stomach," he replied in a last effort at salesmanship, "but do buy it, just for friendship's sake." I did not. But when we huddled together under our common blankets—heads at opposite ends—we seemed to have become friends all the same.

Next morning when I woke up the bunk was wet—wet with the repulsive urine of someone whose daily fill of tapwater had been too much for him. Flinging hot accusations at each other, we soon attracted the attention of our room-mates, lads who had become convinced that evil must be punished. It was found out that the culprit could only have been the Gypsy boy, the newcomer, "an offspring of dirty, mannerless thieves."

A day later, I discovered the real bed-wetter: the Pole from the bunk above, also a newcomer. I also realized that unwittingly I had fallen for the same prejudices that I myself was trying to condemn.

*   *   *

It was already summer. We were engaged in enlarging the "Union" arms plant by another twelve factory halls. The first stage of work was to level the ground, dig foundations and cart away earth.

History books portray slaves as big muscular fellows whose bare chests show beads of sweat. But we never enjoyed such privileges. Toiling in the mid-day sun, undernourished and frail, we had to remain in our prison jackets. To take them off would have seemed equivalent to planning an escape.

Bringing in materials from all over the camp's working area, we satisfied our desire to learn more of it by making detours. Once while dismantling some disused huts near the railway line we chanced to watch trainloads of new arrivals. Jews from Hungary, Holland, Belgium and France—they came with the same hopes as we had had. Crowding around the ventilation apertures of their closed goods-wagons, they waved at us. There was nothing we could say or do for them. . . .

More often than not, the whole transport would go straight to its death, like cattle to the slaughter. Journey's end would announce itself by dark, creeping smoke, slowly rising above the western horizon, from the crematorium of Birkenau.

The guard at the civilian workers' disinfection barracks, the compound abutting on our working site, was in the habit of picking out youngsters to do odd jobs for him.

Once he called me to clean his sentry-hut. While I bent down to sweep the floor he offered me a sandwich. "Here, take this," he said hastily, "but don't show yourself near the window."

Surprised to hear a "thank you" in fluent German, he instructed me to go on with the sweeping until told to stop. Then he became talkative.

"Yes, I am an SS man but I am a human being all the same. Now and then we beat you up—that's part of the job.

"But don't think what's happening over there," he went on, pointing westwards, "is any of our fault. We look at it with the same anguish and helplessness as you do. Officially, of course, we are told nothing, but who can ignore the happenings at Birkenau? Knowing much better what goes on than you prisoners, many of us there go mad. When we joined up, we didn't know what we were in for. Now it's too late. There is no way out for us."

It seemed as though he wanted me to pity him. I still swept the floor, silent and unmoved. Then he ordered me out, shouting as loudly as he was expected to.

Saucy Gert, on night shift, was doing repair-work at the bakery. A good job, it offered opportunities to get bread, throw it over the bakery fence to a waiting accomplice and then smuggle it into the camp. But Gert was not satisfied. He complained of forever being tired and nervous.

"The conditions are good," he confided to me, "but all the same I can't stand it much longer. Night after night, standing on our brick-layers' scaffold and facing Birkenau, we see the fires. It is a sight I can't get out of my head: a flaming horizon contrasting with the dark of the night."

"But you," he went on, "asleep in your warm beds when all this happens, only see the loaves of bread. Believe me, they are no compensation for what we go through."

We pondered over our helplessness. To kill a guard out of spite—a thing we were capable of—would be ridiculous and only bring reprisals. Overpowering the camp garrison by an organized revolt would leave us helplessly exposed to onrushing reinforcements. If the local SS troops themselves mutinied, the Nazis would send in Army tanks.

We had heard about the fight at the Warsaw Ghetto where conditions for a revolt were far more favorable than ours. It was natural, then, that we became pessimists. Slowly initiated by my campmates into the elements of warfare (which I had previously imagined to be a football-match-like affair rather than a science), even I became depressed.

The camp's lone and odd symbol of defiance was Jacob, a big burly Jewish boxer. Reared in Poland, he had toured the world winning fame—it was said—as a trainer. Now his job, anything but glorious, was steward in charge of the punishment cells. We liked him mainly because of his enormous body and the respect the SS accorded to it. They kept him locked up and only allowed him to leave to fetch supplies, his daily trip from Block 11 to the kitchen watched over by a couple of armed guards.

Now and then Jacob was called upon to whip us. Some expected him to refuse. Others, among them the many youngsters who had come to know both him and the punishment cells, said he was gentle. Anyhow they would prefer the lashings of a fellow prisoner to those of the SS.

Another type of fellow inmate whose skills were being turned against us were the surgeons who performed castrations. Officiating at Birkenau, the hell that befitted them, we knew them by their victims, fellow-Jews, block mates of ours.

When summing up friends and foes, the enemy in our midst never escaped attention. Aware that some capos and block elders contributed more to our plight than the guards, we strove to revenge ourselves. Aided by the many camp personages loyal to us, we would harass them until they were eliminated. At our camp we achieved it by blackmail; other camps, tougher than ours, resorted to murder.

Transports of prisoners were being sent away to the Eastern front, to dig trenches. Others, mainly women and Poles, were issued clogs, a fresh blue-white prison garb and dispatched to factories in Germany. Mother's letters had stopped. She too was supposed to have been "sent on transport."

New arrivals, however, had not ceased. Birkenau was crowded with them and room had to be made for them. Once again there were selections. At the evening roll call I confusedly realized that Jews at our block had been whittled down to fifteen, a mere two per cent.

Blonde Gert had died of pneumonia. Saucy Gert, who had found ways of entering the hospital block to pay last respects, asked me if I wanted to come along. I was used to seeing death. There had been dear grandfather, pale and worn with age. All the mourning family had come to his bedside. Then I had worked at the cemetery. Later there had been bodies lifelessly clutching the electrified camp fence. This time, however, it was different. Gert did not have to die. He was young and innocent. He had been healthy and full of life. More than that, he had been our comrade, a fellow-fighter for survival, hoping for a better future. No, I would refuse to recognize death's accomplishment.

No, I could not bear to see his youthful blonde face, his pudgy nose, his thick lips, the straw-colored freckles—lying dead and helpless on an indifferent camp bunk.

No, I would refuse to go!

I told Saucy Gert of my decision. He said that as long as someone went to the hospital it did not really matter if it was only him or both of us.

With Blonde Gert gone, soon to be forgotten, I felt how close we were to the youth of Germany, the sons of our enemy, who too were dying a death against their will. Years ago Blonde Gert had shared a school bench with them. The teacher had extolled the glories of the past, the interests of those who had hired him. Then youth paid the dividends: Blonde Gert entered a concentration camp, his classmates invaded Europe. Now fate had reunited them. One, naked, his striped prison garb already worn by someone else, would be put on a pyre at hidden Birkenau. The others, in field gray, long deprived of their boots, would rot on the wastelands of Russia.

The bitter news deeply upset me and caused me to revise my attitude of stubbornly facing camp life while waiting for it to change.

It urged me to visualize rather than to hope.

My ability to fight the odds much longer seemed doubtful now. Our never-ending hardships had taken their toll, and I had become emaciated and weak. Liberation was a far-off dream and survival a feat for the fittest. In my desperation I started to interest myself in the accomplishments of the daring few who had escaped. To be prepared for emergencies I improved my Polish and memorized our surroundings.

The most spectacular of the escapes from Auschwitz had been the one centering around my former place of work, the blocks under construction for the new women's camp. A campmate who had hoarded gold and other valuables—stolen either from Nazi loot or straight from the new arrivals—decided to make the best of it. Instead of spending it solely on food, he waited until he had enough to buy the assistance of a civilian, a fellow worker of ours. Then one day, he took the SS supervisor's motorcycle and made for one of the unfinished buildings. There, in the sloping cavity beneath the staircase, he had himself built in by his courageous helper, a brick-layer. For five days the area was combed by guards and bloodhounds, but the fugitive had both time and ample cover. His hideout equipped with provisions and a ventilation hole, he stayed on for a week. Then he smashed the brick wall, mounted the motorcycle and raced into the dark night towards freedom.

After that incident all civilians working with us were carefully screened. Some were imprisoned, others sentenced to death.

Most other escapes were unsuccessful and merely a victory for the efficiency of our oppressors. Fugitives caught were brought back to camp from as far as the front lines of the Allies, the haven that had been missed only by yards. Then, hardly alive anymore, they were stood on a dais facing the returning working columns and forced to hold up posters: "Hurrah, we are back again!" "We did not succeed in spite of clever plotting!" "No one gets away from this camp!"

Afterwards they were led to the gallows, which would adorn the kitchen square until the evening after, and hanged.

Despite all, I decided that if a chance to escape offered itself, I would take it. To lessen the danger of being found out, my getaway would have to be solely my own effort with no one to help me and no one to share the secrecy with.

My accomplishment would not fail to be impressive; I would be the youngest prisoner ever to escape from a concentration camp. If unsuccessful, I would, at least, have shown myself to be valiant.

Daily attracting my attention was the outgoing goods train. The wagons, pushed along by toiling prisoners, were lined up in front of the checkpost and left waiting for the engine. Some of them, loaded with boxes or scrap metal, were open ones. Once out of the camp territory, their tarpaulin covers would make a good hiding place. If their destination was far they would carry me into the vastness of Europe: if not, I would have to try my luck in Upper Silesia, plodding to my former hometown, Beuthen. The problem of acquiring civilian clothes did not bother me. Already wearing a shirt without prison markings, I would dispose of my jacket, cut off the trouser legs, and, as a temporary measure, blot out the white zebra-stripes of the remainder with mud. Driving myself on like some haunted animal, I would be a dual personality: a harmless youngster and a reckless fugitive knowing the meaning of capture.

For days I studied the habits of the guard in charge of the check up. With a Germanic sense of duty he arrived exactly five minutes before the train's supposed departure, looked over the wagon roofs and examined the undercarriages. Here and there he lifted up a corner of the tarpaulin but never bothered to untie it. Then he went to the sentry hut—the same that in exchange for a sandwich and a lecture on the helplessness of the guards, I had once dusted—to talk to his colleague. When he heard the whistle of the engine, hardly ever on time, he would re-emerge, throw another quick glance at the wagons and signal the Polish driver to pull them out. It apparently never occurred to him that in between the two check ups someone may have sneaked in. He knew that we prisoners worked elsewhere and had no excuse to be lingering around the shunting rails, certainly not when they were guarded. This, then, was my chance.

Unseen I strode along the row of wagons. It would be now or never. The destination tablet read "Berlin." The flapping canvas begged me to get in.

Then one by one, the wagons rolled away. They moved on beyond the chain of guards—but I had not budged. I had stayed behind.

I had stayed behind, realizing in the last moment that it was not only a matter of courage but also a question of conscience. My plan was an utter failure. There would have been reprisals. If mother was still alive, they would find her.

That evening when my youthful dreams crumbled and I marched back into camp, I was one of the many who had given up hope, yet I could not believe that life could end if one so desperately wanted it to go on.

For the first time the familiar strains of "Colonel Bogey" that greeted the returning working columns failed to inspire me. They rang out like laughter, mocking at our helplessness.

"Work makes free!" said the inevitable wrought iron inscription, looking down contemptuously from over the camp gate. The hated slogan was worse than merely ridiculous, it was sordid irony. Its real meaning was solely in the rhyme the cynics had made about it, the bitter message we so desperately tried to forget about: the saying that "Work makes free, through Crematorium No. Three."

CHAPTER IV

Old Hand

I had pains in my neck and suspected them to come from tonsils. After work I saw the school doctor. "Little brick-layer, you have nothing, it's only a little swelling. Just as you said, your tonsils," he assured me in his jocular way of imitating childish prattle, a habit he stout-heartedly never tired of. "I'll put some of the black paste on it, you know, that kind that's full of sugar, fat and vitamins and it'll soon be all right."

For weeks I walked about with a collar band of precious bandage, but the fabulous ointment failed to work wonders. The paste, whose valuable ingredients had once been discovered by a hungry Gypsy boy who had actually tasted it on a slice of bread, nourished my ailment, instead of healing it. My neck kept on swelling.

"My dear son," said the dispenser of hope and ointments when I could no longer move my head, "don't be afraid, but you must go to the hospital. Go at once, go now. You have got a boil and it has to be cut." This time he was serious. These purulent swellings, maladies of undernourishment, grew to be grotesquely large and quickly multiplied themselves. Widespread as they were among us, this was my first, but a dangerous one, for of all the attractive places of the body this bothering specimen could have chosen from, it had made for my neck, the heritage I was least eager to part from.

The next morning I was strapped onto the operating table, my face covered with a towel. Inhaling the ether, drop by drop, I counted aloud as I was told. Still realizing that I was in a concentration camp and aware that the knife could easily be too long and too impatient for so precarious a neck as mine, I only hoped that my imminent silence would be a temporary one. Then the countings gave way to knockings in my head, becoming quicker and quicker.

When I awoke, they said that my boil, now cut open, had been one of the biggest ever seen there. I did not care. I dragged myself to the lavatory and vomited.

Then I was handed over to the room elder of my sick-block, a male nurse who impressed me by his gentleness. His room, part of Block 28a, had ten three-tier camp bunks, differing from those at other blocks only by their bedsheets. The inmates, mostly old and toothless Poles chosen for their need of care rather than illness, suffered from anything between appendicitis and insanity.

I admired the room elder's quiet, self-confident way of handling them. A German communist who had seen no little of concentration camps, he was no mere nurse; he was a lone prisoner to whom helping the sick had become a way of life. Unlike other camp inmates he seemed to take satisfaction in his job, and—considering how little else there was to be gained—devoted himself to it with surprising eagerness. Whenever there was spare food, he shared it out equally, often dividing his own share among the youngest four of us.

My attempts to make him a friend of mine failed, however. "Please," he would excuse himself, "don't talk with me for so long. The others may imagine I favor you. Sick people are easily irritated and we must avoid their becoming envious."

All that the quiet, boring sick-room atmosphere seemed good for was sleeping, groaning and dying. The visits to the surgery added some variety to my secluded existence, however. There they inserted strings of cotton-wool into my wound, as if stuffing a goose. This, procedure irritating and painful though it was, broke the monotony.

When the wound began to heal I was transferred to hospital Block 21a. The two hundred odd convalescent inmates there, irritable and quarrelsome, spent their time hating each other. As soon as they were well, they started fist fights. After being whittled down by the block personnel, who without exception exploited our infirmity, the food amounted to less than even the usual camp ration.

Aggravating the general anarchy was the room doctor, a German Jew, overworked, ruthless and loathsome. When he thought it necessary he beat us, usually picking out those who did not understand German, the ones he called "dirty peasants." Even I, unoffending as I was to him, was treated harshly. On one of my visits to him he tore off the scab from my wound with such roughness that it opened up again. Then he barked: "Out, I can't waste my time on you. Next one, quick!"

I was aghast to find out that most of our superiors, the people whose intrigues had made our room hell rather than part of a hospital, were newcomers. The very prisoners now imposing their will on us had themselves never seen the harshness of camp life, the common hardship that makes veterans respect each other. Disgusted at the way they treated me, I tried to contact my former protector, the German criminal who had once been so concerned about my being dressed properly. My hope for his help, perhaps justified, was of no avail, however. "He has left the camp," I was told.

At last, after constantly begging for it, I was released. On my way out I took advantage of my last opportunity to look down upon the enclosure opposite our room window, the space between the mystery Blocks 10 and 11—the blocks that many entered but few left. All the secret which revealed itself in the yard between the blocked-up windows that hid cold-blooded executions, painful tortures and cruel experiments, was a rabbit pen.

During my stay in hospital I had missed a lot of news. Camp conditions, I found out, were no better but the inmates had become hopeful.

Hitler's war, it seemed, was nearing its end. Even his own people had turned against him. The Nazis, for the first time, were filling the punishment cells with their own people.

Groups of a dozen or so hostages, freshly arrived from Germany and apparently unaware of their fate, being led to Block 11 had become a daily spectacle. Men, women and children, SS men and high-ranking officers with their ensign torn off, all entered, never to return.

At the same time, along the same streets, singing German camp inmates were marching and drilling in preparation for being "volunteered" into the Wehrmacht, which, in dire need of cannon fodder, had decided to establish a brigade of ex-prisoners.

The future soldiers, anxious to enlist and still more eager to desert, had suppressed their erstwhile scruples by hoping to escape to the Allies.

Somehow—it was said through persuasion—our block elder, too, had joined the "volunteers." At Block 8, the block opposite that oddly enough had become a military training base, he, too, became different. He took to drinking, wandered about the camp in a state of stupor, and avoided his former friends. We only heard of him again when the news came that he had committed suicide. Our stern and strict father, the benevolent dictator of Block 7a, had killed himself.

Our new block elder, a Pole, glum and dismal, had little in common with his illustrious predecessor. We called him "fishhead," for he resembled one both in appearance and talkativeness. Although just as strict, and just as quick to impose a block curfew as punishment for untidiness, he was more of a schoolteacher than a guardian. His sole concern was to run the block. What we did in our spare time and the means by which we thought to survive did not interest him. If, when in trouble, we asked for his help he would shrug his shoulders, smile and excuse himself for being only the block elder of 7a and not the Lord of the universe.

The influence he wielded among the camp personages was insignificant. His German was bad, his voice not loud enough to be impressive and his block one of paupers, inmates who could not raise the bribes necessary to make its representative rich and important. Even we ourselves did not value him. To his dismay we avoided him less out of fear than out of a desire to ignore him.

Soon after my return I went to visit the school doctor, our absent-minded favorite. As someone that felt a personal responsibility for us youngsters, he wanted to know how I had fared at the hospital. I told him all the many details he was interested in. Then he made a confession. He had always realized the seriousness of my swelling but kept it a secret. To shorten my dangerous stay in hospital, so that I would not have to wait for being operated upon, he had dressed the boil with ointments, making it ripe for cutting. I thanked him but he was too busy to look up. With motherly care he was removing the scurf from the infected scalp of a little Gypsy.

*   *   *

The first months after arrival, a prisoner spent his spare time brooding about the future. Then, when he had acquainted himself with all the depressing details of camp life, he would no longer dare to. He would just try to live. Later still, having gone through the many trials and hardships, he would strive to forget.

To us youngsters, the best way to dream ourselves away was to sing. We sang when penned up in our block during the many curfews, whilst having our weekly showerbath or out of loneliness. Our songs were many and varied: Gypsy melodies, ditties about love, folksongs from all over Europe and partisan marches. Those who had picked themselves a favorite would hum it as a kind of signature tune, something they would be known by.

My own choice was a sentimental French song in which a young man reveals to his mother why he had joined the Foreign Legion. "Not because I am a murderer," sings the far-away soldier; "not because I am a robber. No, it is for the love of a girl."

Every time I hummed this, my own private melody, I was overcome with the feeling that, despite all, I was still alive. After a whole year of concentration camp I had remained my own self. Even though I could not see my face, for mirrors were denied to us, I could still hear my signature tune. It was the proof of my existence.

Often when during the evening hours we sat on our bunks, some Russian lads would start to sing aloud. Their catchy songs were so full of defiance and confidence that we could not help joining in. Whether we came from France, Belgium, Holland, Germany, Austria, Italy, Czechoslovakia, Poland, Hungary, Greece or Russia, the stirring rhythm gripped us alike. No matter what our fathers may have thought, to us the rousing tunes that revolutionaries of two decades ago had been inspired by had lost none of their meaning. The message of uniting and fighting the common enemy was not only as appropriate as ever but had now become of vital urgency. Even those who were opposed to communism, like many of the Ukrainians, no longer wanted to stand aside. They, too, somehow joined in the choir.

Among our favorite tunes were "If Tomorrow Brings War," "From Border to Border" and "Steppe Cavalry." Listening to them woke many a sentimental feeling in us. Somewhere in the partisan-held forests of Europe, we imagined, other youngsters would also be humming these songs. Their fight was ours, and ours theirs. They, with weapons in their hands, would sacrifice themselves for those who had been too late in recognizing their foes. We, helpless cattle that we were, could only attempt to survive. All we could do for the common cause was to sing.

Then there were the traditional concentration camp songs. Most of them were little more than German marching songs to which the prisoners had given a new, inoffensive text. Outstanding for its lack of taste was the one about Auschwitz. Based on a favorite tune of our guards, it declared bluntly that "We'll stay in Auschwitz no matter if it snows or red roses bloom." Composed merely because the authorities were keen on having a camp song, it was so repulsive that we only sang it when forced to.

Handed down to us by veteran prisoners were three songs about life at the moorland camps near Papenburg—now a decade old. One said "Where hell is so near the forest border, where the moor engulfs

me, there is my country, there is my home." But its melody, taken
from a German ditty, was entertaining rather than sentimental as it
should have been. The other, "We are the peat bog soldiers and
wear black-yellow dress" was also a failure. Sung to the tune of a
Nazi labor service march, it sounded far too loud and confident.
Only the third song, with both music and words composed by inmates, was successful. Since it was first heard in 1934, at the Boerger-
moor concentration camp, it had become a kind of political
prisoners' anthem everywhere. Its rhythm, though confident, makes
it clear that the struggle would be long and slow. "Far and wide as
the eye can wander, heath and bog are everywhere." "But," it promises to those who sing all the verses, those who persevere, "winter
will in time be past." *

Ten years ago this emotional tune had been hummed by lone
forgotten German anti-Fascists at hidden moorland camps on the
Ems. Now our 400 youthful voices, gathered from all over Europe,
lent it a new vigor. The prisoners' hymn, floating out from our block
to penetrate the dark night, had become a challenge. We knew that
millions of our comrades in the other camps were singing with us.
One day we would be united. Then our songs would go out stronger
than ever before. The tunes of old would not be forgotten. Inspired
by them, we would one day seek out the remnants of our oppressors
and their supporters and bring them to justice.

*   *   *

Working nearby we often watched the roadway to catch glimpses of newcomers. Our attention was turned on the long columns of
women prisoners coming from overcrowded Birkenau to have their
monthly disinfection and shower bath. Shouting at them from a
distance that would make their guards tire of pursuing us, we asked
their nationality. Then hastily summoned countrymen would find
out more.

"Anyone from Miskolc?" the women hailed us. "Anyone from
Miskolc?" our voices echoed in the empty shells of factory halls

---

*See appendix.

under construction. Answering the plea came the running footsteps of Hungarian workmates, folks to whom that town had once meant peace, home and family life. Carefully dodging the inevitable guards, the accompanying SS women and the bloodhounds, they sneaked onto the road to search for acquaintances.

We others looked on. Trudging past came our female counterparts, hardly bothering to lift up their heads to greet us. Dressed in mere rags, their hair shorn, faces worn with worry and despair, they kept their energy—little as it was—for shuffling along the dusty roadway. Weeks ago, I reflected, the same women, clad in elegant fashions, may have paced the streets of Budapest and attracted the glance of many an admirer. Now they represented the lowest type of prisoners, helpless newcomers, suffering a misery which men's hearts would find hard to imagine even. Trying to cheer them up, we bared our shaven heads, waved our blue-white caps, and forced a smile on our faces.

Later, our workmates told us that they had been asked about "children's camps." The women, separated in a special compound for Hungarian Jews, lived right in the holocaust of Birkenau but the scheming authorities—still talking to them about "resettlement"—were keeping them ignorant of it. To many a naive woman inmate, then, bitter reality was no more than a bad rumor, a nightmare she hoped not to be confronted with.

Ogling at women prisoners, wherever they could be seen, became quite a hobby of mine. I wanted to find out what it was that made them attractive. When a group, approaching from the distance, could be identified as wearing skirts, the younger of us, determined to meet it, tried to find excuses for leaving work. The most plausible one was a trip to the three-celled lavatory, a privilege granted but once a day. If we succeeded in delaying this moment until it could be exploited to the full, and were among the first three to sight the skirts, our aim was achieved. Having a keen eye and strong bowels, I was quite a strong contestant. Sometimes the foreman was the first to espy the females but we did not fear his competition. "Three youngsters who haven't already visited the privy may do so now!" the kind soul used to shout on these occasions. To whoever heeded the hint it was then merely a matter of agility.

Enthusiasm for greeting the womenfolk was common to all working groups. Before long, the prisoners lining the road ceased to be lone bystanders. As they grew in number, they became obvious. Our little game came to an abrupt end when, one day, the SS swooped down on us. The chase was touched off by one of the females who happened to be in SS uniform. Spindle-legged and ugly, she nevertheless imagined that it was herself who was being stared at. Her enraged shouts had all the other guards running after us. Pursued around our working site, the new halls for the "Union" factory, we desperately looked for a hiding place. Finally I spotted a heap of empty boxes in which the new machinery had been delivered. One of the containers still endowed with a lid beckoned me to get in. I did.

After some twenty anxious minutes the runnings and shoutings faded away. I extracted myself from my refuge, careful not to be noisy. Then suddenly and unexpectedly I realized that the boxes around me were also inhabited. As soon as all the other fugitives emerged from them we held a consultation. After that we sneaked away, one by one, this time back to work.

The few lads who, having run the wrong way, had been caught by their pursuers, were punished with 25 lashes on the buttocks. To go near the road when women were on it became an offense. But, craving for something unattainable, our efforts to see the females did not cease. Back in the camp, we thronged around the steam-filled laundry barrack in a desperate attempt to see them under the showers. Climbing onto each other, we scaled the walls to reach a lone, high-up window, a misty pane that offered a hazy, distant view of naked bodies. Soon, however, even this precarious pleasure was denied to us. The bathers ceased to come.

Then, one day, I found out that success can come without it being striven for. Dismantling some disused barracks between the railway track and the Birkenau road, we were caught by heavy rain. It meant stopping work and hoping that heaven's gesture would be lengthy. Five of us, having sought the shelter of an abandoned stable, relaxed by listening to the friendly drops tinkling like a melody on to its corrugated metal roofing.

Suddenly our waiting was interrupted by the rushing in of two newcomers who, unaware of us, busied themselves with shaking off the rain from their soaked prison garb. I looked at the contours of their bodies and realized that they were girls, buxom country lasses. Stunned with suddenly finding the object of my youthful imaginations right next to me—and tangible—I just stared at their abounding womanliness.

My other companions, long having learnt their lessons of life, had a hasty few words with the visitors. One was a Polish girl, the other a Russian, and their guard (perhaps afraid of being overpowered) was sheltering in a sentry hut nearby. That seemed introduction enough. The kind rain not being influenced by the lusts of men, we had to be quick. Two pairs hustled off into the second half of the barrack, the straw-filled sanctuary. Myself and the others watched out for intruders. We could not help being envious, but hoped that sometime we, too, would be lucky.

The all-pervading rhythm, the myriads of rain drops knocking in harmony onto the roof, still did not relax its force. Nature is strong, it proclaimed. She offers many a chance. . . .

Returning from work, we often passed the new extension camp, the former building site I had once been so familiar with. Now it was already surrounded by high barbed-wire fences and occupied by an advance contingent of women prisoners who had come to arrange the furniture: seventy triple bunks, a table, a cupboard and two benches to the room. As the few dozen inmates had been picked for their reliability, they were temporarily guarded only by a lone sentry stationed at the gate, an arrangement we exploited to the full.

When passing the fence, we and the girls would throw flowers over it, withered but heartfelt gifts which had been gathered during the midday break, the precious few minutes that remained after gobbling up our soup. We cheered each other by shouting greetings and waving our caps; the girls waved their kerchiefs.

I asked whether they had known any Jewish girls from Germany in Birkenau. "Yes, there are one or two of them," cried someone. Shouting, hands pressed funnel-like to my mouth, I enquired if they knew any women from the transport I had come with. "No, never heard of these numbers," came the reply.

But I was not depressed. I continued to cheer, hailing people who once had meant so little to me. We were not applauding individuals. We were saluting youth, a generation in the growing that would never be conquered.

My boyhood days, when the female classmates prided themselves on being too mature for children like me, and when women were adults, had gone. I now took a natural interest in girls, little as we saw of them.

There were women prisoners at the Union factory, working day and night shifts but the plant was shut off by barbed wire fencing, no stranger being admitted. Although the workers were sworn to secrecy, we knew what they produced by looking at the scrap that in open railway wagons was being returned to Germany's steel mills. The discs punched out of it proved that shells were being made. By measuring the diameter we could even guess what guns they would be used for.

Occasionally we saw women who, recuperating from illness, were employed in a working squad of their own, a group that came to search for weeds. Their job was to scan the countryside for a variety of wild plants which could be used in making medicines or, like thistles, for brewing the prisoners' soup from. Being under guard, they did not dare talk to us. But when stooping their emaciated frames our way to pick some thorny weed, they would show a reticent smile.

The other type of women prisoner was housed right in our camp. On the upper floor of Block 24, above the room of the camp orchestra, there was a brothel: two dozen full-bodied harlots. German prisoners were entitled to visit it every fortnight. Others, excepting Russians, Gypsies and Jews, received the metal entrance discs once every few months. Prominent camp-personages had their favorites, women they seemed really fond of. In return for gifts hauled up by bits of string through an unobserved back window the whores would let them stay a bit longer next time—more than the prescribed fifteen minutes of enjoyment.

Most of these women, from all over Europe, had already practiced the oldest profession before being imprisoned. It was a queer paradox that a prostitute, arrested for being one, had now—catering for guards and prisoners alike—become an asset to the very authorities that had once persecuted her.

They were hardly ever allowed to leave their quarters and only rarely found opportunities to show themselves at the windows. When they did, however, we never failed to watch them. Some of us despised these painted, vulgar dolls, others pitied them, but being fellow prisoners we could not help respecting them as such.

Often, before starting their strenuous evening, they would scan the yard below for prisoners that looked young or very frail. Calling them to stand beneath the window, they then dropped them a ration of bread. It was their way of saying that, despite all, a woman's heart remained motherly.

*   *   *

My friend Saucy Gert, the truest of all, now worked at a large farm near Raisko. It meant getting up before five o'clock, marching a couple of hours, toiling in the fields and then, exhausted, tired and blistered, trudging back, often reaching the camp only after the evening roll call. But working among luscious tomatoes and spicy onions was profitable.

Every Sunday a lone, horse-drawn cart conspicuously heaped with flowers drew up in front of Block 5. Hidden beneath the potted green plants and colorful bunches—with which the authorities' avowed aim of making the model camp "look cheerful" was to be materialized—were sacks of vegetables, the weekly total of whatever the farming squad had been able to "organize." This clever trick often made the farmworkers' room resemble a greengrocers' shop, its inmates bartering away their cherished capfuls of vegetables for even more precious bread. The guards that specialized in detecting smuggling having their day off, it was never found out.

When I visited him, Saucy Gert would always have something saved up for me: a couple of tomatoes to be gobbled up as a treat, a pungent piece of garlic that before vanishing could be rubbed onto many a dry rind of bread, or even an onion, the apple of spice which could be enjoyed peel by peel and would bring variety to a week of camp food.

There was nothing I could offer in return and, as our sharing agreement by which we had intended to help each other had long been abandoned, I felt rather uneasy about accepting his gifts. Generous Gert badly needed his hard-earned weekly two pounds or so of vegetables for trying to help the family. His father had been contacted at Birkenau, his brother at Monowitz.

"When one's family isn't heard of," he used to say, "one fears the worst or hopes for a miracle. Then, when from some camp there is news of their being alive, one feels lucky. But very soon—as their miserable lot becomes worse and worse—one regrets ever having heard about it, for what once had been feared will then be known for certain."

Arriving at Birkenau, day by day, night by night, came large transports of newcomers, Jews from Hungary.

Many of them were transferred to our camp, and the overcrowding forced us to share our bunks. Our new companions stood out from the others for being "Magyars." Living under oppression seemed new to them. Their language, too, was something on its own, having no relation to those we knew of. Trying to make ourselves understood, we spent many an hour striving to acquaint them with the elements of camp life. But we doubted whether they would ever master the art of being an underdog.

Since my arrival, over a year ago now, the total of prisoners having passed through the camps of Auschwitz had doubled. There were now five separate series of numbers: E for Educational, G for ordinary, Z for Gypsy, and A and B for the Jewish mass transports arriving since 1944. "E" prisoners, mostly Germans, lived at a special camp at Birkenau and would be released after "having served their term." All the others, their numbers tattooed on their left forearm, were in "for life."

The marking of prisoners not in the "ordinary" category also showed the letter of the series, so that when on rare occasions the camp administration's political department decided to transfer an inmate from one classification to another it also meant changing his tattoo.

One of these whims of bureaucracy concerned a Gypsy boy I knew, who had become both its victim and beneficiary. Suddenly he had been declared to be a German, an "Aryan" who could visit the brothel and volunteer into the army. His newly-acquired racial companions, however, continued to shun him. "He looks, talks and behaves like a Gypsy," they whispered, "he should have stayed one."

Nor was he influential enough to play the part of a masterman. All he gained by being listed as such seemed little more than a change of number. His old one, adorning his forearm with a Z in front, had been obliterated by crosses. Now he had a new number beside it, more graceful, neater and longer.

Confidently planning for the future, the Nazis were making preparations to absorb millions more of slaves—the many "inferior races" Europe was still full of. Auschwitz was to be enlarged.

New constructions mushroomed all over the camp territory. The demand for skilled building labor became so great that even the thousand former inmates of the brick-laying school could not meet it. Vast new projects were being planned. A foreman of ours had even peeped at the blueprints. They foresaw a living camp of double its present size, a trebling of factory buildings and a new network of roads and railway tracks for the working area.

As a first step towards realizing their plans of expansion, the authorities had introduced a new system of administration. Our camp, the smallest but cleanest, the well-kept show piece for delegations from outside, was named Auschwitz I now. The array of camps at Birkenau had become Auschwitz II, and Monowitz with its subsidiaries, Auschwitz III. It meant that the whole district flanked by the Vistula and Sola was now one unit, a giant concentration camp—a monster to those knowing it, a mere name in triplicate to others.

I had been transferred to a working site called "the new stables." Toiling in the sun, never allowed to take off our jackets, we dug foundations and moved earth. Watching us was an SS man, the works supervisor, sitting lazily beneath a shady tree.

Sometimes—perhaps after having spent too hilarious an evening—the none too eager but aggressive representative of the Third Reich would fall asleep. This would be a signal for the more daring among us to wriggle through the fence of the nearby garden. Anything there attractive to birds, bees and worms also interested us. Berries, flowers and radishes—all were rare and useful. Like the other Polish property within the camp district, the garden, part of a country residence, had been taken over by an SS officer's family. Our small-style looting expeditions, then, were more than beating the enemy by his own methods. "Hitting" without being found out, we would spread confusion—even if only domestic. The Nazi boss, returning home to his villa and seeing the disorder among the flower-beds, would probably blame his own offspring for it.

These, however, were interludes. As a rule there was little to interrupt the monotony of work. Exhausting ourselves with continuous digging, sweating and aching all over, there was only the occasional premium money to look forward to: a pitiful camp mark most of us, like myself, would never be favored with. When sometimes someone received one, he (along with the privileged German prisoners who had accounts from home) would spend the evening queuing up outside the canteen. There, he could acquire mustard, writing paper, toilet paper, cigarette paper, and tobacco made from wood, if these were not already sold out.

Theoretically the premium could be as much as a mark a week. An incentive cleverly used to exploit us still further, this was the utmost 20th century slaves were thought worthy of.

All SS men are shown in yellow, not grey uniform, as there
was no grey colour available. The original SA Nazi uniform was yellow-brown.

"Morning, noon, evening"

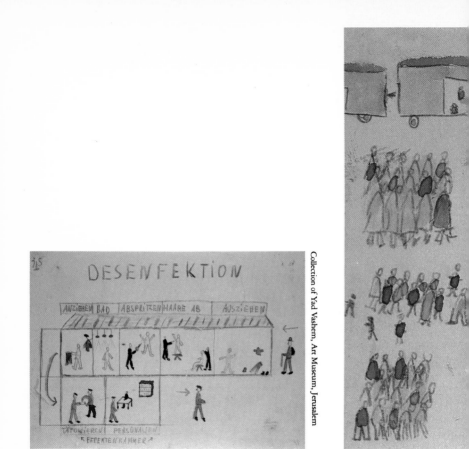

"A number, disinfection"

"Arrival, at the ramp"

"The organisation, armbands at Auschwitz"

An der Rampe
(AUSCHWITZ)

34

"ES STIMMT"   (AUSCHWITZ)

Der Lagerälteste geht dem SS den Apell
Die Blockältesten sind angetreten

"Roll calls, block elders report"

"Roll calls, at night"

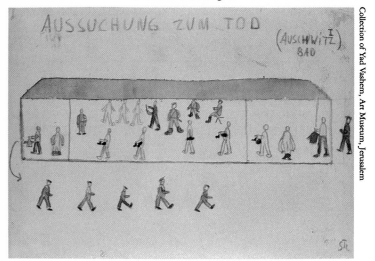

"Selections"

"Sundays"

"Slave labour, our work"

"Dangers"

"Arguments, hunger"

"Music, marching to work"

"New again, surgical department"

"Departure, evacuation"

"Defeat, a day before liberation"

"Victory, selfliberation"

"A new world, American friends"

Saucy Gert had introduced me to a lone newcomer from Berlin, Philip Auerbach, a huge awe-inspiring Jewish fellow in his late thirties whom he wanted me to acquaint with camp life. "Judging by his fat belly and the thick spectacles he wears, he could be a professor," was Gert's opinion, "but you'll find him to be an agreeable chap. He is a bit naive but a grand storyteller. You just listen to the yarns he'll spin you about Berlin."

My new acquaintance had many interesting things to say, and, thrilled by his adventures in the bombed ruins of Germany's capital—told as a kind of serial—I met him every evening. Walking along the camp streets, always peeping behind to ensure that no one was eavesdropping, he unravelled his secrets.

"I am a doctor," he said proudly, "but not of medicine. Being a realist, I studied criminology, which, as you probably won't know, is all about crime and criminals—something quite appropriate for our times.

"Until last month I was locked up at Alexanderplatz prison, where they kept me to help the police in black market roundups. With every bombed-out building a potential shelter for the underworld, and the various kinds of escaped prisoners being able to survive only by turning criminals, we had plenty of work on our hands.

"I had a big moustache, making me look like a real detective, and on outside jobs," he maintained, gleeful as a schoolboy telling of his first cigarette, "I was even allowed to carry a revolver."

My advice to him as a camp veteran was to keep quiet about his past and (as there would be no substitute for them) to look after his spectacles.

"Yes," he agreed, "I'll adjust myself. Besides, I am even aware that former clients of mine, now fellow prisoners, may remember me."

Later, after having slimmed beyond recognition and enlisted the aid of a German camp personage, he obtained quite a good job. Being a criminologist, it seemed, was still proving useful. We ourselves then, two youthful but unneeded advisers, lost contact with him.

With more than a hundred thousand prisoners having arrived later than myself, I had become a veteran, someone who was familiar with all the yearly events of camp life through experience. Many of the prominent camp personages already knew me by sight, and I was now someone they could not help sympathizing with. The youngster every fellow inmate had once been keen on bullying had grown into an old timer who was respected for having survived.

Once, by including me in the list of inmates allowed to write home, even the authorities made a concession to my seniority. Staring at the postcard I had been given, I pondered how best to choose the few, limited words and to whom to address them. Then I wrote about my being well, "hoping that you will send a kind reply" (meaning a food parcel) and sent the message to an old German lady who had been our neighbor. But the few lines I had put my hope in, were never answered. They were torn up, I guessed, before even leaving our camp.

Another time the administration decided to hold cinema shows, tickets being given to Germans and Poles alone. Before each performance crowds of other inmates, Russians, Jews and Gypsies clamoring to be admitted, blocked the entrance waiting for a chance to sneak in. One evening, whilst pushing hard towards the door, my efforts were rewarded. A German imprisoned for being a criminal, who probably knew me, passed by pressing a ticket in my hand. "Go in kid," he whispered, "and enjoy yourself."

My head red with self-consciousness, I entered the cinema, an empty room in Block 2a. Then it started: a film show in Auschwitz, a real talkie. No longer noticing the fellow prisoners we were crowding together with, we hungrily followed the happenings on the screen, a domestic love affair. We were watching careless living, good food, elegance, women and families—a mirage. It was a dream which details failed to interpret; a world so remote from ours that by looking closely it became obscure.

For a while the improvised stage in Block 2a also served for entertainment evenings, concerts with humorous sketches enlivening the intervals, but after less than a dozen performances it was closed down. The authorities, it seemed, had concluded that the liberal assortment of group punishments, in any case cheaper and more effective, would be enough pastime for us.

One of the favorite correction methods was having us do "sport," an ordeal imposed for our "not having worked hard enough." At first it was the capos' turn, dozens of them being led through the camp streets exercising to commandments.

"Lie down!" "Get up!" "Bend your knees, stretch out your arm!" "Jump!" "March!" "Turn around!" "Roll on the ground!"

"And now you bastards," they would be barked at, "to teach you to extract more work from the skunks you are responsible for, we'll do it all over again but quicker."

Next day, the output still not having increased, there would be "sport" for the foremen, the lower ranking supervisors. That still failing to bring results, we would all have to roll in the dirt—accompanied by the grotesque yelling of ridiculous camp songs.

After having been warned to be clean and shiny for the roll call, we then spent the rest of the evening laundering our garb and desperately, but vainly, trying to dry it in readiness for the coming working day, only six hours ahead.

* * *

At long last came the Allied bombers, the first sign that the world around us was aware of our sufferings. Conscious of being itself a target now, the SS garrison hastily prepared dug-outs, painted the buildings with camouflage stripes and equipped itself with helmets and gas masks.

On hearing the wail of the siren, a welcome signal that could be as frequent as three times a day, we left work and, heading for our place of assembly, made sure that no one—being deaf or asleep—was left behind to face punishment as a fugitive. The roll call over, we raced back to camp, keeping up a close formation.

Our squad was the most distant one that had to return. But we did not regret it, for running along the road—exhausted, our feet aching—we would have the satisfaction of watching the hated SS men scrambling for shelter. The mastermen—afraid now and their rifles useless against bombs—were peeping out of the dug-outs, anxiously scanning the sky. Then, less to our liking, the camp district was shrouded over with a blanket of evil-smelling artificial fog.

We prisoners crowding into the camp blocks had no protection whatsoever but were glad about the raids. The building, shaking from nearby explosions, its panes shattering to splinters, was proof that damage was being done to our enemies.

With almost half of Poland having been liberated, the Nazis were becoming uneasy. Selections to pick out death candidates for Birkenau from among the inmates had stopped. Rumors, however, to the effect that gassings were to cease altogether—supposed to have a quieting effect—proved to be false, and transports from South-Eastern Europe, bringing new Jewish victims for the forest of death, kept on arriving.

The attitude of the authorities, as portrayed by their faithful servants the SS, showed a marked change. Instead of "suppressing the inferiors" they now imagined themselves to be protecting us from the "invading hordes from the East." As a last effort Hitler imitating Pilsudski, was trying to turn Poles against Russians. A sentiment-rousing propagandist picked from the Polish brand of Fascists came visiting our camp to enlist his countrymen into a "National Defense Army" that was to ward off the "aggressors." His mission, futile though it seemed, nevertheless netted a handful of followers, just saving its failure, to our surprise, from being complete.

The newly-founded bomb disposal squad, daily leaving camp equipped with digging tools, long hooks and a low-platformed trolley to tackle misfires, was also supposed to consist of "volunteers." Its members, drawn from all nationalities and, perhaps too intelligent to be lured by Nazi talk about "saving Western civilization," had been attracted by the frank and realistic bait of an extra food allocation.

"Chances of surviving Auschwitz, a hydra-headed monster devised by our enemies, are negligible for those who live on bread and water, but a bomb only goes off when tempted," maintained the prison-garbed sappers, secretly hoping that Allied-made explosives, not having blown up their foes, would not dare do that to friends.

At the same time there was news of the German inmates who had joined the army. Herded together, never allowed to leave the battlefield, their company—all former prisoners—had been sent on a suicide mission and wiped out.

Jews arriving from the "rich" countries, like Hungary and Italy, where they had been subjected to clever, calculated propaganda about being "resettled in the East," brought along much of their belongings, often wagonloads full. The owners having been disposed of, it was their chattels that received consideration. Suitcases, clothing, bedding, bicycles, sewing machines, sacks of provisions, bundles of private correspondence, stacks of photographs, rings, diamonds and hidden dollar bills, all went to the sorting barracks to be classified and given the proper respect human beings were not thought worthy of. When the loot had been graded and any name tabs or sewn-in notes removed, it was stacked onto railway wagons to be sent to Germany.

"From Auschwitz concentration camp to Breslau," read the destination tablets fixed to every wagon. "Can it be," we asked ourselves, "that people at the other end, soon to enjoy the booty our modern form of acquisitive society has long been striving for, are ignorant of how it was come by?"

From among the provisions new arrivals had been ordered to equip themselves with many were stale, rotten or "suspected as poisonous" and, accordingly, found their way to the camp kitchen.

Like everything else taken from the mass transports, the foreign-made macaroni, flour, bread and dried fruit were called "Kanada"—possibly because to Europeans that country represented richness and abundance. "Canada soup," then, bringing welcome variety to our diet, was a bread soup which depending on its manifold ingredients—chunks of fruit, cake, sandwiches,

newspapers and often even leather and nails—would be either sweet
or bitter.

Workers of the "Canada" squad—the prisoners sorting out
loot—managed to acquire some of it for themselves, to "organize."
Daily exchanging cheaply acquired camp-boots for pairs of good,
solid leather shoes, wrapping bedsheets around their waists, pushing
golden watches up their rectums, hiding jewels in their nostrils and
lining their caps with foreign banknotes, they soon became finan-
ciers that lesser traders had to look up to with respect.

At camp the goods were passed on to other operatives, receiving
a commission hardly worth the risk, who would barter them to
civilian work-mates in exchange for alcohol, butter and cigarettes.
Three cigarettes—the money of the black market valid all over
Europe—bought a day's ration of bread: 350 grams. Butter was
reserved for buying capos, foremen and block elders, while brandy,
in great demand but hard to smuggle through, was used to bribe
richer camp personages and SS men.

Naturally, on returning from work we were subjected to a
search, a daily procedure in which one person in about fifty was
thoroughly inspected and the rest threateningly looked over for
suspicious bulges. If one was caught, it meant being brutally beaten
and then for the rest of the evening having to stand between the
fences, hemmed in by wire grids six feet apart, humming with
dangerous charges of electricity.

*   *   *

The brick-laying school and myself had moved to Block 13a. Its
apprentices, all new now, were mainly Jewish lads from Hungary,
youngsters from fourteen to sixteen. Like naive Little Kurt—long
since vanished—they, too, clung to their pleasant childhood and
took little interest in the cruelty around them. But watching them,
unperturbed and balanced as they were, was a pleasure, something
to cheer us up.

A few, having had a Zionist education, entertained us to tunes
about pioneers in Palestine, about a man called Trumpeldor who,
unlike Jews in Europe, had fought before dying—sentimental

melodies recalling an ideal which old-time prisoners had long forgotten.

"Sleep quiet, Valley of Jezreel," sang the clear youthful voices, helplessly muffled by a roomful of dusty, straw-filled camp bunks, "sleep quiet, wonderful valley, we are your guard...."

Another little group that never tired of showing themselves to be cheerful—mainly, also, because it earned them an occasional extra bowlful of soup—were a few Gypsy lads, rhythm-conscious Romanies who spent their evening at the "Birkenweg," the "camp-promenade" facing the treble row of barbed wire fence, dancing and singing to remind us of days gone by.

I now had enough time to listen, for, having given up vainly begging for food, I no longer limited my attention to inmates from whom favors could be expected but endeavoured to meet them all, to watch their various habits and try to understand them.

Opposite our working site, the new stables, was a rest house for SS officers, a "Fuehrerheim." As in all SS living quarters, household work was in the care of a religious sect called "Investigators of the Bible," women prisoners who, when faced with weighty supplies such as sacks, boxes and barrels, would call us in to help. Hoping to snatch morsels of food, we were so eager to show ourselves useful that on seeing the weekly provisions-cart draw up at the mansions we would sneak up to it and try to attract the women's attention by grotesquely pointing at ourselves.

Once it was my turn to be favored. Precariously balancing a case of wine bottles on my youthful shoulders, I passed the servant's entrance, climbed down the dark stairwell and entered the supply vault. Letting down my load and lifting my eyes, I was confronted with a sight I had thought existed only in fairy-tales. Stacked along the wall lay endless rows of bottles, the choicest wines of Europe. Hanging from a rack were plucked geese, hares, sausages and fragrant, juicy, mouth-watering hams. An elderly housekeeper with a bundle of keys tied to her blue-white prison frock pushed a piece of cooked chicken into my pocket then bade me return to work.

On my way back I threw a glance at the rooms upstairs. Furnished with a luxury befitting kings, they lacked neither rugs nor paintings.

Yes, the masters of the master race, their greed satisfied, had reason to relax in their armchairs. Their starving slaves, plenty of them, were cheap; their well-trained sons, no fewer of them were dying "to serve the fatherland."

Of the "Investigators of the Bible" sect, imprisoned for their stubborn pacifism, only the women had survived. Mostly Germans or Poles—their avowed honesty having been cleverly exploited by the authorities for their own benefit, the cause of the war gods—they now served the SS as cooks and housekeepers.

Apparently incapable of hurting even their worst enemies, the "Bible women" were entrusted with positions of such responsibility that the restrictions imposed upon them were merely symbolic. Slaves rather than prisoners, they were attached to SS living quarters within and beyond the guard-surrounded camp territory, housed there, and free to move about the district whenever their work required it. Seeing a prison-garbed woman queue up at the village shop was just another odd spectacle the surrounding population had become used to. The prisoner would neither engage in conversation nor try to escape, for her pledge would be kept with all the religious fervor she was capable of. Even if she broke it, there was nothing to be gained.

We fellow prisoners respected the devotees of the Bible mainly because they helped us. But they deserved more, for their attitude to life, obscure though it seemed, showed courage. To them, God was far from being the heavenly judge who demands holy wars and forgives the sinners. "Only our own conduct can be our savior," they acknowledged bravely and stubbornly. "Through it He reveals Himself."

Under the shower we would look at our scars, liberally littered all over our flabby skin, study them, compare them. Signs left over from boils, abscesses, skin diseases, sometimes even lashings—each had its own characteristic place, shape, size and color. We all had them. In the winter of 1943 the crop of assorted abscesses, the curse of undernourishment, had been greater, an epidemic invading the whole of our bodies. Before that it was worse still. Now they thrived mainly on our legs. When poking our fingers into our calves left a hollow mark on them, it meant that, in addition, we had dropsy; that we had become a living sponge. "Those damned swellings," said the veterans, "come from drinking too much putrid tap water. If you lads don't sleep with your legs up it'll spread to your hearts." "Stop drinking or you'll blow up like a balloon."

There was nothing funny about it. Excepting air, water was the one food we received without being whittled down to starvation rations, the only element we were still free to enjoy. Deprived of the washroom tap, we would wither like shrivelling flowers—ugly ones nobody was interested in any longer. That would be worse.

Other phenomena repulsively brought to light by bathroom nakedness were the red, sore bodies of the newcomers—those still unacquainted with the persistent fleas of a concentration camp, who had scratched themselves until they bled. Several of them had already become infected by scabies—the minutest of vermin from which toiling, sweating prisoners, once afflicted, could do next to nothing to save themselves.

Typhus and fevers—typhoid, spotted, scarlet—were taking their inevitable toll with frightening regularity, seconded by the no less deadly diarrhea and dysentery. "It's the dirty food," argued the sufferers. "It's our weak constitution," said the others.

"Don't drink! Danger of epidemics," warned placards hanging over the taps, the valves guarding the cherished chlorine-flavored wetness, the treasure that so generously dispensed cooling, refreshing nourishment.

"*Eine Laus dein Tod,* a louse is deadly," shrieked the enamelled notices fixed to the walls of the rooms, showing a large, neat portrait of the beastly sucker. For the first time, we now had lice, tentative visitors from mice-rat-and-bedbug-ridden Birkenau where competition was sure to have been fierce. Every Sunday now, after roll call, we queued up for vermin inspection, carefully cleaning out the seams of our clothing beforehand, in case we be accused of spreading diseases.

One of these parasite hunts proved to be another abrupt step forward in my steadily-increasing experience.

Shirt in hand, trousers down, I approached one of the inspectors, a fellow prisoner who, armed with a magnifying glass, would look me over for body lice, head lice and crab lice. But, grinning with amusement, he only lifted his lens to look close into my eyes. "Oh, so that's you, old fathead! Still alive and kicking, eh?" exclaimed a Slovak-accented voice. It was Ello, the gay lad who had once been deputy room elder at Block 7a. "Next time," he whispered, "save yourself the bother. I'll cross you off the list, like the block personnel, without seeing you. Old hands like you can be trusted to crack the lice by themselves."

Going back to receive my daily soup, the warm, filling liter to bribe my belly with, I glanced once again at the lads still lining up for the inspection. One after the other, I looked at their bared forearms that prominently displayed their camp numbers. They were all higher than mine, most of them newer by over a year. It was true. Only a handful of block inmates exceeded me in seniority. I had become an "old hand."

CHAPTER V

Moving On

One autumn day in 1944 an unexpected motorcycle came rattling on to our building site. Its rider, an excited-looking SS man, dismounted, called for his colleague, the supervisor, and exchanged a few hasty words with him. "State of emergency." "Send them back to camp, immediately." "Report to the barracks."

By the time when, running at the double, we reached the camp gate the guards already wore steel helmets and had taken up positions at the air-raid dug-outs. There was a strict curfew. "All the working squads have been returned," gasped our block mates. "Didn't you know? Birkenau is burning!"

Waiting for signs of news, we nervously paced our room. In the afternoon something unprecedented happened: we were issued our rations in advance—one and a half loaves of bread to last for six days. Our fears became intensified. Even influential prisoners with up to eleven years of concentration camp life behind them seemed to be afraid. People had become tense and irritable.

Then night came, but we sat up on our bunks, silent, uneasy and pondering—now and then straining our ears for sounds from beyond the fence, rustles that might well have become ominous.

By noon next day we had returned to work. The imminent danger was over. But our fears had been fully justified, for, when the true story trickled through, it revealed itself to be a plot more daring than we had thought possible.

A working squad at Budy, 100 Russians and Jews, had over-powered their guards and escaped. At the same time, either to di-vert attention or, by causing a panic, to facilitate more escapes, other prisoners set fire to one of Birkenau's crematoria.

The Budy group, trudging through the woods, headed for the spurs of the Carpathians, the partisan-held mountains five hours' march away. Only a fortunate few, however, reached them. By the time they had come to cross the last serious obstacle, the Vistula, it was already guarded by speedy patrol boats. So was the Sola, the tributary parallel to it. At every crossroads and bridge were threatening checkposts.

Faced by a cordon of military backed up by collaborating po-lice units, and pursued by ruthless SS men with bloodhounds, the bulk of the brave rebels had no alternative but to surrender. Then they were massacred.

The crematoria had burned down completely. Its work would be taken over by the other two. The revolt had failed.

Later, the weapons the Budy squad had started their revolt with were traced to the Union plant, the ammunitions factory which employed prisoners. Three young girl workers, it appeared, had smuggled out a pistol and enough explosives to blow up all the cremation furnaces.

Unknown heroines, their fate was to be hanged. The execu-tion took place at the women's camp. The highly emotional in-mates, witnessing such a gruesome spectacle for the first time, were deeply stirred. Once ordinary housewives, they now faced all the brutal reality that turns the wheels of history. Suspended from gal-lows, four yards high, swung the lifeless bodies of three teenagers—lone casualties in the fight for liberation the world over; to their fellow women—gallant examples of courage and determination; to youth—an honor.

At the men's camp, victims of reprisals being many, public hangings were staged about every other month. When someone had escaped, the first to suffer were his relatives, then his work-mates. I had seen it being enacted on the squad of brick-layers, neighbors of ours. Lined up, one hundred of them, still not sure of the reason why, every fifth was told to step forward and taken away as a hostage.

Once a mass hanging of twelve Poles was meant to be a great spectacle of intimidation. But it failed and developed into an unexpected show of defiance. The roll call over, we were supposed to march past the gallows, but we were hungry, tired, and in no mood to suffer caprices. It was already dusk when the first columns received orders to turn left and march towards the kitchen square. But, even to our own surprise—they refused. Meanwhile the inmates assembled in the rear became impatient and rushed for the safety of their blocks, guarded by brick walls. When the others followed suit, the show was over—stolen, for the first time, by ourselves.

*   *   *

I was transferred to the new squad engaged in building private air-raid shelters for SS officers living at the town of Oswiecim.

Our daily trip to work, accompanied by half a dozen guards, took us past the outskirts of the camp and along four miles of country roads. It never failed to be instructive, acquainting us with the nearby hamlets and the layout of many an SS encampment (the distant, elaborate "statistical office" being one of them). But more interesting still for herded-in prisoners was the town itself.

Our first shelter was for the commander of the Raisko farming region, an *"Obersturmbannfuehrer."* The preliminary stage for the brick-built, concrete lined, underground hide-out the Germanic potentate would soon be forced to descend to, was 100 cubic yards of excavation. The project had top priority, and as we had been picked as fast workers, this meant digging at speeds which can only be described as frantic.

Often the magnate paid visits to ensure that his safety was being properly toiled for. No, it was no fairy tale, but he, the prince, arriving in a black carriage drawn by a couple of white horses, descended, pulled at his gray uniform to straighten its silvery epaulets, tightened his white gloves and then proceeded to inspect us, aided by the inevitable monocle—the symbol of Prussian perfection. I was quite glad that manners forbade him to address us. Nor did he think our guards worthy of being talked to. The next day he would send a note, "reminding those concerned that quick completion of the shelter was of the utmost urgency."

For building the walls, blue clinker bricks had arrived. Unloaded at record speeds, they were thrown down a chute, with myself at the receiving end four yards below. Arriving there like some hard, sharp-cornered missile, they bounced vigorously into our bare hands and then had to be stacked. They came in their thousands. Protecting ourselves against their blows with bits of paper, hard to find and quickly worn through, was futile. Nor was there time to look out for bricks that overturned, dropped off the chute and then came hurtling down on us. Our bodies covered with bumps, our arms bruised, hands bleeding, we tried desperately not to give up—for when the days of unloading were over it would be an easier place to work at.

During the midday break—an hour now, for our guards' convenience—we climbed out, filled our stomachs with a liter of soup and sat on the grass, gazing at our surroundings. A few yards away were two bungalows whose occupants, Polish civilians, did not dare to show themselves. But when our guards were busy eating their lunch, we would sneak away to the garden fence and wait for some of the inhabitants to notice us. Often they did, giving us fruits and receiving letters for our kinfolks outside.

A well-developed Polish girl of about twelve who paid visits to sprawl on the flower-dotted grass and to play with a big, equally contented-looking dog, greatly provoked our youthful sentiments. She must have come with a purpose—either of her own or of her parents. But we could not find it out. We could only stare at her, watch the carefree, undisturbed way she moved her white, well-shaped limbs and envy her freedom.

My own existence in this world exceeded hers by a mere two years. Only a dozen odd yards of grassy field separated us. But our civilization had drawn a line on it—two brown stones, a foot high in all and fifty yards apart. Beyond them we would be shot.

When, except for another two layers of bomb-protecting concrete roofing, the shelter was finished, we experienced our first out-of-camp air-raid. All twenty of us were herded into the dark, newly-built vault, where we sat on its moist floor, leaned against the supports of the wooden framework and waited.

From one of the houses, a radio blared out the raid report: "Bomber formation heading for Blechhammer." It was an industrial district, another sweat shop which drew its cheap slaves from concentration camps. Shortly afterwards, the bombs probably having hit the target, the announcer bellowed: *"Die amerikanischen Angreifer wurden siegreich zurueckgeschlagen."* To convince his audience that American planes completing a mission 700 miles from their base, and now returning to it, represented a victory for Germany, he then put on the much-worn record of the Wehrmacht's march of triumph, specially kept for occasions like these.

My workmates, all Russians and Poles, enticed me to find out whether the guards would let us rest till the all clear signal. I groped my way to the shelter entrance. The opening, sharply outlined by daylight from the stairwell, was blocked by a figure reclining between the doorjambs.

"Entschuldigen Sie bitte, ich moechte etwas fragen," I announced myself. Jerking into attention, the figure made for the steps, groped a rifle and cocked it. Again I proclaimed my intention, this time gentler still. *"Oh, Sie sprechen Deutsch?"* queried the surprised guard, visibly relieved. Then he hurried up the stairs, looked out, returned and told me that his colleagues were out of sight. The interview was granted.

"We were damned frightened that the lot of you may try to escape," he addressed me. "I don't trust these Russians. One never knows what they are hatching, with these air raids tempting them. Four rifles handled by men far too old for military service are no match for a horde of sturdy lads. If we returned without you, one need not guess what our superiors would do to us—and don't forget we, too, have families."

He opened his breast pocket, pulled out a photo of his wife surrounded by three young children, and showed it to me. "They hope ever so much to see me back."

"Actually I am a newcomer, one of those who had no inkling of the place's vileness," continued the wearer of the ill-fitting, dilapidated SS uniform. "It is a bad job, especially now that it no longer protects us from air raids. Our lot is hardly better than yours. What do you think they make all these camp extensions for? Now that they have finished with the Jews and Gypsies, they'll round up the Slavs. When these will be done away with they'll start picking the inferiors from their own people, old and useless ones like myself. A friend of mine who studies all these new books about race and destiny says that is what they are aiming at."

At this point a continuous, penetrating wail interrupted him: the all clear signal. Quickly, without comment, he resumed his position of authority. *"Heraus! Schnell! Zur Arbeit!"*

Perhaps there was some truth in what he believed about the plans of his leaders. He had only forgotten that it was no longer necessary to round up the Slavs. They had come on their own and were knocking on Germany's door. Not as underdogs, however, but as conquerors.

Our little construction squad moved on to a second shelter and then to a third.

The townspeople, not daring to look at us in public, still made detours around our working site. But even so, Oswiecim had become familiar to us. We knew her the prisoner's way, by her facade.

Her homes being in a world apart, we were acquainted with her streets. Patches on the asphalt paving seemed gay, drainage grids along the gutters bright. Houses, the red, brick-built symbols of steadfast citizens, appeared to be hearts. Lanterns, high-up globes dotted with vacuum bulbs, were eyes looking down on us.

The work was hard, and the lengthy way back to camp strenuous. But, unlike the other prisoners, we had many opportunities to get acquainted with our surroundings. All the various checkposts, administrative centers, officers' villas, isolated farm buildings, SS camps and railway sidings, otherwise unattractive or even repulsive, had to be learned about.

Eager to prepare ourselves for emergencies, we memorized their lay-out and watched out for changes. Almost daily we noticed something new. It made us glad, for we had become useful. We were confident now. Any scrap of information passed on to our camp mates was more than merely valuable: it was ammunition in the fight against our cleverly enforced ignorance.

With only a few disheartened old men to guard us, it seemed easy to escape from the squad. But no one attempted to. Why should we endanger ourselves, now that it was our cause that was winning? We went on mixing concrete. Attacking the huge heaps of sand and gravel, as if they were our enemies, we savagely hit them with our shovels and flung them into the ever-rotating mixer. It did not occur to us that unwillingly we were helping to build the Nazi Empire. It was only our youth we were aware of, the dynamic urge for progress that could never be wrong. Besides, someone had told us that chunks of earth harmed the concrete and had to be removed. We were determined to do the opposite: to feed the mixer with as much muck as possible. It was just what we had been looking for, a way to resist the foe.

Once, on our way to work, we met a group of girl prisoners from Birkenau. Judging from their muscular legs, most of them were Russians. When they shouted slogans at us, we were convinced of it. Our feelings were running high, and we replied with even greater vigor. They waved their kerchiefs, we our caps, but our longing was one. Whether we had been born on the shores of the Atlantic or the plains of Mongolia, our fiery, unquenchable youth was the same. There were shouts of *"Da Zravstvuet—!"* "Long live—!" (That, *"Krasnaya Armiya"* and *"Na Stalina"* was about all I could make out with my poor Russian.)

The guards, perceiving only an unintelligible noise, tried hard to stop us. It was useless. Neither they nor their leaders could put back the clock of history. On the contrary, they were hastening it.

Then the girls took the road forking off into the valley and, separated by a shrub-covered embankment slowly rising in height, we parted.

* * *

I had returned to the squad building the stables. Our job was to finish the interior, to cover the floor with a herring-bone pattern of clinker bricks, to fix the fodder cribs, plaster the mangers and line the attic with panels of cemented wood shavings. It was the pleasantest place of work I had known. As needed materials never arrived in time, much of our day was spent "waiting for them." Also, the elderly foreman, through my talking English to him, had become a friend of mine.

"When after the last war I found myself on the German side of the border," he told me, "they used to look down on me as *'Wasserpollak'*; when I returned to Poland, they snubbed me for being a German. Then in 1939 it suited the Nazis to make me a *'Volksdeutscher,'* but they soon regretted it and put me in prison." "And now," I interrupted, "you are a Pole again." "Yes, a good one, and glad of it too."

Half our workmates were civilians, craftsmen from Poland and Czechoslovakia who had signed on for two years and more.

"Again they have put sheep's fat on the sandwiches," they would proclaim, abandoning their lunch on some window sill where we could not help noticing it. "Damn those kitchen people. Even rats wouldn't nibble at food like this."

But, except for these occasional, greatly appreciated gifts, the civilians did not dare show their sympathies openly. The only prisoners they talked to were those trusted few they bartered with.

We had unwelcome guests now—the SS men in charge of the horses. Drunkards, lazy and vulgar, they had taken over the two rooms at the far end of the barn, from where they came swooping down on us, trying hard to frighten us away. They abhorred having to live under the same roof with us, but their colleague, the building inspector, would not listen to them.

"The workers will stay till they have finished," maintained our SS-uniformed boss. "If they do, we'll kill them, all the stinking lot of them," cried the enraged stable boys. "They make a mess of the place, steal turnips and frighten the horses, and you, you gullible ass, want them to go on with it."

Some days later the guardians of the stable, drunk as usual, came rushing in on us, swinging whips, fingering pistols, and cursing both us and the civilians. "We'll teach you to cheat us, you *Schweinehunde!*" One of them grabbed me by the neck, stared at me and then shouted to me to continue my work. I raced off, climbed up the ladder into the attic, and was glad of my quickness. Below, the commotion went on.

In a corner, leaning against the sloping roof I met the foreman. "Well," he said, "I expected it; they'll never recognize him." "Whom?" I queried, taken by surprise. "Didn't you know?" he grinned. "One of our lads sold them brandy and, when they didn't pay up, he threatened to denounce them to their superiors."

The Warsaw rising had been squashed. The hostages, men, women, and children—the population of whole streets—arrived at Birkenau. Fellow inmates from Poland busied themselves looking for acquaintances and finding out details.

Again feeling linked with the world outside, now about to be liberated by the Allies, we pleaded with our civilian workmates to bring us newspapers—to wrap their sandwiches in the latest "Voelkischer Beobachter" or its stereotyped Polish equivalent.

Dressed in our blue-white uniforms, our bald heads covered by flat, round prison caps, we crouched over spreading heaps of moist building sand and drew maps of Europe on it, lining in the war fronts.

Considering that the Allied effort already had the blessings of nearly the whole world, and that it had many powerful backers, the progress of the armies of liberation seemed disappointingly slow. With the Nazi extermination policies as an inevitable impulse to our far-away friends, we had expected a "Blitzkrieg" in reverse, the quick crumbling of the few Fascist legions by the onrush of a well-equipped, determined army having the utmost support of the population. In the East, we realized, the Fascists and all they stand for had been driven back 1,200 miles but the Allies that had landed from the sea were still somewhere in France and Italy—despite the western tip of Germany being only 100 miles from the Channel. No, it didn't seem like the total war we had hoped it to be.

We youngsters, our minds far less occupied than those of grown-ups with worrying about our families, craving for women, and recounting the good food we had enjoyed, rarely thought of the past. It was the present we were concerned with: our fellow-prisoners from all over Europe we wanted to understand and to learn from. They would be frank with us for, unversed in politics, we were unlikely to inform on them. Nor did we take offense as quickly as the more biased grown-ups.

I enjoyed observing other people's attitudes and customs. No habit, however strange, I reasoned, could be repulsive if no fellow human beings were actively hurt by it. Only planned, premeditated evil deserved to be condemned.

For myself the thrice weekly one-and-a-half ounce stick of margarine was something to be spread on bread, evenly and sparingly. To some of the Russian country lads, however, it was something like a frankfurter, to be gobbled up on its own, bite by bite.

For me, hitting someone meant being angry with him, but with the Greek boys it was a play. They called it *"Klepsi klepsi"*—a nickname given to stealing. The harder you slapped your blindfolded playmate's face the more fun there would be in watching him try to recognize you from among the crowd of grinning bystanders, all doing their best to look guilty, and if he did, it was your turn to cover up your eyes and guess who was hitting you.

Then there was the Jewish boy from Belgium, a mere child in his outlook. Before being sent to Auschwitz to become my neighbor, he had never made his bed, never washed his clothes, never sewed on buttons, never darned socks, never cut bread, and never left home without asking for permission. "At home," he confided in me, "I had a big head of hair and mother combed it for me every morning ever so carefully."

At first, after lights-out, his small, frail body rolled up in a pair of rough, flea-infested blankets, he used to cry. "If you really want to help me," he begged, after I had vainly tried to comfort him, "do make my bed in the morning. I'll never manage it on my own and I so dread being punished by everyone for being untidy." I did. Perhaps it would have been better to let him manage on his own, but I doubted whether the cruel camp life would wait for him to become independent.

Maurice, too, was a character on his own. A young Greek Jew, tall, stringy, red-haired, freckled and snubnosed, he was the symbol of optimism. I first got acquainted with him when, trying to baffle us with a puzzling question in mathematics, he was surprised to find an equal before him, even though our interests were different. Instead of wasting his time looking for food and acquaintances, Maurice was determined to go on learning and educate himself. Our crowd talked about camp news and the war, but he spent his evenings with a Polish friend of his, a professor, who in exchange for lessons in ancient Greek taught him Russian, Polish and Czech.

I had met a former workmate of mine, an unusually well-educated Ukrainian, and grappling with our language difficulties, we were having a talk about the things that worried us. My bitter criticism of his compatriots was quite a challenge to him.

"They are callous robbers," I hissed, "cads, hated and despised, bullies who do not even shrink at attacking the 'Mussulmen' weaklings." "Everyone does that," he countered, "and you certainly can't expect peasant lads to be sensitive about it. Their stomachs are much bigger than yours and hunger teaches them to be ruthless. They surely wouldn't swallow those rotten vegetables from the kitchen dump if their hunger was to be borne lightly." "Yes," I interrupted, "I know, but they should concentrate on thieving from the camp supplies and the stores like the rest of us, and not on get-

ting their neighbors' bread ration." "It's easy to be a smart aleck,"
he admonished me "and you aren't even that, you're just being
naive. Have you ever seen a Ukrainian holding a job that is good,
one where he can smuggle something back from? No. They neither
speak German nor Polish, so how do you expect them to be clever at
scheming? Do you think peasant lads, who hardly know the value of
money, are the kind to go in for black-market affairs? Not likely.
Their only asset is their brawn and that, naturally, they use to the
full. Your compassion for those being robbed is also out of place,
kid. People who save up their bread to trade it for things like tobacco, deserve no better. Anything not eaten up at once is surplus, so
don't worry yourself if it goes to those who need it."

Aghast at my acquaintance's attitude, I stubbornly maintained that stealing from fellow-prisoners could be nothing else but
a crime. ". . . a dastardly crime," I cried. "No bigger than those the
others commit," said my equally aroused opposite. "It's an open
secret that the Germans in their cushy jobs as block personnel take
away part of our rations. That's allowed, eh? The Gypsies sell cigarettes they have skillfully poked out half the tobacco from. The
Jews will cheat you on anything and everything. That's ruthless,
too. Or isn't it, because you do it more pleasantly? Our people are
rough and outspoken, they do the same, only by force, rudely and
frankly."

I still had ammunition to reply with. "You can't convince me,"
I shot back undauntedly. "They are repulsive hooligans, nothing
Russia can be proud of, a bad advertisement, indeed!" "Well,"
came the reply, remarkably quiet but sneering, "ask those lads
about the Western world. Go on, tell them that what they have seen
of it is civilized."

We paused awhile. The Ukrainian—a little unfairly, I
thought—had cornered me with something I was too young to
judge. Then, to my relief, he changed the subject. ". . . next time
you start arguing," he broke off, "remember that gentle cheating
and open robbery smell the same to us."

I talked to a fellow-prisoner, a Pole, who worked at the butcher's. "It is nearly impossible now to get rich by smuggling out sausages," he told me, "all our 'organizing' methods have been found out and controls are strict." One of the ways of "organizing," I learned, had been to cause the drains to be blocked, to call in the sanitation squad and have them poke out the muck with long cleaning rods so that when at the inside end the rods came wriggling in through the inspection hole, all the partners had to do was to hook a few sausages onto them.

Much of the meat had found its way to the sausage factory because at Oswiecim it had been condemned as being unfit. "Sometimes there are even worms in it," said my acquaintance, "something really sickening to look at."

Next Thursday accordingly, when we received our twice-weekly allocation of sausage, a worker's ration of 100 grams, I struggled hard to keep up my determination not to be reminded of its ingredients. Previously the relative merits of spiced black-pudding, liver sausage containing fish bones and jellied pork sausage—the three traditional camp varieties—had greatly interested me. Now I no longer dared to pass opinions on them. When thinking of where they came from, they all seemed to be a disgusting, repulsive fraud; but when considering where they were to go, they still appeared to be a cherished luxury, a treat we counted the days by.

* * *

Officially, the stables had been completed now. Our little construction squad had been disbanded, much to our despair. The autumn winds heralded yet another camp winter. Dared we face it at a bigger, harder place of work where our being newcomers would be exploited to the full? We racked our brains trying to find an alternative.

A dozen of us, the remnant of the former "new stable" squad who had been unable to find another more or less agreeable job, were assembled at the unemployeds' place, in order to be assigned to unload railway trucks—the slavery of the materials yard I already once had had a taste of. It was dawn, a few minutes past six.

One by one, accompanied by metallic marching music, the working squads were marched out of camp—"specialists" leaving behind a dozen haggard, useless, unskilled ones like myself. I felt as helpless as on the day of my arrival.

Then, completely unexpectedly, our foreman, the one that knew English, suggested that we, too, start marching out. He had a plan but would not reveal it. "You leave that to me," he said hurriedly, already placing himself in front to lead us on. "If we don't take the risk now, they'll send us off to become 'Mussulmen,' to unload bags of cement running at the double. Come on lads, all I ask you is to march smartly. Don't forget: hands and caps pressed to the seams of the trouser legs; short, quick steps!"

"Kommando Aufraeumungsarbeiten Neue Pferdestaelle 12 Mann, Voll" yelled our spokesman when we had reached the gate, "cleaning-up squad, new stables, 12 men, full." The guard on duty scanned the list. He had never heard of such a squad and could find no record of it anywhere. Nor was there any, but our foreman soon accounted for it.

"Yes," agreed the SS man, carefully adding our newly created squad to his checklist, "if you have left a dirty mess at the place you'll damn well have to clean it up yourselves."

Our trick had worked. At noon the foreman would look for our former SS-supervisor, convince him—if at all necessary—and have our squad legalized. Work would not be lacking. We would beautify the stables: level the earth all around, fill up the cracks, touch up the whitewash and climb up the attic rafters to look for leaky roofing tiles. Any duty-conscious SS supervisor would be satisfied by that.

The twelve of us, now perhaps the smallest and pleasantest working squad, were glad to be back at the stables. Warm horses, soft bales of straw, heaps of turnips, the penetrating smell of fodder, and a roof over one's head were not too bad to spend the winter with. We even felt attached to our surroundings. We had sweated to build, now we would try to enjoy. Our foreman friend, too, was satisfied. He had been promoted to sub-capo, and certainly deserved this honor for his cleverness.

My second winter in camp seemed far more endurable than the first. I was less hungry and no longer afraid of the cruel world around me. It now lay before me like an open book, waiting for youth to tear away the few pages that were spoiling it—to rebind it with a strong, unbreakable cover of equality and comradeship, to brighten it with the achievements of progress, to gild it with an unquenchable determination for justice.

Often, now, the room elder sent me along to the kitchen compound, to act as spokesman and persuade the head cook to allocate another vat of soup to us youngsters at Block 13a. Sometimes, drawing heavily on that part of the brain that stocked polite, German eloquence I succeeded so that, much to the envy of the other blocks, we could feast on noodle-with-milk diet left over from the hospital.

People had begun favoring us young prisoners. Everyone was eager to show himself helpful, now that supplies were being bolstered by the provisions the well-supplied Hungarian transports had brought along. A good name could be had for little sacrifice and, with the war drawing to its close, the adults around us were quick to grab the opportunity. Last year, bewildered, younger, we had been on our own. Now, hardened, experienced, we scorned those who then had shrugged their shoulders at our sufferings—those who called themselves men, but were really blind cattle about to drown in their own filth. We no longer needed their paternal considerations.

Then there was Leo Voorzanger the Dutchman, a new friend of mine, twelve years my senior. Measuring a lanky six feet, flatfooted and clad in grotesquely large shoes, frog-eyed and wearing a dilapidated pair of glasses held together by string, gentle and full of pleasant memories of Scheveningen, his peaceful home town, he was the ideal figure to make fun of. But jolly Leo did not mind. On the contrary, he took pride in being the object of laughter. "All right, lads," he would concede. "All right then, you say I should sing something to you, because I am called Voorzanger. All right, there we go," he cried, his big feet tapping out a jazz rhythm, his shifting eyes full of glee. "Hey, baba ree bop—!"

Those of us who said that the Dutch are musical were right. At home Leo had played the saxophone—"The shiny thing that comes next to Holland and my wife," he told me. Leo was also an enthusiastic patriot, even now that the Nazis had found that the Voorzanger half of the family was of Jewish origin.

I greatly liked easygoing Leo. He made a good comrade, frank and trustworthy. In addition he knew a thing or two about cooking—handy now that I robbed the docile horses at our place of work of a turnip a day. On Sunday evenings, when the lone stove in his room was not littered with toast, he would make soup on it, a delicious brew of turnips, bread and an occasional onion.

Surrounded by cold, snow-covered fields, our lucky secluded little squad at the stables hardly merited the attention of the roaming SS supervisors, so that our relative independence was rarely interfered with. Of the twelve of us, one was a foreman, two lookouts, and another two spent half their time plodding back and forth to the camp to fetch our soup.

Once, together with a young Polish Jew, it was my turn to get the soup. Pushing a wheelbarrow with a thermos container strapped to it, we were stamping along the icy road. "What do we do when we arrive at the gate?" I asked my companion. "Don't you worry. Leave that to me, and for heaven's sake don't do anything else. Just keep on pushing the barrow," said he. "It's not the first time I've gone for soup, so leave all the reporting and standing attention to me." Within sight of the camp he again reminded me: "Remember what I said, you go straight on!"

When we reached the checkpost, I did, and, marching neatly while at the same time carefully balancing the barrow, I passed the gate. But I did not get far. Someone from behind was vigorously boxing my ears, shouting: "How dare you damned *Schweinehund* ignore us?" I was thrown onto the paving and kicked at. The barrow overturned. Crouching on the ground, trying to ward off the blows, I perceived glimpses of running feet—jackbooted ones of more SS men rushing towards what was for them a scene of entertainment. "I'll teach you for that!" shouted the fierce gray figure above me.

Then an SS officer came and asked the guards what I had done. Someone said that I was only a harmless *Schweinehund.* "Take your bloody barrow off the roadway," shouted another, "how dare you block the traffic!" "Get away from here, bastard!" I raised myself and gladly did as told.

My perplexed companion, pale with fright, his fair skin whiter than ever and myself flushed and bleeding, pushing the barrow like a drunkard, entered camp. Our fellow prisoners stared at us but they had little to ask about. Silently we made for the nearest washroom.

When I had cooled down and quieted my anger, I asked what had happened. The SS man who was to check us in, unable to trace our little-known squad on the lists, had told my companion to stop. He in turn was supposed to have transmitted the order to me, but in his excitement he forgot and let my unaware self, my eyes fixed forwards, march straight into camp without being registered. This, in the code of the SS, was an offense exceeded in seriousness only by leaving without being registered. Being so, I had come off lightly, I realized.

A few minutes later there was another surprise. "You nearly got us into trouble, this time," mumbled my companion, opening the container and extracting two packets of black market butter from it. "Didn't you rather?" I replied, unpleasantly aware of what his nervous forgetfulness had been caused by. It had taught me yet another lesson.

* * *

By permission of the SS, or perhaps by order, a Christmas tree had been erected at the camp—a huge, rustling mass of green twigs with colored ribbons, glittering globes and electric candles. There being no black-out, it was to shine like a beacon of hope, but we could not bring ourselves to like it. There just was too much irony about it.

This Christmas, unlike last year's, had been declared a holiday. We did not work, received extra allocations of soup and bread, and, for once, stopped worrying about being hungry.

Saucy Gert invited me to Block 5, where more than a hundred people had crowded into a little room to celebrate. In the far corner was a table with a small, poor-looking Christmas tree on it. Few of us still believed in religion, but it was comforting to know that, at this moment, people would concentrate upon thinking of their fellow men.

Would those surrounded by their carol-chanting children remember us? Would the many devout ones that filled the silent churches be remembered of us?

We started singing solemnly and impressively. "Holy night, holy night. . . ."

A German camp veteran next to me was weeping. It was the twelfth time now he had heard this song battling against the cruel walls of concentration camps.

Most of the assembled were Germans, all veterans. Saucy Gert's superior, the capo of the Raisko farming squad, a former German criminal, pushed himself through the crowd towards the table. As patron of the gathering he wanted to say a few words to us.

"Comrades," he addressed us, "today, in the year 1944, it is Christmas again. We think of Jesus. We think of our families. We think of those who have left us. . . .

"In our many years of trial, we have often come near the verge of despair. But we kept on hoping, confident that one day the spirit of the Lord will prevail. Today, on this memorable day, we not only hope, but know for certain, that the next year will bring us the decision we all so anxiously have been waiting for. Let us spend this Christmas with the conviction that the forces of brotherhood, love and self-sacrifice will be victorious. Let us look forward to a world of equality and peace.

"When, with the will of the Lord, on the Christmas of 1945, we shall be free men again, let us not forget, then, all those we are gathered with now. However far apart, let us recall what we had wished for. Then, as now, may our conscience guide us—"

We had listened neither to a Christian nor to a German, but the voice of a bitter, hardened concentration camp inmate. When it had faded we joined in to sing: *"Wir sind die Moorsoldaten."**

After Christmas our hopes were brighter than ever before. Only a very few transports were arriving now and the SS was unexpectedly quiet towards us. Again there were chances of a quick liberation, for the Soviet armies were expected to start their long-awaited winter attack within a few days.

On New Year's Eve I had an invitation to Block 16a. When I arrived, the room was already filled with dense smoke from *"Ersatz"* tobacco; the inmates were sitting on their bunks, their feet dangling down to the wooden frames below and tapping out rhythms on them. At the end of the gangway sat a "band": three Dutch Jews with a drum, a violin and a saxophone they had borrowed from the camp orchestra.

Towards midnight the listeners climbed down from their beds and started to dance—waltzes, foxtrots, polkas, all within the bounds of the three-yard wide corridor between the bunks. A few busied themselves imitating women, others drew laughter by jerking the lower halves of their bodies, sportively thrusting them back and forth. Everyone—except perhaps myself, a non-dancer, watching attentively from the third, upper tier of a bunk—was doing his best to be funny. Then, with the three sweating musicians playing jazz, they danced lively solos. By the grace of God and by the birth of Christ, it was now 1945.

A week later, rumor had it that the camp was to be evacuated to the West, but no one seemed to know when and how. Meanwhile we went on working. Otherwise the whole district would become paralyzed. Without the prisoners at the supply depots, without those manning the various maintenance squads, Auschwitz would cease to exist.

*See appendix.

Our little squad, too, continued to work; to trudge its way through the cold Polish winter to the far-off stables, to enjoy the warmth of the horses, to hide itself amongst the bales of straw, and to contemplate things to come. While the other squads still counted a few hundred, or even a few thousands, ours had shrunk to six—half a dozen *Schutzhaeftlinge* (protective custody prisoners as the authorities ironically chose to call us) whom, to our luck, no one bothered much to supervise.

Some months ago, the Nazis, finally realizing that their cause was lost, had ordered all major construction work to be stopped. Every second one of the many buildings littering the camp working territory had been left unfinished.

It was we who had built them. Written on the foundation concrete were our names; hidden among the bricks were messages to those who would survive us. One day the world would know.

The bare walls stuck out like ruins, row after row of red bricks surrounded by a vast sea of lifeless snow. Where there should have been roofs and windows, sat deep cushions of white snow—triumphant like conquerors. An icy wind whistled through the empty shells. No one had been near them for a long time. There was not even the faintest sign of footprints.

The uncompleted structures looked as grotesque and odd as the ideas of those who had ordered them. Like antiquities, they would soon be relics of a culture that had killed itself—a way of living that was a path of death, a system that had failed.

It was the day of our departure, early in the morning. Long queues of people waiting to leave the camp coiled around the blocks. The block personnel, under SS supervision, busied themselves burning index cards. Feeding the pyre came the documents from the administration barracks.

First we were led to the bath at the vast, newly-finished disinfection and laundry building just beyond the fence. At the still uncompleted de-lousing wing, we saw an array of heavy metal doors lying on the icy ground—doors that could no longer be fixed, doors of gas chambers whose purpose had been planned as "manifold."

With ourselves marched off to another place, all this would be left behind.

Our beds which, being the only things to call our own, we had become so fond of, would also be left behind. Carved on their wooden posts and boards were our names and numbers. How often had I spent the evening lying on my sack of straw, reading the fading chronicles of people who had slept there before me? No more beds for us now: only two blankets, rolled up and slung diagonally over our shoulders, to take refuge and dream on.

Then I queued up again, for hours. I had lost contact with the friends I wanted to be together with. Near the gate, surrounded by guards with fixed bayonets, were carts full of provisions. Each of us received two loaves (the ration for eight days) and a tin of stewed steak. Every third was given a 500 gr. packet of margarine. They were supposed to have shared it, but quite a few took the treasure and disappeared. Others, rightly or wrongly clamoring for their shares, busied themselves threatening from among the precarious owners of fatty, yellow slabs all those who were likely to be intimidated.

It was already dark when I passed through the camp gate. I had done so some 800 times before, but now, on the 18th of January, it was for good. I was marching out of the vast territory of Auschwitz for the last time.

We passed a detachment of guards with heavy machine-guns. None of them looked sympathetic.

Then, joining the long columns that slowly moved along the dark country roads, came the women of Birkenau camp. Some of them could be recognized as looking old. "There you are," said someone. "I told you so. We are not going to be led far. Otherwise they would not drag along the old ones." "Probably they are marching us to another camp somewhere around here," argued another. "Who knows how many places like Auschwitz there are by now?"

The moon had come out. We were trekking along the road parallel to the Sola River. There were guards on the right, on the left, behind and in front. Liberation had just been a dream. It would come to Auschwitz, yes. But not for us.

CHAPTER VI

Finale

The column seemed endless. As it crawled along the road, it was joined by prisoners from the subsidiary camps. At every crossing there were more of them. We were moving on without a stop, the fast ones in front, the old and slow behind.

At first we had marched in rows. Now we were shuffling along like a herd, tired and exhausted.

Lining the fields on either side of us were lone heaps. I had noticed these ever-recurring landmarks before but now, by the dim light of the rising moon, I recognized them. Lying on the snow huddled up in their blue-white prison-coats were lifeless bodies.

One had a ripped open cardboard box next to him—empty except for a bundle of letters, fluttering in the icy breeze.

Had the owner been too slow or too quick? Who, later on, had been the daring thief? Or had the body itself been the thief?

My head was humming with the words that had once decorated the walls of Block 7a: "There is but one road to freedom; its milestones are obedience, diligence...." The guard, before pulling the trigger, must have heard the same in his ears. How else could he have sworn blind obedience to those to whom humanity was nothing but exploitable cattle?

I looked away from the heaps. I tried not to think at all, and staggered along like a drunkard. All that mattered was to reach our destination.

At dawn we reached a road junction. Beyond lay hills, at the left a village, and to the right an icy field littered with squatting, slumbering prisoners. On our being told to join them I sprawled onto the trampled-down snow and quickly fell asleep.

Soon, however, loud shouts woke me up again. An excited messenger, sitting on a motorcycle, his legs apart, one hand on the handle bar, the other gesticulating vehemently, was arguing with some officers. He seemed to be a Wehrmacht man from the front, who had come to warn them of Russian observation planes. Then the officers shouted at the guards and we were hustled into the nearby farmyards.

I pushed myself into a warm barn. It was already crowded with men from the other camps, but before they realized my intrusion I had climbed onto a haystack and was asleep. Then someone tapped my shoulders: "Wake up, kid, the old woman at the farmhouse has just invited some of us in to have some food. You'd better hang around there in case she asks another lot to join her."

The Polish peasants, I reflected, were courageous—much more than we had expected them to be. When we passed their villages, stubborn old women stood at the curb handing out milk—even at night. That they were beaten by the guards, who were infuriated at not receiving such favors for themselves, did not deter them at all.

I did not care, however. Food or no food, kindness or none, I wanted to sleep.

After a bare four hours' sleep we were chased out onto the roads again. Not wanting to burden myself with things that anyhow would not save me, I left behind my blankets. Of the provisions that were to last a week, only one loaf of square, dark army bread had remained for the strenuous task ahead. It was tucked in beneath my armpits, for my fingers were numb with cold.

There was no longer one continuous marching column. Plodding along the country road were several independent detachments, some quicker, others slower. If the guard was decent he would allow the weak to wait for the column behind. Or was it that the stragglers were to join the silent landmarks we had seen?

Everyone was endeavouring to walk near a "good" guard. If the rifleman really was "good," he would even shout: "Keep on moving. It's only a few more miles now and it sure ain't worthwhile giving up now. I'm tired too, but we'll have to make it."

Our guards, although frequently relieved and equipped with plenty of marching provisions, liked to pity themselves. Self-pity, it seemed, had become a virtue in Germany. To make it worse, they made it a pretext for having us carry their baggage. "Come here, boy," they hailed us, "take my rucksack for a while, it's getting damned heavy for me."

There were also the old and sick among us asking to be helped. My feet were blistered and aching, but I could not refuse to do my share. Having someone support himself on my shoulders had become routine. More than that: when I asked to be relieved, I never sounded impressive enough for passing on the burden.

It was dark again, and we had ceased to be of any particular age, nationality or prominence. We were just figures trudging through the night.

It was the second night of our long march. Hail and snow were driving into our faces. We were hungry, but our fingers were too numb to grip the cherished bread that was hidden in our pockets.

About midnight we passed a churchyard. I was not squeamish about cemeteries. Two years ago, when I was barely thirteen, I had myself dug graves and already then had walked around tombstones after dark.

Even this deserted little burial-place would not merit the attention of ghosts, I reasoned. If there be any such creatures they were right among us. I looked forward and behind. True, I seemed to be surrounded by ghostly shades—hordes of them.

Then, suddenly, something happened that shook me up. Even the various kinds of ghosts would surely not have ignored it. From the East, behind the woods, fiery trails were shooting into the sky, plenty of them. They rose and fell again.

Someone shouted *"Katushas."* I remembered now. It was

not ghostly shades that surrounded me, but people the like of whom I had known for nineteen months in the concentration camp. Katusha, the Russian multiple rocket gun, was not new to me. We had heard it being sung about so often that it had become synonymous with victory. It was a dream no longer. They were coming now.*

Our lips were closed to keep out the cold, pressed together to retain their warmth. But again I perceived the tunes we had sung about the Katushas—this time from that part of my being where hope is stored. "We'll bring Katushas...." " "Good luck to you, Katusha!"

Thirty minutes later the sky to the left of us was still il-luminated by rockets. They had penetrated our hearts. Turning from despair to confidence, we had found new strength. "Come on, comrade, pull yourself together," we encouraged each other, "we might be liberated any hour now."

A group of two dozen women prisoners and their guard were seen moving along a footpath winding itself through obscuring shrubs to the woods beyond, where the rockets came from. A guard of ours, spotting them, shouted across the field: "Hey, you, where are you taking your flowers to?"

"Don't worry, I know the district," came the reply, "we won't get lost. We are just taking a short cut to get there quicker." I myself never found out what he meant by "there." But, judging by the look of it, I wished them good luck for their adventure.

The attitude of the guards had changed remarkably. They now told us that we would be marching on till a railhead was found from where we could be evacuated westwards.

Here and there, the requisitioned sledges we were pushing, heaped with the luggage of the guards, became resting places for the weak. Some others, whose legs had failed them, were pulled

---

*I found out later that it was the beginning of the Russian offensive which ended with the encirclement of Breslau.

along the snow lying on mere planks.

We had reached a railway station. Dazzled by the bright lights that illuminated the sidings, we slowly passed a greasy black engine. It was standing near the road, blowing off steam, and the driver leaned out of the cabin, unperturbed. "Nothing doing anymore," he kept shouting at us in a strong Polish accent, "our line has been cut. The trains have been overdue for hours now." The Katushas, it seemed, had been more than nice fireworks.

Then we passed the town of Pless, where my great-grandfather had lived. In the market square we met a group of Birkenau women prisoners who were squatting around the fountain, resting for a while. We wanted to join them but had to move on.

The town's inhabitants were asleep, doors and windows covered with shutters. No one seemed to notice us as we shuffled along through the dark, narrow, cobble-stoned streets. Only the dogs in the backyards, howling a strange greeting, were interested.

Later the road rose into the wooded hills, turning and twisting, and sapping our precious energy.

A mysterious silhouette stood out from the forest. I recognized it to be a hunting lodge, some three stories in height. Decorating the high gables were elaborately carved roofing timbers. They were barely visible and only very few of us may have noticed them; but, possibly because of this, they greatly intrigued me. How could people have worried about such unessential nonsense?

Those who had set up this forest residence could, at the same time, surely not have concerned themselves with their needy fellow-beings. Why, then, should I expect them to care now?

The landscape became Upper Silesian: coal mines and pitheads. Some mines worked night shifts and stood out like beacons from the otherwise blacked-out countryside. Others seemed deserted. I remembered the time, six years ago, when coal mines were my favorite playgrounds, when I had tried to climb the slag dumps, when I had admired railway engines. It was all so different now.

Adjoining one of the mines was a concentration camp. Both were deserted. I scanned the barracks. The windows were broken, the walls charred. The streets were littered with burned-out furniture, blankets and eating bowls.

Had the inmates been liquidated? Had the SS tried burning them alive? Had there been a revolt? Or was it vandalism for its own sake?

Our column, dwindled to a mere thousand, kept dragging itself on. We had passed more railway sidings but our destination remained as uncertain as ever. Again there was forest around us. My eyes grew dim and I walked in a trance. I may have had determination, but my legs, alas, were only those of a boy.

The guards were firing over our heads. I would not have noticed it if they had not used tracer bullets, which woke me up a bit.*

I no longer recognized what was going on. Silhouettes that lined the horizon seemed to be rows of tall buildings. Moments later they appeared to be the outskirts of a forest. Then again I imagined we were in a town.

Finally our column stopped. The shadows I had moved along with came back to life. It was dawn. Ahead of me was a sea of prisoners moving slowly towards a tunnel. From the far end of it rose clouds of smoke. High-ranking SS officers moved about surveying us. Our guards had left us, saying that this was the destination.

Some of us, trying to escape, were shot down by sentries that lay inconspicuously in the surrounding fields. One of the victims, still wearing his yellow armband, had been a capo.

Again the snow was dotted with heaps. This time death seemed to have been violent, for the shapes, in their striped garb, hugged the ground as if they had wrestled with it, and there was blood.

Morale was at an ebb, the rumors frightening. No one returned from the tunnel. We could not see the far end but sensed that it was bound to be ominous.

Jostled by the pushing crowd I descended the funnel-like

---

*Later I was told that there were partisans in the forest. The Germans had fired for the sake of effect.

slope. The decisive moment had come and I wanted to be prepared for it—to fight to the last. I dropped my precious loaf of bread, loosened my belt and flung away the useless metal mug that was tied to it. My hands free, I was ready now.

Luckily, however, my youthful imagination turned out to be wrong. The far end was nothing but a railway station. The smoke had risen from an engine shed. We had arrived at Loslau, the railhead to the West.

By the rays of the rising sun, I now found some acquaintances of mine, exhausted like myself but still adorned with "luggage"— blankets, shawls, bowls, mugs, loaves and, here and there, even carefully-saved tins of meat. "Where did they snatch your blankets, boy?" they hailed me. "At the farmyard when you were asleep??" "Eaten up all your bread, too, eh?" All I could answer was a meek "Yes." I was too ashamed to tell the truth.

Then we were ordered into the open goods-wagons that waited along the platform. There appeared to be no more of us than two train loads full. Arranging ourselves into neat rows, legs spread apart gripping the neighbor in front, we squatted on the dirty floor boards and fell asleep. When the train pulled out, we jerked backwards and bumped together, but I barely realized it. I had spent myself. Of the last strenuous fifty hours only four had been devoted to rest.

In the late afternoon I raised myself to look over the wagon walls. The district was familiar. Back in 1939 I had passed it sitting in an express train munching sweets. On our left, running parallel to us, was the Oder. I had never tired looking at it, and could stare at it for hours. I had known it since birth, drunk it, dipped into it and crossed it in a rowing boat together with Aunt Ruth. Even now it was fascinating.

Our hunger was immense. On stopping at small country stations, we begged the railway men to fill our metal eating bowls with snow. The icy fluff, more or less white, had become a delicacy, and the type of bystander willing to hand it to you a subject of study. At some places even workers with Nazi Party emblems in their buttonholes were helpful. Elsewhere, however, often throughout a whole district, our requests were ignored.

To expect sympathy at the bigger stations was futile. Platforms were crowded with suitcase-laden German civilians clamoring to be evacuated westwards who, on realizing that the so-called "subhumans" were being given preference to them, threw spiteful glances at us. It must rightly have hurt the pride of the many pompous, arrogant wearers of brown SA uniforms that dotted the impatient throngs, to have less privileges than mere prisoners. "Will there still be time?" they must have asked themselves in despair. "Will there be enough wagons to take unproductive civilians?"

In ordinary circumstances, people fleeing their homes are sympathized with. But those Germans who queued up in front of the guarded railway stations deserved no better. They had had all their lives to think about imperialism, or *"Lebensraum"* as Hitler chose to call it. Again and again there had been warnings as to its consequences, yet the nation of *Kultur* and science seemed to like it. The striving Germans, goaded on by Fascism, were not satisfied with having to toil for their successes; they wanted slaves, Jews to take valuables from, dead bodies to strip clothing from, and human bones for making soap. Now it was over, and the murderers of yesterday were clamoring to be rescued, to be saved for the sake of all the virtues they themselves had never had the courage for. They would claim to be educated, kind, polite, cultured, clever, intelligent, straight, clean, accurate, hard-working, home-loving, animal-loving, European, Western, Christian and pious. After the defeat they would try to enlist the help of everything and anything. But they would not dare to ask for justice.

From what we saw, the German population imagined itself to be immensely important. Ourselves, mere under-dogs, only deserved to be despised, or, at the utmost, to be pitied by them. But the proud Teutons were wrong. The many intellectuals and "dangerous ones" that would decide the future of Europe were on our side, among us, wearing prison garb.

Already now we were determined to stage a show of strength. Whenever, in the surrounding fields, we spotted fellow-prisoners we yelled greetings and wishes for a quick liberation. The guards, two to the wagon, were helpless. They neither risked provoking a revolt nor felt entitled to stop the train.

Near Breslau, where oddly enough work was still going on at new embankments and extension lines to the railway, we passed many more toiling prisoners—inmates of prisons, concentration and labor camps, prisoners of war from Russia, Poland, France and Belgium, conscripted laborers from the Ukraine and Czechoslovakia, men and women.

When we slowly moved past a storage depot where prisoners ran at the double unloading sacks of flour, our defiance reached its climax. Someone started singing; not the camp ditties with which we had once proved ourselves to be alive, but songs which were awake, vigorous, determined and stirring. We joined in, wagon after wagon. So did our comrades at the depot who had stopped work and lined the ramp to greet us.

At the far end of the stores an irate SS man busied himself chasing his flock of prison-garbed beings back to their jobs.

"Arise, ye starvelings from your slumber...." Drowning the protesting shouts of our guards were the strains of the "Internationale." It was the only song known to all of us, the only hymn none of the bystanders would fail to recognize. It was no particular favorite of ours, but appropriate.

Of Breslau we only saw the shunting yards—the endless fields of rails, the criss-cross canopy of electric feeder cables—the overhead steel-wires, cut, dangling down loosely, telling of a recent air-raid.

Awhile later we arrived at a fence-surrounded expanse of barracks which, hemmed in by wooded mountain slopes on one side and by the single railway track on the other, was unmistakably a concentration camp. I felt glad, for I could not have stood it much longer. We had continuously been exposed to the bitter cold for nearly a week, and our provisions, supposed to have nourished us with 350 grams of bread a day, had all been gobbled up. It was three days since I had last nibbled at a crumb of hard, frozen bread, two since I had swallowed some mouthfuls of snow. But the SS officer who, in the loud manner so characteristic of his kind, came to meet our train, did not want us. His camp, he shouted at the commander of our guards, was full up and we should be taken elsewhere.

The train jerked into motion and pulled out again towards the main line.

When, after less than an hour, we reached a village, the guards opened the doors and shouted their traditional *"'raus!"* I jumped down onto the gravel below and, my knees shaking with weakness, joined those who waited to be marched off. But some I had shared the open wagons with, stayed behind. Many who for days had been sitting on the floor no longer had the energy to raise themselves. Not a few of those sleeping quietly in the corner were dead.

Then we trudged through the village. On the left were old farmsteads, on the right rows of new bungalows, most of them unfinished. The road-sign read: "Gross-Rosen."

At a bend, the road was blocked by a big horse-drawn cart full of hay. On top of it, at the reins, and in front of the nearby barn, we recognized French prisoners of war—talkative Latins who, quite unimpressed by our guards' shouting to clear the way, wanted to know all about us.

I asked what they were saying. "There is a concentration camp a few kilometers down the road, but they don't know how its prisoners are being treated," someone translated for me. "Most of their talk is about being home-sick." "And what was that they were shouting?" "They are wishing us good luck and say we should forget our troubles and be full of spirit like themselves."

After passing some large stone quarries where, standing out from its bright gray walls, there scurried figures in blue-white prison garb, we reached the camp gate. From there by the vigorous commands of "left, right! left, right!" we rigidly marched onto the vast *"Appell Platz,"* the roll call place, and then along the road leading to the barracks. On either side were large flower beds.

The plants were so well looked after that they could have competed in the most luxurious of garden shows. Yet they seemed ugly, cold and militaristic—mere dots in painstakingly symmetric patterns that, implanted on square plots of earth, were designed to divide off the SS buildings from the wretched shacks of the prisoners.

Then we left behind the flowers. On our right was the fenced-off women's camp, its ragged, haggard inmates, also having arrived from the East, shouting messages at us in Hungarian. On our left, under curfew, lay the men's compound, rigidly supervised by guards and criminal block elders. Ahead, at the end of the road, was another gate and beyond it our destination: some fifty widely spaced barracks embracing the rough hillside, the extension camp. Next to it threatened the inevitable crematoria.

"Gross-Rosen," they called this uncanny conglomeration. "Great Roses," indeed.

*　　*　　*

I had been pushed into Block 40, a bare wooden floor surrounded by walls, enclosed by a roof and approached by a precariously supported ramp, two yards in height and covered only by tree trunks two feet apart. The ramp was dangerous—perhaps purposely so—and a constant cause of accidents. Being driven out to the hours-long, thrice daily roll calls, we slipped and fell on it—often right through. At one of the blocks, at night, under the blind onrush of some one hundred warmth-seeking inmates, it had collapsed.

People were nervous, irritable and unwilling to cooperate. In the evenings, when after the noisy, troublesome issuing of blankets we were looking for a place to sleep, the floor never seemed big enough. At night when we groped our way to the lone pit in the loamy ground outside that was the lavatory, we risked being shot at. On coming back we would find our sleeping place occupied by someone else. Then, unless we felt strong enough to be aggressive, we could only wait at the door until the next lavatory-goer had to give up his place.

Even those hugging their precious part of floor without ever budging from it, had anything but a quiet night. There was not an inch of stepping space and people trying to pass the mass of sleeping bodies rarely bothered to take off their shoes. If you slept near the door you had to lie on your hands, else they would be trodden upon.

In the distance, now, we already heard the roaring of gun battles. But even that failed to have an effect on the many unsociable characters among us. The agents of hell kept on being devilish fiends.

Before their imprisonment, I found out, most of them had been quite respectable persons, well-mannered family men. They went to church, or to synagogue, and their only sins were committed when, on rare occasions, their business demanded it—for business was business. Afterwards, forced to live under abnormal conditions among people of different tongues, intellects and ideas, their outlook had changed. God, the one they had built their hopes on, the one they had put their trust in, had shown that he took no direct interest in their sufferings. The reaction of the disillusioned ones, no longer bound by scruples, had been violent. Knowing that the system of each-for-himself had reached its climax, their fellow men—beings they had never really cared about—were just ignored now.

When you reproached someone for his vile, loathsome behavior he would excuse himself by saying, "Camp life is camp life. If you want to survive, you must be ruthless." Their saying of old, it seemed, had somewhat undergone a change, but the story was an old one. It had come right from the prehistoric caves and jungles by way of Fascism: "Let all others suffer, as long as I myself survive."

We young people knew well who was degrading himself. But we did not feel depressed. It was not our concern to defend the past. Ours was to look towards the future.

We now lived on a daily ration of 300 grams of bread and a spoonful of jam. Three times a week there was half a liter of luke-warm soup—flavored water whose main ingredient seemed to be salt.

Obtaining this pitiful measure of soup was quite a procedure, for it usually arrived at night unexpectedly. The moment our block elder was notified by the camp-kitchen (the sweatshop that despite its 24-hour day was far too small to supply the 80,000 new-comers) that our allocation was ready, he would start looking for volunteers to fetch it. At first, conscious of the extra quarter liter it earned them, people had been willing to help. But soon the incentive for trudging through the cold, slippery camp laden with heavy vats began to seem ridiculous. It did not warrant giving up our sleep and risking our health. So we preferred to be picked by force—to be chased around the block by the infuriated block elder who kept shouting that if we did not collect our soup the kitchen would stop supplying us altogether.

One night, when my dodging the block elder had not been clever enough, I too was sent for soup. Was it to be as dreadful an ordeal as people said it was? I did not trust rumors.

The twelve of us took the carrying battens, the U-shaped iron vat supports, and strolled dreamily through the sleeping camp. Instead of roads there were steep, winding footpaths, slippery with slush and littered with boulders. On our left, heaped in front of the crematoria, lay piles of naked bodies, frozen blue. We looked away, scanning only the descending ground ahead lest we slip on it.

Our destination, the gate leading to the main camp, was already blocked by some 300 others who had arrived before us. Looking down on the impatient and hungry throng cornered in by a separate barbed wire enclosure were glaring searchlights, perched on poles. From the central tower beyond the main gate there shone more lights—an array of big projectors, eight in all, that were hung onto it, side by side, like enormous pearls in a chain of unworldly glitter.

At half past two, after we had waited for over an hour, the crowd became livelier, shouting and excited. The vats had arrived. One by one they called the numbers of the lucky blocks that were to receive them. But the frantic bystanders could not endure seeing food carried away for someone else. Like human hyenas they pounced upon the open vats of soup, some trying to dip in their caps, others attempting to push their heads into it. Here and there we heard piercing yells, fierce and hysterical.

Then they called for our block. But when we had jostled ourselves to the gate and finally stood before the steaming vats, we were suddenly faced by another little group, who also claimed to represent Block 40. It was an obvious fraud, yet by the time the kitchen people made up their mind another half an hour had passed.

After that, we picked up our precious soup, two to a vat, and made our way back, led by a brawny Ukrainian who threateningly swung his spare carrying batten to ward off thieves. Careful not to spill the hot brew onto our feet, we climbed the dark, treacherous hillside, slowly, skillfully, step after step. Every now and then a rowdy eager to get at the vat tried to kick our legs to make us fall. Elsewhere we slipped of our own accord through sheer panic. I seemed far too weak for the heavy vat. My knees were trembling but I had no choice. I was a mere number no one cared about, a slave entitled to live only as long as I was useful.

Finally we arrived. The block elder was furious about our having spilled so much. Then, still shouting, he turned to the sleeping mass of inmates in order to wake them for dinner.

Being the latest of the newcomers, we, the inmates of Block 40, were not working yet. Half our day was spent standing to attention at seemingly endless roll calls. The rest of the time we passed by walking about camp and anxiously looking for some friendly companion we could talk to.

Many of our camp mates were as yet unacquainted with the planned, continuous intimidations that were practiced in concentration camps. Organized mass killings were new to them. Up to now they had seen only labor camps, places where work may have been harder than at Auschwitz but where the surroundings had been civilian. There had been no criminal or hardened prisoners among them and they had been grouped according to nationalities. As a result, their outlook on life had shaped itself differently from ours. They lived and thought as secluded, unbalanced individuals, either helplessly lost or aggressively egoistic.

I saw only very few youngsters and knew none. Talking with adult companions was a hopeless enterprise, for they soon let you feel that they were depressed. The tragedy of having lost their families was an all-pervading shadow, too big to be ignored even for minutes. When I dared to mention the future they would be aghast.

Long-term prisoners—those who had not heard from their families for anything up to 12 years—were different. Mostly they were socialists, people who believed their sun to be too glorious for anything to overshadow it. Even in their darkest moments they had imagined it to be shining. I knew them, for their like had often helped me. "Not out of charity," these odd people had said to us perplexed youngsters, "but because we have our obligations." Now that their sun was rising they had all the more reason to concern themselves with the young. Aware of this, I was determined to find some of them. But my scanning the haggard, indifferent faces around me was useless. The benefactors had gone. They had been sent "elsewhere"—or murdered.

Unable to find diversion among the motley crowd, I absorbed the details of the camp scenery, and, there being no one to talk to, listened attentively to the thunder of the gun battles.

The guns sounded nearer now and had become loud enough to disturb our sleep. Rumor said that we were to be evacuated again, but camp life went on as usual. Working squads, driven on at feverish haste, still toiled at the construction of new barracks.

Hauled up the steep hillside by a noisy power winch, their wheels squeaking, came dumping trolleys laden with building materials. At one of the unfinished barracks stood a furiously rotating concrete mixer. The floor was being laid. Five workers, stripped to their waist so that the wintry air would cool their sweat, shovelled away frantically at a heap of mortar. Those at the far end of the room, loudly clapping their trowels, shouted for the exhausted wheel-barrow pushers. Near the entrance stood the watchful capo, his left hand circling back and jerking forward to remind his fellow slaves to be quick, his right fingering a long, black whip. Around us, less penetrable than ever before, stretched mile after mile of lifeless, snowed-in barbed wire bulwarks charged with deadly electricity and cordoned off by a wide, low belt of entanglements. Behind it threatened slowly pacing guards, one rifle-carrying gray-coat to every fifty yards of silent snow.

This and this again was our landscape, the only one for us. Eleven years ago some lone prisoner had even composed a song about it, the "Moorsoldaten." By now this moving, sentimental melody had become the concentration camp anthem. Looking at the seemingly endless rows of fencing I could not help humming it:

> *Up and down the guards are pacing*
> *No one, no one can go through.*
> *Flight would mean a sure death facing;*
> *Guns and barbed wire greet our view.*

*   *   *

The hilly, stone-littered camp site, together with my youthful desire to explore it, took its toll now. My left shoe, the precious companion that had served me for thousands of kilometers was falling apart. Its sole was hanging down and stubbornly refused to be fixed again. I tried mending it with rare bits of string, rusty iron ends and twisted remnants of nails. But it was useless. The shoe had ceased to be one. Clinging to my left foot was nothing but a dirty gray monster that gaped at me like the threatening snout of a crocodile.

Any hour now they would drive us out for the long-expected, long-feared evacuation march. Despair and rage overcame me. Everything on earth and in heaven seemed wicked and vile. More than that: it begged to be punished for its own evil.

I limped about the frozen rubbish heaps, dug at them with my numb fingers and hoped to find something resembling a shoe.

Others, too, were searching the dumps. Torn prison clothes, broken spoons, leaky eating bowls, fragments of cement sacking, splintered spade handles—all of it looked useful to desperate camp inmates. With luck there might even be shabby remnants of garments taken from the bodies of the dead.

Then, towards evening I finally dug up what I was looking for: an oval object, flattened out by the weighty rubble above it, frozen together and encrusted with earth. It seemed to be a shoe, but before I could find out someone shouted *"Das gehoert mir!"*

The prison-garbed figure that had been lying on the other side of the heap came crawling my way. When he reached me, still not raising himself, he threw a stone. Seconds later he bit my wrist. The cruel ruthless teeth buried in my lean flesh were those of a madman: a human beast in search of loot, a prying animal whose jacket was filled with an amassed junk of everything rummagers come across—sticks, wires and paper. Before me was a being who might once have been a professor lecturing at a University on the law of private property, but was now a creature that for the sake of a slice of bread would have murdered me in my sleep.

I hit back the way it deserved, kicking it in the stomach. The beast rolled back, defeated.

A few days after the shoe affair I was walking along the trolley track—the two dark rails, standing out from the snow, over which with clockwork-like regularity rolled lorries full of sand. The lorries, passing steadily at five-minute intervals, had become something to measure the time by, a spectacle I could watch for hours. It even reminded me of home, of pit railways and coal mines.

Suddenly, however, my dreaming was interrupted. Someone had come up from behind and put his hands over my eyes. Helpless, I waited for my pockets to be searched. But my attackers only laughed. They could hardly be wanting to tease me, I reasoned. My camp-mates were all strangers and the short, sausage-like fingers pressing onto my cheek were far from friendly.

Then my mask was removed. Before me, patting my shoulders, was a squat little Russian with a smile on his broad, round-featured face. Around us stood three more like him, the other lorry pushers. "Don't you remember?" he cried, hugging me like some old woman welcoming her long-lost son. "It's me, Wajnka, Wajnka from the brick-laying school!"

I remembered now. It was one of the Wajnkas, the one who had left a year ago, the silent lad who was so obstinate that people avoided him. But that did not matter. Both of us had changed. We were old friends now, veterans.

There was much we would have liked to tell each other, but the lorry had to move on. I joined in pushing it.

Then came the foreman and we had to part. "They, too, are coming," stammered Wajnka in a mixture of Russian and broken German, pointing to where the guns were thundering. "*Etom nashe.* They are ours. You, I—comrades!"

* * *

It was the last week of January 1945. We were given scanty rations of bread and margarine, led off to the station and huddled into the cold but already familiar open goods wagons. Minutes later, accompanied by the quieting click of the wheels, we pulled out, leaving the Breslau countryside to the East. The thunder of the guns, too, seemed to be moving with us. At some places it was even louder than it had been at Gross-Rosen, and here and there along the railway line steel-helmeted soldiers were digging in already. The ponderous war god, angry, desperate, and in the throes of death, was returning to the fields he had been reared on.*

During the night, with the cold, rushing air quickly penetrating our emaciated, thinly-clad bodies, I woke up with a painful urge to relieve myself. Carefully stepping over my sleeping, curled-up wagon mates I reached the guard. Taken by surprise he jerked his bayonet: "*Was willste!?*" "*Ich muss austreten.*" "*Austreten willste, Kackvogel? Wenn de willst kannst du gaenzlich austreten.* But if you ask me, get onto the buffers."

There being little choice, I climbed down the wagon walls, balanced myself on the buffer piston, pulled down my trousers and

---

*The closing by the Russians of the "Breslau pocket" was completed by the 4th of February.

bent my knees.

The next thing I remember was my being in a strange corner of a wagon where no one wanted to know me. I found neither my place nor my blankets. I wandered about tapping at the wrapped-up bodies and looking for someone familiar. They whispered to each other that I was mad. My telling them that I had been to the buffers and then lost my way only seemed to prove their convictions. The less sleepy ones even kicked me. "Get away with you, you loony ass."

Finally, quietly and inconspicuously I squeezed in somewhere and fell asleep again.

Was it all a dream? Or was it a trance? Or had I returned to the wrong wagon? I never found the answer.

By dawn we reached Leipzig. It seemed badly damaged but alive. From the cellars beneath the ruins children came out with shopping nets and buckets to join the early queues for bread and water. We stopped at the terminus. The station hall was not only intact but as busy as it would have been in peace time, during summer holidays. Buffets and newspaper stands were being wheeled around. Platforms were crowded with well-dressed, healthy-looking civilians. Here and there people strutted around in uniform or with swastika armbands. They all seemed to be content and accustomed to seeing ragged, haggard prisoners. Except for a few, who were whispering to their neighbors, none of the bystanders appeared to be interested in us. They evidently knew all they wanted to.

Some of our German comrades wanted to tell the onlookers who we were, but we proudly decided that it would not be worth our while. Anyhow, those who needed to be told—the children—would be instructed by their parents that we were "a bunch of criminals."

A little pig-tailed girl, her neatly ironed black skirt whirling over a pair of agile, clean, blonde legs, came running towards the train, followed by her mother.

"Look Mummy, so many faces," she cried pointing to our wagon, "there is a young one. And over there another one."

We youngsters felt proud. If the adults ignored us, there still remained the youth. Would the little girl remember us?

Opposite stood a hospital train, modern, spacious and well equipped with loot from all over Europe. It was being received by a flower-bearing delegation of Red Cross sisters. We called to them, begging them that they bring water to the sick among us. But they too shut their eyes. Civilization had decided that their role would also be a farce.

Then we slowly rolled towards a siding, some miles out of town. There again was a hospital train, this time separated from us by a mere three-yard width of gravel. From the kitchen wagon delicious odors escaped. We saw the pots and pans—the luxurious compartments, the soft, white beds.

Limping along the strip of gravel came a soldier, his leg bandaged. Soon there appeared more of them. They wanted to know why honest-looking people like us wore prison-garb. We told them. It seemed news and they looked impressed. "We lads at the front knew little of what really went on back in Germany," said one. "So that's what we have been fighting for," mumbled another.

Our train started to move. The soldiers scrambled back to their compartments. They were throwing something out of the windows. It was falling into our wagon too. I looked: sweets, boiled sweets wrapped in cellophane.

I wondered. Could the lesson learned on the Eastern front from the "Red barbarians," painful though it was, have been more convincing than the drill at home from their kinsmen the nationalist, Nazi schoolteachers?

We had arrived in Weimar, at the eastern end of the main goods station. It seemed that we were going to wait there. The engine had left and so had most of our guards.

I scanned the new surroundings, a vast railway yard on one side, beyond and behind, and on the other, some meters away from us, a road. Along the road were gardens, but just opposite our wagon was an impressive building. It was the engineering college. Through the large windows I could spot the students, lads of about eighteen dressed in suits and neckties, sitting in front of a chalk-marked blackboard. A bell rang and they jumped up, raced down the stairs, busied themselves with their sandwiches, laughed and shouted. They had a world of their own, a universe of rules and figures, books and traditions, regular meals and sound sleep—at a time when for five years boys even younger had been perishing on front lines and in concentration camps. Then the air raid siren started howling. The students, grouped into classes, marched in an orderly way to their shelters.

High up, from the west, came rows of silvery little crosses, leaving long white trails on the blue sky—bombers. A scout plane, flying a little lower, drew a circle of vapor around us. I looked about me. There was silence. The engines were standing idle, people had gone to hide themselves. Afar, the planes were diving down now. The noise of the explosions was drowned by a strong wind, but at the outskirts of the town, rose dark clouds shot through with flying debris. Another bunch of vapor trails appeared in the sky, this time heading towards the station. Soon we were rocked by explosions. The storage sheds were hit. Our guards ran for the shelters. We opened the wagon doors and dispersed, some hurrying across the rails towards the town, others crawling underneath the train.

Only I remained, alone in the open wagon. To be crushed by derailed railway wagons or to be buried among Nazis underneath some collapsing building, I reasoned, was nothing worth running for. I took three spherical eating bowls, left behind by my companions, stacked them together, put them on my head and crouched into a corner. My big red helmet must have looked queer, but there was no one to be amused by it. Besides, the time for merriment was over. Bombs exploded all around. It was raining rubble.

When the bombers had passed, I shook off the dust and looked out. Some rails beyond stood a train full of turnips. It was being pillaged. Later on, one by one, came our guards, shooting to demonstrate their alertness. They seemed to have drunk tea and rum in the meantime.

We rushed back to the wagons. Crowding was less now. Many had escaped. Some had been killed.

When darkness set in, the train, coupled to a puffing little steam engine, was pulled along a one-tracked branch line. Kept awake by the moaning of the wounded, I stood in the wagon-corner and watched out for any change of landscape. A trail of smoke hung over the wagons and blew into my face. It was black and dirty but warm.

In less than an hour we had reached our destination. Those of us who still had enough energy jumped out. We would have helped our ailing companions but there were too many of them.

On the ramp waited men in blue uniform, black berets and tidy polished jackboots whom we thought to be members of the fire brigade, or auxiliary troops. They ordered us into rows of five and marched us off. By the light of a street lamp I looked again at our new guardians. Their armbands read: "Lagerschutz." On their breasts were prison numbers like ours. Beyond we already saw endless double rows of lamps—the familiar charged, barbed wire fence.

We passed what seemed to be the buildings of the camp administration. In front of one of them stood a cannon—somewhat old-fashioned, but a monster all the same. Was it there merely to intimidate us?

Then we reached the camp. As in Gross-Rosen, the entrance was through a passageway. Over it was the main watchtower. On either side spread wings housing guard rooms, offices and prison cells. Adjoining it stretched the inevitable large *"Appell Platz,"* the roll call square.

"Right or wrong, my country," "To each his own," read the tablets fixed to the entrance building. We had arrived at Buchenwald, the place political prisoners from Germany had been taken to.

* * *

After a day's wait in a huge tent came our turn to queue up for disinfection. Next to us waited a group of Gypsy prisoners, inmates of Buchenwald. I talked to them. They were about to take their monthly bath and to be deloused. Lice, it appeared, were plentiful in Buchenwald. One of the lads, there since 1944, had also been to the Auschwitz brick-laying school once. "Don't ask me about the other Romany boys," he sighed, "it's such a while ago. I don't know what happened to them. There are only four of us now."

When we reached the disinfection building, we surrendered our clothing, our shoes and whatever other property we may have had. Cherished bits of paper, pencil ends, nails, strings, spoons and self-made knives—all had to be parted with. Then we were penned into a room with tiled walls, and waited. We lay, sat and stood there for hours. It was hot. Our naked bodies stank and sweated. Those near the windows would not let us open them, for fear of catching pneumonia. We were thirsty and cried for water, but no one seemed to bother about us. The door was locked. Prisoners from the camp were forbidden to enter the disinfection compound. Those in charge of it seemed busy with the earlier arrivals.

Finally after ten hours of self-made torture, when many had fainted and could no longer raise themselves, we were let out again. There had been a delay, we were told, for the air raids had cut the water supply.

We were going through the reception procedure now. It was nothing new to me. This was the fourth concentration camp I was entering. Our hair, bristles that had grown to a full proud inch, was cut by irritable, overworked Frenchmen handling machines that badly needed cleaning, oiling and sharpening. After that we dived into a tank of sharp, biting disinfectant. It clung so obstinately to our burning skin that even the warm shower which followed failed to wash it off. In the next room, at a table, sat an SS doctor. Running past him at a distance of four yards was called medical examination. For the sake of the card index someone also measured our height.

I was handed shirt, jacket, trousers, socks and shoes. There was no underwear. Dressed, I entered the registration room. A clerk in prison garb pushed a form towards me. "Fill it in yourself." The questionnaire seemed rather out of date. Eight years had passed since the first prisoners were registered. 127,157 had come before me, not counting those prisoners who had taken over the personal numbers of the dead. Most youngsters, fearing to be declared "unfit for work," were in the habit of registering themselves as older, but I, besides having once been educated to be honest and upright, never believed in cheating fate. My age was fifteen, my profession brick-layer. Date of arrest: June 28th 1943.

The clerk, a German political prisoner, took the form and scrutinized it. "So your father is fighting for the Allies." "Yes, I hope so," I replied proudly. "Don't ever think that no one cares about you here," he went on—like some hotel proprietor welcoming a guest. "This is Buchenwald and here we feel like comrades for each other. Ever since the camp was built, we, the political prisoners, have done all we could to improve matters. One of our achievements, for example, is the *"Lagerschutz."* Instead of SS guards we have our own camp police, people we can put our trust in. It cost quite a struggle to attain this and now we need cooperation from you newcomers. I hope that you, too, will find your place among us."

I told him that I was Jewish and anyhow would not enjoy any privileges. But that did not seem to interest him. "Here we are all alike," he continued. "Do you really think that the few lousy privileges they allow to us Germans make us any the happier? They only embarrass us. Don't worry about how the SS classifies you. The will to cooperate among ourselves, so that we may survive, is stronger than the Nazis."

Later that night, escorted by camp police, we trudged to a shed. There we received some soup. We had not eaten for two days, but, occupied with the many new impressions around me, I had forgotten that.

Afterwards we went inside and sat on the floor, in rows, with legs clutched around our neighbors, the way one rides on a toboggan. That kept us warm. We had to, for the shed's windows were without panes and an icy wind was blowing through them. At the door, watching us, sat a Lagerschutz man. In other camps his orders would have been to intimidate us, but here he seemed to have been told to help and merely see to it that trouble-makers cooperated.

Perhaps, I reasoned, it was true that our new prisoner superiors could be trusted. My first impressions of them, even if contradictory, had been favorable. Then I fell asleep.

In the morning we were taken to what was called "the cinema"—a large hall filled with benches which, judging from the wall fixtures, had been used for gymnastic displays and film shows. There, lying on the floor, crowded, cut off from the other prisoners by wire fences and camp guards, we spent our weeks of quarantine.

Then I was sent to the "little camp," the new extension camp built for newcomers from the East. It lay on the roughly-cleared hillside below the solidly constructed main camp, consisted of wooden barracks of the "Birkenau" type and was divided by wire fences into seven separate compounds. Three barracks were filled with the sick, three others with invalids. The remaining ten were crowded with those on the waiting list.

My new home was Block 62. At first I slept on the cold, moist floor. Later I was allocated to a bunk. I already knew these square wooden contraptions, called "buxes," from Birkenau. Then they had been filled with sacks of straw, blankets, bugs, fleas, lice, mice and five inmates. Now they were mere trays of bare boarding but housed ten of the human species. One had to lie on one's side like a tinned sardine, without moving. Turning over or lying on your back was impossible. The width per person was less than a foot. On waking up—the unpleasantest moment of all in a prisoner's life—hands and feet were numb, backs aching. Where our thighs rubbed against the boards, obstinate and persistent abscesses grew.

Our block-mates, mostly Ukrainians and Poles evacuated from labor camps, were just the opposite of the righteous Buchenwald prisoner the clerk at the office had boasted about. Every night they staged bitter fights. In the morning they would carry off the wounded, battered and bleeding. People knifed each other over petty quarrels and there was no one to restrain them. Even I had "bought" a knife. It was not even sharp enough to cut bread, but it was big and impressive.

The block seemed a den of wild animals, beasts that howled, robbed and killed. In the dark when they had to relieve themselves they used their eating bowls. By daylight they stared at each other with eyes of hate and suspicion. They were decaying in mind and body. Some had already been certified as mad and "sent away."

In the evenings, after the roll calls, we were given discs with which we could draw our rations on the next day. We held them tight lest someone snatch them. We hid them in the seams of our clothing lest our pockets be pilfered. They meant life or death. After hours of queuing up in front of the already familiar cinema, we would exchange them for one liter of watery soup and 300 gr. of bread. Four times a week there was 25 gr. of margarine, twice a spoonful of jam or white cheese, and on Sundays a much dreamt-about 50 gr. of sausage.

As at Auschwitz our meeting place, the sanctuary where we could smoke and exchange the latest news, was the lavatory—a hut with a large open tank. We perched around its edge like birds on a telephone wire, carefully balancing ourselves and looking out for any block elders that were likely to disturb us. Luckily the lavatory was in our compound, and if we found our way across the stone-littered mud in the dark we could use it even at night. People in other compounds, however, had to wait for their fixed visiting hours.

The washroom was less popular. It was opened for half an hour in the morning, but the water was icy cold and there were no towels. All the same, every time any of us youngsters met there we would surprise and greet each other with a cold, generous splash. "Wake up, boys," we shouted, "you want to be alive, don't you?"

One day, suddenly and unexpectedly, we were driven out to work. They took us to a field littered with stones, told us to pick them up and stack them on a heap some 500 yards away.

The way to the heap was lined with guards. At first I naively thought they had come to take us back to camp again, but I soon found out that they, too, had come to "do something." It seemed that someone—on earth or in the heavens—had divided them into five distinctive groups. The first passed their time shouting at us to keep up running. The second bawled at us for taking stones which were not heavy enough, making us drop them on the way and run back to fetch bigger ones. The third group amused themselves kicking and hitting us. The fourth thought up games: things like running competitions, obstacle races, making us run blindfolded, telling us to balance the stone blocks on our heads. Only the fifth group appeared to be inactive. These gray-coats sat underneath the trees, about a hundred yards away, clutching their rifles and dreamily looking on. If any of us approached them, they would shoot.

That evening, on returning to my barrack home, I was bruised, blistered, exhausted and depressed. But something kept me from despairing. I had seen the surroundings—the hidden, mysterious machinations encircling us, the unknown every new-comer was so afraid of. Now that I knew it, I could fight it.

On the way to work I had memorized the lay-outs of vast SS living quarters: the solid barracks and the fashionable villas. For every hut in the huge concentration camp there seemed to be three buildings beyond the fence. The SS barracks could hold a garrison of 15,000. But that was not all. Buchenwald seemed to be a country of its own. There were parks, stylish villages, a zoo, a bear pit, an aviary, a riding hall, a concert hall and more—all for the pleasure of the masters of the master-race. For us there was an abundance of ammunition plants, factories making parts for V-2 rockets, and stone quarries.

They said that our having to work was something temporary. The authorities were supposed to be aware that our long trek from the East had weakened us. It was a big lie—like the one about our being "protective custody prisoners." We went on toiling, day after day, week after week.

With the continuing work came more new experiences. We were sent to clean up a wood, a place which looked as though a bomb had fallen on it. It was beyond the camp's working territory so that we had our own chain of guards who, as was their habit, were hiding somewhere amongst the trees. The SS men had ordered us to pick up all the stones and fallen twigs, and then left. I was alone, rummaging about in strange woodlands. Lingering in my mind were stories about how prisoners were tricked into being "shot while escaping." For every dead body in prison clothes, the guard would receive prize-money—5 Marks, a packet of tobacco and three days' leave. Then I heard shots. But now they no longer surprised me. Jumping through the underbrush, my heart thumping violently, my eyes looking only ahead, my ears strained for voices, I raced back to the assembly place.

Now I knew that when Buchenwald veterans talked about their experiences, they were not exaggerating in the least. I had tasted that history myself.

How had these "old numbers" from Germany managed to survive? I wondered. They must have had something great to live for. But what could it be that seemed great to a haggard, despised prisoner shut off in secluded concentration camps? Was it victory? But then, the political faith he may have believed in had been banished long ago, and his leaders of old murdered. Until three years ago the Fascist creed of his oppressors had seemed invincible.

* * *

It was March 1945. Our purpose in life seemed to be nothing but exasperating, tiresome waiting. We waited for our liter of soup, for the roll call, for a free place at the lavatory, for sleep, for the lukewarm rays of the sun, for spring, for someone to defeat Hitlerism and for liberation.

Often as a punishment for something trivial, we would even have to wait to be let into our barrack of crowded sleeping bunks. After the roll call, standing at attention, we would be left in the creeping cold of the evening. Then all that we could do was to dream of other things.

My imagination seemed to have become expert. Longing to go to sleep, I thought of the moment when, stumbling over the mud littered with stone and rubbish, we would all rush impatiently towards the small barrack door, and the glad seconds when I would climb into my bed to lie on planking and be pressed by the warm bodies of my neighbors. Hungry, I would appease my stomach with dreaming about food, of liver sausage, blood sausage, garlic sausage, Bologna sausage, frankfurters and salami. Above all, however, I would water my mouth with the thought of Sunday, when, clutching 50 grams of camp sausage, we too would enjoy a royal feast.

We were being divided into groups to be sent away to branch camps. Speculating as to which of these new places were the worst, people tried evasion and trickery to avoid them. But it was useless, for conditions were bad at all of them. The innumerable subsidiaries of Buchenwald stretching from Eisenach to Chemnitz, and from Coburg to Leipzig, were hardly more than large slave cages.

At Dora, Ohrdruf and Ploemnitz the inmates dug tunnels for big underground factories that were to produce V-2 rockets. These flying bombs represented Hitler's last trump card. With them blond, cultivated Germans would kill thousands of equally blond and cultivated Anglo-Saxons. It would be irrelevant, then, if they also cost the lives of a few thousand emaciated outcasts reared in forests, caravans and ghettos.

When it was my turn to be sent off I, too, trudged to the hospital compound to face the selection board. I must have been little more than a meager skeleton, for, to my surprise, they decided that I was to stay in Buchenwald. This time, quite unexpectedly, my weakness had been useful.

Excited by my luck, I ran back to where we had undressed ourselves, to pick up my clothing. My cap and shoes had been stolen. All that could be done was to take somebody else's. The only cap left was a green one. I pondered whether this color would match the rest of my motley garb. To be strikingly dressed meant attracting attention, and I could not afford to be picked out by the SS guards. But I had no choice. I grabbed the green beret, put it on and hurriedly paced back to our block—alone, hoping to remain unknown and unnoticed.

One day I saw a boy of four, the saddest character I had ever come across, abnormal in his physique, behavior and speech. He staggered along like some weak, wounded animal and uttered cries in German-Polish-Yiddish gibberish. "That," I was told, "is the kid they keep hiding from the SS. His father brought him here in a rucksack. Every time there is an inspection they gag the poor devil and tuck him away underneath the floorboards. What a life!" I asked whether there were more children. "Yes, there is another one at the main camp, at Block 8, the children's block. All the other boys are at least twelve." At Block 8, I learned, lived about 100 youngsters, mostly Poles and Russians between the age of fourteen and sixteen. Several of them were attached to influential camp personages and quite openly played the whores. As a result they were as jealous of each other as women. "There also is a youth block at the 'little camp,' " I was advised. "If I were you, I would try getting transferred to it."

At long last I was sent to Block 86, the home of some 300 to 400 youngsters. The block elder, a blonde Polish Jew with years of German concentration camps behind him, received us according to custom with a noble-sounding introductory speech. He seemed very concerned about his proteges and repeated what I had already been told at the registration office. The block elder of 7a, back at Auschwitz, had also been well-wishing but had bawled at us like a dictator. His equivalent at Buchenwald, however, appeared to be a friend.

I was happy to be back among youngsters. It was the pleasantest block I had ever been to. Even the SS man who came to receive the roll call did not bother us, as for some reason or other our block elder had succeeded in being on good terms with him. Most of my block mates had come from labor camps and were Jews. In my room they hailed mainly from Poland, in the other from Hungary.

Those of my bedfellows who since 1939 had lived in secluded ghettos knew little of the world around them. Their lot had been much harder than mine and they had witnessed great tragedies.

But they had been too young, too ignorant, to grasp what was happening to them. They had reacted by retracting into a kind of shell, a mental barrier that kept them isolated. Everything beyond it seemed hostile and did not merit contemplation. To the ghetto youngsters the unknown was something they could not or would not think of. Naively suspicious of "foreigners," some of them even suggested that I might be a German spy.

There also were two German Jews. Friendly, educated chaps, they would have made ideal companions. But I avoided them. Their pride in being "Germans" and "Westerners" repulsed me. Nor did anyone else like them. All they earned for their stubborn haughtiness was contempt and general ridicule.

Our various backgrounds led to several differences between us, but our quarrels remained petty ones. We were young and would try to understand ourselves. At the worst we would feel sorry for each other for "not having grown up yet."

During the day we perched ourselves on projecting rocks and tree-stumps and tried to catch as many life-giving sun rays as possible. They were becoming warmer now. The last of the tough, perilous concentration camp winters was surrendering to a spring of hope. Soon it would all be different.

Once we youngsters at Block 66 even received Red Cross parcels—gifts from abroad addressed to French and Dutch prisoners who were no longer alive to enjoy them. Their arrival meant fervent excitement. We loudly argued about the supposed contents, and worked out how these treasures would be divided, hopefully imagining that all the lettering on the tins was French for some kind of meat delicacy and watering our mouths. We dipped our spoons into the sandy mud and polished them, clutched our eating bowls, tried to spot solitary places where the relishing of luxuries would not be interfered with and impatiently waited for the moment of their distribution. In the end, however, with everyone holding his share, all the agitation quieted down to admiring your neighbor's portion, which compared to yours, was bound to be marvelous. Those who had received cereals searched for twigs and implored the block elder to lend them his cherished cooking pot. My own luck in the lottery remained limited to a tin of sardines without a tin-opener, that had to be divided between five of us.

Then there was the hobby of our block elder, something he had thought about, founded and made a success of: a choir. If one wanted to be among his favorites and be given preference when his friends at the main camp had allocated us an extra vat of soup, one had to sing for it.

"Obvious, undisguised extortion," mumbled the unmusical elements of Block 66. "The old crow seeks fame. It's not enough that he's a clever manager. He wants to be a conductor and composer as well—all at our expense."

"They deserve their second helping of soup," proclaimed the rest of us. "They work hard enough for it." "Hear, hear!" echoed one of the youngsters. "Let's see one of you spending the evenings shut up in the washroom and practicing. And, besides, it's all for your benefit." "Quite so," announced a bright lad, "they only know to grumble. Come to sing with us? Never. They sleep in the evening. If they get up, it's only for the lavatory. And there all they do is stink."

The choir met after bed-time so that its new songs would remain a secret to us. Once, however, I had a chance to eavesdrop. It was close to midnight. Quite unperturbed about the acid remarks people like me had bestowed on them, I groped my way to the urinal. The washroom next to it was locked and illuminated, and emitted a catching tune—a fascinating chord repeated again and again as on some broken gramophone record. They certainly worked hard in there. I sneaked to the door so that I might also hear the words. But someone must have seen my shadow. "Get back to bed, spoilsport," they cried. That then was the end of the concert for me.

Back on my bunk, however, I meditated, for the tunes had so impressed me that I could not sleep. I must have misjudged my roommates. They seemed to have emerged from their shell of isolation and now appeared to me like young people everywhere. More than simply that, they sang with such vigor and conviction that others would be encouraged by them. I felt glad, extremely glad. For the first time in years there were friends around me, true friends. The chords I had been listening to were far from being part of a missed concert. No. What I had sneaked in on had merely been a preview of the beginning—a glimpse of the glorious symphony of youth.

* * *

The long-awaited day had come. There was to be an entertainment evening for the choir's debut. Even SS men had been invited—possibly in order to give our adventure legality.

Impatiently sitting on benches that had been improvised from borrowed bunk planks, we waited for the guests. Our room, measuring hardly eight yards by ten, was filled with hundreds of spectators. Everyone craned his neck to see the door and the adjoining stage, supported by soup vats. It looked promising. Then came a few V.I.P.'s from the main camp, friends of our block elder and half a dozen SS men, some of them officers. They sat down in the front row that had been reserved for them, and the show started.

The program consisted of songs, sketches, acrobatics and solo dances. Every nationality was doing its own. First came the Polish youngsters with a song about how life was to be like in the new, rebuilt Warsaw. Our applause was wildly enthusiastic. We clapped our hands rhythmically in unison like the muffled clatter of railway wheels. There were calls and whistles. More likely than not, this was to be the farewell party to each other and we knew it. No one would stop us saying what we wanted to. The SS visitors understood little of what we were singing about. Oddly enough, however, they, too, seemed to be cheering us.

Afterwards the Russian boys trooped onto the stage, to show off their muscles and their famous, tradition-rooted choir singing. They were only a handful, but their voices were strong. Sounding through the packed room came the cherished words of Stalin, Red Army and Sovietland. Any of the present SS officers who may have believed that Hitler had succeeded in re-educating these vigorous and determined youngsters must have been greatly surprised. I knew these lads when, nearly two years ago, they had arrived at Auschwitz. Then they felt far from certain about the cause of their motherland. Some even seemed disappointed about it. Now they praised it. Their confidence had become stronger than ever before, their zeal and loyalty unquenchable.

The last but biggest group of performers was the Jewish lads from Poland. To begin with they chanted about ghetto life, about mothers, rabbis and learning the Bible—a moving portrayal of the Yiddish-speaking people. Following this we heard the sad laments of people being led to their death, the story of doom, helplessness, and despair. It was a picture of dismal self-pity that only a Jew could draw.

Suddenly, however, the singers changed their attitude and we jerked into a mood of hope and determination. They had started to sing the melodies about the future, the songs they were proud of, their own songs. The stirring tunes I had been eavesdropping on during my nightly sneaking tour had come into the open. The muffled words that had been whispered in the cold, hard-walled washroom, the verses written by unknown fellow-prisoners, were clear and vigorous now. "Oh, how they will suffer for having laughed at us," proclaimed one of the songs. Others told of the time when all men will be free and equal. "Then our children living in a better world, one that is sure to come, will find it hard to believe what their fathers tell of the past."

Our gray-coated visitors sat perplexed. It had all come so unexpectedly to them. They had not prepared themselves for being mentally imposed upon. They had wanted to laugh. I scanned them to see their reactions. Their skull-and-crossbone decorated uniforms seemed less weighty, less polished now. Some nervously scratched their heads. One officer started to wipe his glasses.

They must have understood a few of the Yiddish words. Besides, the performers they had seen were far from what the Nazis and their friends all over the world would have wanted them to be. There had been no stupid Polish peasants, Russian barbarians or timid, sidelocked, Bible-chanting Jews on our stage. There were only dynamic and defiant youngsters seeing the future and wishing to build for it.

Then our unified young voices had finished with the glimpses of past and future. The show was over. Prisoners and SS men rose, stretched their limbs, and left.

It was as though we all lived in a dream. I wondered. Perhaps we were.

*   *   *

April had arrived, and with it the thunder of Allied guns. Our compound, at the exposed lower fringe of the camp, had become a gathering place for eager watchers, people who would spend their day anxiously looking down onto the vast plain below us for any signs of the approaching liberators. Among them were prominent personages from the main camp, armed with concealed binoculars. They had little to be afraid of, for by now the SS seldom entered the camp without our being aware of them previously. The end, good or bad, was near. It would only be a matter of days.

Someone shouted that there were tanks in the distant fields. "I can't spot them yet," replied one of the visitors, twiddling about with his precious binoculars. "Let us have a look, then," we cried. One by one we were honored with a magic glimpse of the silent, far away and miracle-hiding countryside, but our efforts were in vain. I, too, proudly took hold of the field glasses. Unconvinced as I was, I painstakingly scanned the valley, the stretch of gray country-road, the fields, the hedges. The only thing resembling tanks—or anything else that may have heralded our liberation—was a group of haystacks.

Later, after rumors had it that the camp was to be evacuated, the SS authorities issued a declaration. "The inmates of Buchenwald will remain in their camp.... it will be in your own interests to keep on being disciplined and to obey orders.... With the arrival of the American army you will be handed over peacefully and in orderly fashion." It seemed reassuring and we felt happy.

One of the nights, when I was returning from the lavatory, an unpleasant 200 yards walk across the rugged, darkness-enshrouded hillside, I heard strange voices in the block elder's room. Although it was well after midnight, he seemed to be entertaining visitors. They talked about Poland and their home-towns. One of them, oddly enough, appeared to be speaking English. This attracted me. I pressed my ear to the wall and listened. His voice was very weak. It crackled and was disturbed by whistles. I flushed with excitement. There was no doubt about it, I was listening to a hidden radio set. All that apparent interest in remote Polish villages seemed clear to me now. It was a gathering of camp personages who had come to hear news. While they talked to drown the radio noise, someone was scanning the ether for details of Allied successes. They had picked upon our block because it was the farthest away from the SS barracks, secluded and inhabited by inmates who were too young to be informers.

I strained my ears for local town names, proud to be among the privileged listeners. Before long, however, I was joined by other lavatory-goers. To them it all seemed something that I could translate so that they might discuss it loudly and excitedly. But the block elder, too, wanted a say in the matter. He opened the door and persuaded us to return to our bunks.

After that, I listened in night after night. Sitting on the floor and leaning against the wall with the voices of the Allies behind it, I laboriously tried to grasp the news. Next morning the "rumors" would fail to surprise me. When, twig in hand, camp mates drew maps on the dusty ground to show us the front line, it would be familiar to me. It also proved that the mouth-to-mouth news service had worked efficiently. What I had been told on my arrival seemed finally to have become true. "Do not think you are forgotten, our comrades are on the alert, even if you never notice it."

Before long, however, our quiet waiting time came to an abrupt end. The loudspeaker system of the main camp had announced an order and was repeating it again and again. "All Jews to the gate." To us it was passed on by our block elder. Struck by the ominous news, we relapsed into disillusionment and fear. What had happened to some of the Eastern concentration camps shortly before their liberation was well known. We sent a scout to the main camp to report to us. When he reached the roll call place, at the gate, he found it to be empty. No one had persuaded himself to go there. The order had been disobeyed.

In the afternoon they declared a curfew and staged round-ups. SS search parties were seen roaming about both the main and the little camp. They came as far as our lavatory, but not further. It was already dusk. For today they were satisfied. *"Das Hauptlager ist judenrein,"* blared the loudspeakers. All the Jews from the main camp, together with most of their brethren from the little camp, had been led off to a separate tent compound.

Next morning we again had an unexpected surprise. The ones that were said to be on the alert without us ever noticing them, had acted. Their bold determination had come out in the open. Our block elder received a parcel of red, black and green colored cloth triangles, and in a matter of minutes all the Jewish lads were adorned with the new recognition marks. The boys from the ghettos became Poles and Russians—political, unsocial or criminal ones. I myself became a German political prisoner. Our block too was *"judenrein"* now.

The familiar Yiddish had vanished. My room mates only talked Polish and Russian now. Their knowledge of these newly-acquired mother tongues was anything between poor and fair, but the Buchenwald SS guards would not notice it. Anyhow the standard answer to all questions being asked would be the good old *"Nix vestehn Deutsch."* I, however, was odd man out. My new role as "Aryan" was far from playing the ignorant. German prisoners, as a rule, were well dressed, looked healthy and lived in a block apart. I, then, would be asked about my being different from them and my explanations would need to be exact, self-confident and convincing.

In the evening, that day, I was mercilessly teased. "Come on," shouted my roommates, "let's see you playing the bully. Don't forget you are German now and if you aren't rude we'll lose all respect for you." "Hey, *Deutscher,* can't you take me with you when you go to the brothel next time? I'll pay you, you know, half a liter of 'A-1' camp soup." "If we'll stay here for long they'll be making you block elder, *Deutscher*." "Be a sport mate, do a nice snappy *'Heil'* for us." "The Fuehrer will be sorry to see you here among all those foreigners." "Yes, why don't you write to him?"

In their eyes a German and a villain were the same. It would have been tactless to suggest otherwise. The lads wanted a good laugh and I was the last to refuse them. *"Reichsdeutscher politischer Schutzhaeftling Nummer 127158,"* I bellowed, "wishes to complain about these dirty Pollaks for mocking our fatherland. Number 127158 begs to be transferred to more civilized surroundings, where German is spoken."

Then, after greatly having enjoyed ourselves, we went to bed. Someone patted my shoulder: "And don't forget to snore like a German!"

*   *   *

Contrary to what we had been led to believe, Buchenwald was being evacuated. The first to go were the Jews from the tents. Then came the Czechs from the main camp. Some transports left by rail, others by foot. Their destination was said to be either Dachau or Mauthausen—both concentration camps in the South, where the Allies had still been unable to cross the Alps.

For a whole week now we had been fed on nothing but bread and artificial honey. Day by day we became weaker and hungrier.

In a desperate search for food I managed to smuggle myself into the main camp. But I was disappointed. Many blocks were empty already. The few confused inmates that scurried about the camp seemed busy racking their brains for means to avoid being evacuated.

Streets were littered with the belongings of those who had left—cardboard boxes, parcel wrappings, old newspapers, photographs, letters. The cherished, carefully-guarded and smuggled-in possessions prisoners had thought made them rich, lay thrown onto junk-heaps. I took a stick and searched the rubbish lest it contain something edible. But it did not. There was only paper, paper everywhere, fluttering in the breeze and turning over like leaves in a book. I looked at it: stacks of hoarded camp money, useless blue mark bills and equally useless red two mark bills; a card covered with clumsy handwriting, red censorship signs and a postmark giving the name of some obscure Polish village; scraps of dirty, stained paper with old-style German letters carefully drawn by the hand of some unknown intellectual. Curious as I was, I picked up one of them, a little one, and read it: *Wer nie sein Brot mit Traenen ass, wer nie die kummervollen Naechte an seinem Bette weinend sass, der kennt Euch nicht, Ihr himmlischen Maechte.* Then there was a dividing line and under it *Kennt Ihr das Land wo die Zitronen bluehn, wo man statt Frauen Ziegen Liebt . . .* Was it a quotation or something original? I did not know.*

My rummaging having proved useless, I returned to the relative safety of our block. Next morning I was out again, this time to the vegetable gardens. The large, barbed-wire surrounded plot abutting on our compound, that supplied the SS with vegetables and flowers under the care of prisoner gardeners, was being looted. A daring dozen of starvelings, I among them, had cut an opening into the fence and busied themselves plucking spinach leaves. Bent down, I tugged away at the stems and greedily heaped what I expected would make a grand salad meal into a cardboard box.

Occasionally I looked up. The distant woods were being attacked by American dive bombers and started to raise columns of dense black smoke. I grew so enthusiastic about this that I thought of nothing but Americans and spinach leaves, spinach leaves and Americans. Then, still absorbed in my dreams, I suddenly heard shots. Running across the field came a pistol-waving SS man, a monster who either wanted to satisfy his hunting instinct or resented being deprived of next week's spinach dinner. Panic-stricken, we hurried over stubble and ditches towards the opening in the fence. But I

*One is a citation from Goethe, the other a parody.

was weak. My ill-fitting shoes hurt my toes, I limped and could not run fast enough. As a last resort I dropped the cardboard box with the precious collection of leaves. But that, too, was of no avail. The enemy came nearer and nearer. Then a wooden club swished down on me. Instinctively I ducked my head and absorbed the blow with my left forearm. "Stay where you are, you ass face, or I'll shoot you," shouted my attacker as he made for his next victim. Upon that I bent my back, in case I would be too easy a target and, like some hunted animal, raced towards the fence.

Back at the block, I nursed my bruised and swollen arm. I felt like an utterly defeated fool. After all these years of trial I had risked my life for a few hundred spinach leaves. My escape had been a narrow one. I had lost both the eagerly-awaited salad and my cherished cardboard box.

Next day, April 10th, our compound was also to be evacuated. We hid ourselves wherever we could—in the cavity between the boarding and lining of the hut-wall, in the dark, musty and narrow space below the floorboards, underneath and inside our stuffy sacks of straw, or huddled up in some stinking vermin-infested manhole—and refused to leave our block. Soon, however, we were cordoned off by camp police. SS guards came rushing into our room with the inevitable whips and revolvers. Resistance ceased and we trudged up the slope towards the camp gate.

In the main camp I desperately tried to rush past the cordon of camp police. "Be sensible, kid," they quieted me, "most of the other inmates have left already. We ourselves are also leaving today. By eight o'clock in the evening the camp is supposed to be empty. Only those at the hospital will stay behind. Besides, are you all that sure that the last transports to leave Buchenwald will be the safest? Go on, kid, join the rest."

They persuaded me to join the group waiting some yards from the roll call place, between Block 3 and 9. As I squatted on the pavement, in expectation of the things to come, we were passed by long columns of silent, worried-looking camp mates on their way to the gate. They knew that beyond it was the unknown. Only a sunburnt

Gypsy lad seemed confident. Eagerly pacing amidst rows of companions much taller than he, he called us to join him. "What are you waiting for? Come along with me. I am a Gypsy and glad to get out of here into the open air where the birds sing. It's good to belong to the countryside. Farewell, comrades, I am off to freedom!"

We stayed behind and kept on waiting. "There aren't enough guards," said one of the camp police. "Your turn will come when the contingent that led off the preceding column comes back to take another one."

Then the air-raid siren started howling. It was glad tidings to us. Traffic on roads and rails would stop. The evacuation would have to be delayed. Overhead buzzed a fragile-looking American reconnaissance plane. German anti-aircraft guns had ceased to exist long ago, and it came down low enough for us to see the head of the pilot. We anxiously expected him to drop something—weapons, food or, at least leaflets. But he did not. All he brought was suspense and expectation.

Afterwards came hours of silence. People sat on what had once been garden plots, in the shade of adjoining blocks. All movement had ceased. None of the guards had returned yet.

By evening there was still no news. The all-clear had not been sounded. When it was dark, we slowly trickled back to our blocks. Less than half my roommates had managed to return. Everyone was confused. We only knew that this night was to be decisive. For a whole week now we had said so and evening after evening hoped that we would wake up to be liberated. But now it seemed final. Whether there was to be a future or not, the decision about our fate was imminent. As we lived on the fringe of the camp with the open plain below us, there was much argument about our being vulnerable. The thin wooden boarding of our block afforded no protection at all. The few hiding places behind solid concrete walls were too small for all of us. We stayed awake and speculated about stray rifle shots, bombs and shells until early in the morning. Then I dozed off.

When we awoke things had not changed. There was a curfew and a disquieting silence. What went on at the gate, the place at which the administrative buildings were situated, was hidden to us by the sea of barracks that was the main camp. For the last twenty hours we had been without news. It was two days since we had been issued our last 300 grams of bread with the usual spoonful of artificial honey.

At noon we noticed a howling we had never heard before. The Germans called it "tank-alarm siren." The moment of decision had come. We scanned the valley below us. At the outskirts of the wood we saw a hurriedly moving file of steel-helmeted gray-coats, SS guards retreating with ammunition boxes and machine-guns. Some time later we spotted more of them, in still greater hurry but armed only with an occasional rifle. Then the landscape was quiet again, and the uncertainty continued.

I put my trust in the comrades of whom it had been said that "they are on the alert even if one never notices it." Should there be an attempt to annihilate us they would act. Their numbers would be inadequate, I feared, but their resistance fierce. We were not defenseless. We would fight.

It was between three and four o'clock, the date April 11th, 1945. We waited in suspense and with unprecedented tension. No one talked anymore. Some lads lay on the bunks and stared at the ceiling. Others gazed through cracks in the wall, onto the valley.

Suddenly there were shouts, from the opposite direction, from the main camp. They became louder and louder. We rushed out to investigate: our compound was lifeless as before. "Look at the gate!" shouted someone. I lifted my eyes and searched for the pyramidical roof of the main watch tower that stood out from beyond the main camp. The crooked cross of Fascism had gone. Fluttering from the symbolic flagpole was something white. The moment we had so anxiously been longing for had come: the cherished victorious minute, for which our German comrades had been waiting for 4,453 days and nights, was here at last.

* * *

There were tears and jubilation. A white flag fluttered over Buchenwald. But it was not a flag of surrender, it was a flag of victory. It was not a victory for an army from over the ocean but a self-fought victory. Nor was it a mere military one. It was a far-reaching victory—our victory.

PART THREE

A NEW WORLD

CHAPTER I

A New World

Proudly flying over the main gate was one of those rare bed sheets from the camp-hospital—a dilapidated white rag that after years of adorning dismal sickbunks had become historic. Buchenwald was free. As soon as we had sighted the American tanks, we had seized the watchtowers and liberated ourselves. The Allies, in hot pursuit of what remained of the Wehrmacht, had by-passed us, but we had been ready. "The comrades who are on the alert, even if one never notices it," had acted quickly, smoothly and effectively. While we in our secluded compound had waited and anxiously counted minutes of fear and uncertainty, others had cut through the fence. First to break out into freedom had been those with guns in their hands, the daring few that fanned out to seek the enemy. Then, in desperate search for some far-off hiding place, had come criminals, traitors and informers.

When the few of us, who the day before so narrowly escaped being evacuated, lay down to sleep that evening, we did so in the comforting luxury of security. The time for our being helpless victims of reprisals had passed. We took no chances in guarding our liberty. There were armed comrades in the streets, the watchtowers, the dugouts, the former SS barracks and the surrounding woods.

In the morning, as we woke up into freedom, it was as though we were reborn. I had never experienced that feeling of independence before. Nor had I ever known about being free. For us youngsters it was the beginning of something new, a new life, a new world, a new era.

The old chains had been broken. Sooner or later we would have to forget our lost families, to grow up and become good citizens. The tasks facing us would need to be solved with the same determination that had helped us survive. Our Polish, Russian and Czech comrades would go back home to prove that if there can be total war, there can also be total reconstruction. Many of the Jewish youngsters would make for their ancient homeland in Palestine, where they would have to show that deserts can be made habitable. "The world cannot supply food, shelter and happiness to all its evergrowing population," I had once been told at school. But the past, and all it stood for, had crumbled ignominiously. Together with youth everywhere we would help to disprove that theory. To achieve this, we would have to cooperate and remember our common sufferings. After all, we had not lingered in concentration camps as individuals, but as youngsters unwanted and forgotten. Millions of our Jewish comrades had not even been allowed to embark upon this bitter struggle for survival that was over now. They were murdered—monstrously and wholesale—before even having had a chance to realize it. Thousands of boys who had been our camp-mates, block-mates, roommates or even bed-mates, had perished, regretting ever having been born, with disappointment and anger in their hearts. They hailed from all over Europe—some even from Asia—and their beliefs and emotions were different and many. But they had come to be part of us. In our memories they lived on, and what they had wanted to say we would have to say. That was another cause to unite us. If only we were confident and determined, we would succeed.

The sun was high on the horizon. I had slept enough. I had pondered enough about the future. I now had to see the present. My legs were little stronger yet, but I dragged myself out into the camp. Old people say old age is creeping in on them. In my case I felt the reverse. Weakness and frailty were creeping out. Soon I would be agile and young again.

The camp was as busy as an ant heap. Everyone wanted to see

everyone and everything. Groups of proud ex-prisoners with newly-issued rifles were doing drill. It was our own-equipped, own-planned and own-organized army, all clad in blue-white prison garb. No wonder we lads envied those who belonged to it.

By afternoon a reconnaissance plane hovered over our compound. It had American markings but we, nevertheless, regarded it with suspicion. We knew enough about Nazi trickery. The guardsmen loaded their guns and pointed them skyward. Then the pilot dipped wings. "He's saluting us," cried someone with wild enthusiasm. "It's an American, a real American!"

In the evening a contingent of American infantry arrived at the gate. The first GI to enter it, they said, was being carried shoulder-high all through the camp. People yelled, sang and shouted. Precariously I pushed myself through the crowd. From beyond, among a sea of blue-white, striped prison caps, bobbed an egg-shaped brown helmet and close to it an equally brown pair of marching boots. The American! At last I had spotted him. I shouted also. So did he. Maybe they were hurting him. Maybe he was becoming dizzy. But he was ours now: we were glad he was yelling.

* * *

As the days passed, the food became more and more plentiful. The changeover from 300 gm. of dry bread to unlimited quantities of goulash soup was too quick. It brought us diarrhea, uncontrollable and pitiless diarrhea. The stagnant brown pond in the lavatory pit threatened to overflow. Everything around it, together with the footpaths leading to the blocks, was contaminated and sticky with whatever it was that the bowels of a starveling make out of warmed-up Hungarian-style tinned goulash.

Lavatory attendants, whose job had once earned them a much sought-after extra liter of watery camp soup, no longer showed the slightest interest in their profession. Nor was there anyone to cart the stinking mud to its once traditional destiny: to be manure, to grow into vegetables which would be gobbled up by 100 per cent Aryan supermen whose purity was vouched for by two Ancient-Teutonic-style S's on their uniforms. All we could do now was to ask for volunteers. We did, there were volunteers, and the first, perhaps somewhat unfitting problem that freedom had put before us was solved.

*   *   *

Those who felt strong enough for it explored the countryside, and after a few days relaxation I also dragged myself up early in the morning to join the wanderers. The dusty path to the nearest village, the shortest of our excursion routes, was thronged with groups of slow-walking ex-prisoners. Our spirits were high. The air was filled with the smell of spring; the fields were green, moist and dewy. There was much I wanted to do. But I was too weak as yet. I merely hobbled along like some aged pilgrim.

Upon reaching our much-talked-about destination, the village square, we made for its pump, put our heads under it, doused ourselves and then admired the old-fashioned cast-iron water-spout for its ornaments. Some, amidst peals of applause, stripped naked and dipped into the pond. "If a female shows herself," they cried before plunging in duck-fashion, head down, behind up, "tell her we are ducks." "But what do we tell the ducks?" "Tell them to get roasted." The traditional pond occupiers, however, were nowhere to be seen. Perhaps the grotesque impersonations of their successors had frightened them off. Perhaps they had already exchanged the cold blue surface of the pond for someone's plate.

Then for want of a suitable companion—or any other youngster for that matter—I strolled along on my own. Observing things and being inquisitive were old hobbies of mine and now that we had been liberated, I could concentrate on them without being disturbed.

The country population, I discovered, was frightened. They moaned about being maltreated by us. If in their eyes the confiscation of eggs, milk, butter and potatoes represented maltreatment they were right. To feed the many sick among us, the camp kitchen badly needed these fresh farm products. We had to get them, even if this meant using threats. True, there must have been excesses against the German population around us, but I failed to hear of murder. Corpses could be seen only at Buchenwald. Even now the survivors were dying of disease, exhaustion and undernourishment.

Down one of the deserted village paths came an old, sour-faced woman carrying a pail of water that seemed far too big and heavy for her. I was determined to exploit this opportunity in order to embark on some excesses of my own now. "Tell me," I somewhat naively encountered her, "where does one get eggs here?" *"Da kommen Sie zu spaet, die sind alle schon weggestohlen. Mit Ihnen kann man ja reden, Sie sind ja selbst Deutscher."*

Her unexpectedly frank reply so astonished me that I momentarily forgot my designs for acquiring eggs. *"Sie,"* she had said to me. When I left Germany for the world of barbed wires I had been a mere *"Du,"* a child. Now I was a *"Sie,"* a man. Moreover, she had put her trust in me because she thought me a fellow-countryman.

"No," I said determined, "I am no German, I am from Buchenwald." *"Ja, Sie sehen aber vertrauenstwuerdig aus.* Tell me, why do they treat us so terribly? What have we simple countryfolks done to deserve that?" "Nothing. You haven't done anything. For eight years you have lived next to Buchenwald and merely looked on." "But an old woman like me couldn't have helped anyhow. I can hardly fetch water any more. All the family have left me. The pigs, the goats, the chickens have all been stolen. The SS, the Americans, and your people, all have been plundering us."

Complaints about anything and everything rained down upon me. She quite forgot that it was her own children who had been causing them. Before me stood an ugly monster that was helplessly unaware of being one. I had to get rid of her.

"All right," I stopped her, "I am in a hurry. Give me that bucket, I'll carry it home for you." *"Danke, danke, Sie sind sehr anstaendig.* Perhaps you may like to be invited in for the evening? There'll be a friend of mine, a young woman who will surely take great interest in you."

"No, thanks." I had seen enough of the villagers for today. Having carried the bucket to her ivy-covered cottage, I put it down at the dilapidated garden gate and left.

Later I met a German ex-prisoner who also was looking for

something or other. "It's disgusting," he said. "The whole village is besieging me with complaints. They say that, being their countryman, I should intervene for them. True, I am their countryman. But they all forget that, as a German, I know much more about Buchenwald and the Nazis than those foreign comrades they are complaining about. Yes, even if their moanings were less exaggerated and less trivial I couldn't bring myself to help them. I remember 1933, I remember them well. It's only a pity they are all scared, unimportant little peasants around here, for everyone of significance or holding positions has fled. Be sure they knew why. It was only Buchenwald they did not know about, these bastards."

On my way back to camp, in one of the fields, I spotted a group of excited-looking Russians and Poles. I joined them, driven by curiosity: *"So to yest,* what's going on here?" Lying on the ground between them was a man dressed in what had once been a uniform. *"Dolmetsch,* come on kid, translate for us." The huddled-up, dirty image of a man was shaking with fear and whimpering: *"Italiano, Italiano kaput, kaput!"* He pretended not to know any German. But on hearing that I did, he tugged at his ragged breastpocket and yowled *"documento, documento."* A stained, sweat-wetted army paybook was pushed into my hands. It was of some German auxiliary unit; his nationality was given as *"Italiener."* I told him that he was in the Buchenwald district—a territory which prior to the arrival of the main American occupation army we ourselves administrated—and under arrest to have his presence there investigated, but he must have understood little of my explanations.

As we dragged him along he started to moan a new version of his German-Italian lingo. *"Italiano nix tun, Italiano kaput, nix tun."* It could either mean that he had not done anything or that we should not do anything to him. That he no longer was a proud ally of the Nazis but "kaput" was obvious.

When, on arriving at the camp, he was led away by two armed escorts in prison garb, he nearly fainted. Ordinarily he may have deserved to be gored like any other Fascist pig. But we were the proud victors now, and the young, enthusiastic guards with their fixed bayonets possessed soldierly discipline. He was merely being taken to the barbed wire cage to join officers, SS men and Nazi officials, captives that had been caught in hiding, during the skirmishes or while still unaware of their defeat. If his love and admiration for the military was as great as that his German colleagues had confessed to, he might even enjoy it in there.

*　　*　　*

Our French comrades, whose government was sending them buses and planes, had already started to leave for home. The rest of us were transferred to the former SS barracks or to the main camp. I was allocated to Block 29, the block of "German politicals." One of the oldest barracks in camp, it had become a kind of hotel now. Its boarders, all veterans, some camp personages, others well-known personalities from pre-1933 days, were away most of the time, either at the administration offices or on outside missions.

Other newly-acquired comforts included cupboards, good, clean blankets, books, stacks of news sheets from S.H.A.E.F. (the Supreme Headquarters Allied Expeditionary Force) and wonderfully useful 100 watt light bulbs.

When my block mates came in for supper they did so mainly to talk among themselves. It was only natural that they liked to hear their voices free and frank after all these years of fear and suppression. They revealed many an interesting thing to me. I discovered that the brain behind Buchenwald's resistance efforts had been a so-called International Camp Committee. Its pre-liberation members had, in the main, been German and French left-wingers experienced in organizing and underground tactics; its secret arsenal— a few rifles and pistols, gas masks and spyglasses. But the same moment the famous white flag had been hoisted, our force was equipped with machineguns and mortars. Now the committee was the supreme camp authority. Its heads represented all the various nationalities. The number of its armed guards ran into hundreds. We patrolled the countryside to round up former SS men and to discover hidden Nazi stores. Trucks in search of supplies for the camp kitchen travelled as far as Erfurt and Jena. The population—apparently for other reasons than mere political ones—were scarcely eager to point out the carefully-concealed emergency stores, but we searched woods and cellars till we found them, a whole chain of them. One hide-out, a cave whose present character the local people really would not have known about, contained wine looted from France. Another was stacked with tinned Hungarian chicken.

It was said that at the hospital compound, which had now been taken over by the Americans, they were issuing milk-with-noodle-soup. I was keen on milk and liked sweet things, and the thought of seeing soldiers from over the ocean greatly fascinated me. Next day, then, early for fear of missing anything, I walked down to the sick blocks. Gladly aware that my walking quicker than my companions was a sign of returning health, I eagerly made for the hospital kitchen, joined the already forming queue and sat down on the pavement to wait.

"You are early," wisecracked someone from among the few in front of me. "They don't come to work till eight, don't bring the milk till eight thirty and don't start cooking till nine thirty. If they'll get finished by ten, we'll be lucky. I know from experience." "But never mind, kid, it's worthwhile," said another, whose complete, natural baldness and missing teeth lent him a perhaps unwarranted seniority, "it's made with butter, you know. And it's only supposed to be for the sick."

Bored with waiting, I fixed my glance on the hospital gate, through which anything that could change the monotony would have to come. I studied the lone American sentry as if I were his commanding officer—his high-laced boots, his tucked-in trouser-legs, his slightly off-level ammunition belt, his fluttering brown tunic, his jolly face and his equally jolly egg-shaped helmet. Then I heard the noise of engines. Racing down the roadway from the camp, chased by clouds of dust, came a few army ambulances. "There they come," cried the one who had seen it all before, "it's eight now. In half an hour they'll bring the milk cans." The guard that had looked so sluggish and unconcerned, jumped to attention and saluted. The hospital yard was getting busy.

Later I spotted white-coated surgeons that talked American, and more ambulances. Hanging onto one of them, and pointing out the way, was someone I seemed to recognize. He was a big fellow, flabby skinned and wearing glasses. My goodness! It was the doctor of criminology—the Berliner that back in the Auschwitz days of 1944 had so puzzled me by being both shrewd and helpless. "Dr. Auerbach!" I yelled, "Dr. Auerbach!" The ambulance stopped. *"Was schreien Sie denn so? Was wollen Sie von mir?"* "Don't you recognize me anymore, Auerbach? We were together in Auschwitz, together with Gert, Saucy Gert. Don't you remember when you arrived? When we talked to you every evening about camp life?" *"Nein, ich erinnere mich nicht.* Drriffe on."

The car rolled away. Yes, I could quite imagine him now, the doctor of criminology, back in 1943, hanging onto a car that instead of dusty brown was polished green, whose driver wore the sparkling, piked helmet of the Berlin police instead of a jolly, round American Army one, when instead of red crosses there were swastikas. No wonder the Herr Doctor had not liked to remember the past, the dark days of Auschwitz when the crematoria loomed on the horizon, the evenings he had told me of his exploits as a police agent.

But maybe I was mistaken. I asked someone the name of that big, busy fellow. "It's Auerbach," I was told, "Dr. Auerbach, liaison officer to the American medical corps."

*   *   *

Time moved on. The district administration had been taken over by the Americans, the Buchenwald army disbanded. Several Allied missions arrived to study the horrors of German concentration camps.

They inspected the crematoria, saw the stacks of bluish, emaciated bodies, visited laboratories where prisoners had been scalped to provide lamp shades and beheaded to make shrunken miniatures, heard about the mechanism of gas chambers and were shown a height-measuring device with an adjustable hole in it for shooting unsuspecting "prisoners of war" through the head during medical inspection. The ladies and gentlemen of the visiting delegations were shocked. Their conscience must have been rather uneasy about it all. They had come when the battle was over and won. Now their whole concept of Western civilization was being challenged.

Where had all these eager humanitarians been in 1937 when Buchenwald was inaugurated? Even during our final struggle, eight years later, no effective aid had been given to us, for our well-wishing visitors apparently had relied on their German colleagues to do so. It had taken them twelve years to grasp the reality of concentration camps and four years to realize Hitler's war-time extermination policy. Would they, in their lifetime, understand the changes in us, and in the world as a whole, that had happened since?

The Americans also brought the local German population to visit us. They were rounded up in Weimar or other towns, loaded onto trucks, assembled on the former roll call square and addressed by an officer's voice strengthened by a loud-speaker. Then they followed the loudspeaker van through the camp and trudged past our shabby barracks as if on some pilgrimage or funeral. Some even looked as if it was a pleasant trip to the countryside for them. A few girls, dressed in short skirts, giggled. They were too young to be vicious, I thought, they only lacked tact. What annoyed me were the Hitler-time police and railway officials' uniforms I saw. If their wearers' professional pride had really been exceeded by a dislike of things reminiscent of the Nazis, they would have discarded them. As it was, they had not even bothered to obliterate all the swastika markings.

We did not like these guided sight-seeing processions and when some, who thought them an insult, threatened to attack them, they ceased.

Our pleasantest visitors were American soldiers on leave. They arrived in hordes—young, frank, jolly and talkative. Above all, however, their pockets were bulging like that of a mother kangaroo. The tall, brown-clad, Yanks were loaded with chewing gum, chocolate, cigars, cigarettes, cameras and flashlights, and made no secret of being generous.

Eagerly clutching their sparkling cameras, they came to invade our sleeping quarters. "Do you mind chums? Just a little snap-shot for the folks back home." "With pleasure!" We lined up arm in arm and smiled.

"Chunggum?" whispered an aged inmate whose begging and munching habits were incorrigible. Jokingly one of our visitors tugged at his shirt-pocket, took out a strip of chewing gum, bit off half and offered it to him. But we were too busy to laugh at this. The room was buzzing with talk about the front line, homes beyond the ocean, the Allies, the Nazis and concentration camps.

"We've got to move on now," called a soldier who had a peculiar combination of sloping and curved stripes on his shirt sleeve. "Who's responsible for this room here?" "I," said a frail-looking German intellectual, whose eagerness to sit in a corner and absorb long-missed books had recently caused him to be named room guardian entrusted with ladling out soup and sweeping the floor. "O.K. boys, empty them out." Dropping onto the table came bars of chocolate, strips of chewing gum and packets of cigarettes. Then they pushed a bunch of cigars into our room steward's breastpocket. "That's for you personally, for seeing that everyone gets his share."

Once unknown and forgotten, Buchenwald seemed to have become the hub of the world. It was our world, a new world. Our time was so interesting that the days were far too short for us. We contacted other liberated concentration camps, invited women, considered taking on jobs in Weimar and prepared ourselves to return home again. Overhead, day and night, hastening the end of Hitler's Germany, hummed long trains of American supply planes.

In our block, shut up in their rooms, sat camp veterans drawing up reports on Nazi crimes. Much of the official data collected by them was new to me. I discovered that the population of Buchenwald had once been bigger than that of Weimar. The survivors amounted to 20,000. Since 1937 51,000 people had died in Buchenwald. Another 15,000 comrades had perished in its subsidiary camps. Transports which had left the day before liberation had been stoned, shot at and massacred. After we had already occupied the administration offices there had been a phone call from Weimar for the SS commander. The requested platoon of flame throwers had arrived, it said, and was waiting for transportation.

We did not want to forget. On the contrary, we felt an urge to set what we had witnessed on paper and to tell about it. I, too, was gripped by that desire. If we who had experienced it, I reasoned, did not expose the bitter truth, people simply would not believe about the Nazi ogre. I asked my grown-up colleagues for paper and pencil. Then, armed with a stack of abandoned swastika-imprinted questionnaires of the Nationalsozialistische Deutsche Arbeiter Partei and a few stumps of colored pencil, I embarked on sketching camp life. Scenes of days gone by became vivid again—the arrival, the selection, the punishments, the food, the diseases, the endless rows of fencing, the work, the roll calls, the winter, the revolts, the gallows, the evacuation, the *"Katushas."* One day, when I was a man, I would keep them as a souvenir.

Buchenwald's cinema hall held crowds again. Usually they came to see glamorous American Technicolor films, full of unintelligible words and foreign attitudes. But one day they congregated for something quite different. A Jewish remembrance service was being held. An American Army chaplain, a rabbi reared in far-away Brooklyn, issued small pocket-size prayer books. On either side of the improvised altar stood tall white candles, behind them brown-uniformed Jewish-American service-men. Filing into the hall, thoughtful and heavy-hearted, came the survivors of European Jewry. Many had nearly forgotten about their historic heritage. But this was a day of remembrance. We all wanted to greet and thank those who had fought to liberate us. We all had our lost families to pray for.

* * *

With the opening of a regular train connection we at once set out to explore Weimar. To be treading the pavements of a town again like any other free citizen was so proud a feeling for us, that only few abstained from it. Day by day we arose early in the morning, hastened to the station, rushed to the small branch-line-type railway-wagons, pushed ourselves into the stuffy, crowded compartments, and rolled into town—the lucky insiders singing, the latecomers determinedly hanging onto doorsteps or balancing themselves on the roofs.

On arrival our first concern was to pace the few kilometers to the central food office, to queue up, to register, to receive a temporary ration card and be given a small allowance of expense money. Then we strolled off on a spree, to meet later on at some restaurant, park or brothel.

I had planted myself in front of a vast, abandoned building site at a deserted square somewhere between the center and the railway station. Long rows of white, fluted columns stared at me. Some were covered by equally cold and unemotional lintels, some stood bare. Others had only been finished to three-quarters, half, or quarter their height. It looked like the drawing of the Acropolis that I had once spotted in an older friend's history book. Probably it was one of Hitler's projected huge memorial halls.

Rather distracted by the wild, gripping jazz tunes from a nearby army loudspeaker, I looked for something I could earn muchneeded pocket money with—a saw, a hammer, chisels, or the like. On one of the small stone pillars near the mason's yard, to my surprise, I spotted a darkish ball. It turned out to be a bronze Hitler head. When I was about to inspect it more closely, however, I was suddenly interrupted by a deep, American bass voice: "Get away from there, kid!" I jerked back and turned around. Sitting on one of the pedestals was a huge flat-nosed Negro soldier. "Get back on the road."

Having returned to the pavement, I switched my attention from the smoothly-combed, metal Hitler head to the fuzzy, abundantly fleshy one of its self-appointed guardian. It was only from a circus seat that I had seen the like of him. He shook his body rhythmically to the melodious jazz tunes and hummed something about "loving a baby."

Queer, I thought, just as grotesque as the bronze head. Then he fed a bullet into his revolver, took aim and fired. The Hitler head tumbled and banged onto a stone slab. The fuzzy-haired one laughed like a madman. When he had finished, he wiped off his sweat, giggled, went to the pillar, picked up the bronze, enthroned it again and reloaded.

The narrow streets of Weimar looked sleepy. Here and there, one saw collapsing walls and piles of rubble. Goethe's house, too, was in ruins. Schoolchildren lingered about in the parks. Better-off town people, together with disguised, jobless Nazis, crooks and criminals, sat in coffee houses and restaurants. Some, whose consciences were particularly troublesome, even masqueraded as liberated camp inmates. Nazi fanatics busied themselves with arson. The new town police, mostly former German Buchenwald prisoners, hurried from one check-up to the other. If one saw Americans, they usually raced along in jeeps, hooted or sounded their sirens, and terrified the pedestrians.

Not a few of us went to Weimar merely to be with women. The arrogant German females of yesterday now walked about shortskirted, barelegged, and available for a few cigarettes. We picked them up in fashionable cafes or waited for them at side street brothels. Payment was in goods. Many of us youngsters embarked on their adventurous trips with a packet of margarine or a wrapped-up sausage under the arm. More often than not, they then returned with a good dose of venereal disease.

My own amorous exploits, however, were limited to two, both of them unsuccessful. One was a high school girl in the park. She wanted me to sit on the lawn and talk to her. For this, naturally, I had neither patience nor time. The other lived above a restaurant. I met her on the staircase and she asked me whether I knew some American film show we could go to. Then her mother called her. I stared after a thin pair of fifteen-year-old legs climbing up the stairs, heard a door thrown into its latch, and she was gone.

*   *   *

It was the first of May 1945—my first May day. Former inmates who had settled in surrounding towns and villages returned to celebrate with us. Our dirty, old barracks were hidden in a sea of fresh white slogans.

The Russian compound looked like a fair-ground. Its streets were overhung with garlands and its blocks vied with each other for the best hand-painted Stalin picture. The prize-winning portrait, crude, but done with obvious care and patience, measured an impressive two meters square and hung above their reading room barrack flanked by flowers, a bald Lenin and a bearded Marx.

German blocks displayed the proud notice "We are coming back" and pictures of Breitscheid and Thaelmann—two who, like most other former socialist members of Parliament, would not be coming back anymore. (One the leader of the Social Democrats, the other of the Communists, they had both perished in Buchenwald.) Other banners read: "We remember our 51,000 dead." "We thank our Allies" and the short but forceful "Never more!"

Our Spanish comrades hardly had enough room around their lone block for all they wanted to say. "You are going home, what about us?" they painted on its wall. "Fascism is not dead yet, Franco lives!" "Now Franco is Enemy Number One!" "We shall not give up!" "*No pasaran!*"

My room mates were certain that I, too, would be joining them for the May Day Parade. They showed me a stack of boards painted with the names of some small German provinces. "There are no survivors from these provinces, so someone else will have to carry them. What about you? You are tall and would look rather impressive marching on your own."

I hesitated. "Brandenburg," read one of the large red banners that already had a fair number of followers assembled behind it— the same letters that had once said "SS division Brandenburg," the very same province that had reared divisions of murderers. I had little in common with these letters. But the flag around them was red, the same flag that others of Brandenburg sons had believed in before they perished in concentration camps—shot in unknown marshes, gassed in distant wastelands, silenced for ever. It was the flag enthusiasts in the far-off Russia of 1918 had ridden to victory with; the flag that to its followers had been fluttering even in their darkest hours, when only minutes away loomed gas chambers. No, I did not dare desert them.

I grabbed one of the lone boards with the name of a province and was shown my place in the marching column. Then we paced off towards the gate. A small hunchbacked German socialist next to me, who had survived the rigors of Buchenwald by being a tailor, chirped: "Left! Left! Left!"

We assembled on the camp square, each column behind the flag of its homeland—Poles, Russians, Czechs, Yugoslavs, Hungarians, Rumanians, Austrians, Germans, Norwegians, Frenchmen, Belgians, Dutchmen and Spaniards. In front of us, near the fence, was a huge stage, marked May 1st, 1945. On it stood a boarded trapezium trisected into upward radiating strips, painted with the colors of England, Russia and America, and decorated with diagonally-spaced portraits of Churchill, Stalin and Roosevelt. From high-up poles, gently stroking the liberated clear blue sky, fluttered all the colorful flags of Europe.

To begin with, we saw a symbolic play about Buchenwald, its dark past and its liberation. Afterwards the platform was filled with guests from abroad and we listened to speeches. We paid tribute to our dead, thanked the Allies and affirmed our solidarity. We also pledged ourselves never to forget our common sufferings. "The remnants of our suppressors and their supporters must be brought to justice." Our applause was powerful and enthusiastic.

Then the band started playing and, one by one, the columns drew past the saluting base. The square that, with the Nazi flag towering over the entrance gate, had for eight years of daily roll calls been filled with helpless prisoners, now held triumphant crowds parading with the proud banners of their homelands. Its vast expanse of asphalt, which had heard the moans of thousands after thousands trudging to their death, now resounded with the victorious marching steps of the survivors.

Countless striped blue-white trouserlegs flapped in unison. The band struck up anthem after anthem. Hundreds of red May

Day banners were raised.

Finally it was our turn. The big flag in front of me, that had been making a nuisance of itself by incessantly and obstinately tickling me on the neck, was lifted up at last. My neighbor, the hunchbacked little socialist, blew himself up, thoughtfully moved his leg in readiness to lift it, arched his tongue, anxiously looked at the feet of those in the front row, and then uttered a proud, melodious "Left!" The column moved forward. "Left! Left! Left!"

There were wide empty spaces between the marchers, to represent those who had not survived to join us. Someone intoned *"Brueder, zur Sonne, zur Freiheit."* My little neighbor wiped his eyes.

Soon we all would be heading for home, I thought. If we had none, we would be looking for a new one. Some of us would become ordinary working people, whose past no one cared about. Others would return to become members of Parliament or even Ministers. That impressive May Day at Buchenwald, however, would turn into a cherished memory—something we would be reminded of year by year.

Our column approached the guest platform. We marched neatly and stiffly. To my right, on the flag-surrounded platform, I spotted a row of Army officers—Americans, Russians, Frenchmen, Englishmen and others. When we drew near they saluted.

I, the haggard, shabby bearer of a little painted board with the name of some obscure province on it, I, the forgotten youngster that for years had been rotting in concentration camps, was being saluted! My cheeks flushed with excitement. Then a newsreel camera was turned on me.

*   *   *

I had stopped travelling to Weimar, for I disliked the coffee house atmosphere. Instead, I walked about the camp, listened to the radio, looked at books and newspapers, and tried to impress the Americans with my English.

On one of my trips around the blocks, when I passed the elderly inmates who spent their day sitting on the curbs and talking to each other, I noticed someone young among them. He sat in the sun, drooped his head and dreamt. Next to him lay a bundle tied with string, as if he were a vagabond. I bent down to see his face. It was long, angular and frightfully thin. His sharp, prominent nose looked familiar.

I woke him up. Then we recognized each other and shook hands warmly. It was Gert, the dark one, a brick-laying school friend of nearly two years ago, who had just been released from hospital.

I was glad to have found him. Only three of my block-mates were my age: one was mentally disturbed, the others sought their luck among the adults. I badly needed suitable companions, and Gert was more than merely an old friend. He was intelligent.

Buchenwald had become gay. There were women from surrounding labor camps, girls from Weimar who had sneaked in to earn cigarettes, and frolicsome Americans on leave. In the evenings they all got together to dance, to drink, and to fondle till early morning.

Once, when the nightly accordion tunes kept me from sleeping, I went to investigate where they came from. It was a paper-garland-decorated barrack room, lit by dim reddish lamps and filled with long-legged dancing couples. They seemed tired already. In a corner, leaning onto a table with empty beer bottles, sat an ugly-faced, drunken blonde. Next to her was an American soldier in miniature, one of the camp kids who had become the mascot of some local army unit. Except for signs of rank and the American brass eagle, he wore a full army uniform. One of the tall and real soldiers came up to him, patted his shoulders and whispered: "Still keeping an eye on her, kid?" "Sure!" exclaimed the proud mascot, anxiously squinting at the drunken female.

During the day we listened to the loudspeakers. The program—news, announcements, personal messages and music—was chosen by the camp committee to cater to the various nationalities, and continued from dawn till midnight.

At a meeting attended by delegates from other liberated camps we even suggested forming a volunteer corps. But the Allied advance was quick and our victorious friends no longer needed help.

The final collapse of Nazism was expected any hour now.

The week after May Day was crowded with farewell celebrations. One by one, the different nationalities took leave of their camp comrades and left for home.

The German inmates said their good-bye to Buchenwald in a cold, concrete-lined hall at the laundry building. Some, who had already left, came back for this occasion, together with their families. We ate, drank, heard songs and saw sketches.

Then came the climax. "Now we'll sing you something new, something of our own," announced the line of prison-garbed veterans that had stepped onto the stage. Their faces looked old and worn. Their camp numbers showed them to have been in Buchenwald for close to eight years. They were the veterans of veterans, and had wanted to surprise us by forming a choir of their own.

Unsere Strasse fuehrt zurueck
Wir kommen wieder, Kameraden, unverzagt!

Eyes filled with tears. Some of the women went outside. "Our road is leading back," echoed the refrain, "we are going to return, comrades, nothing will dishearten us!"

Our Russian camp mates gave their farewell performance in the huge former SS theater. I just managed to crowd in and to swing myself onto some vacant spot on a banister. The stage was filled with talented singers, ballet dancers and acrobats. Some of this talent, I dimly suspected, must have been imported from outside Buchenwald. People sweated and accompanied the booming, vigorous Russian dancing steps by clapping their hands, shrieking and whistling. Everyone—except the guests of honor in the front row and those who, like me, had to balance themselves precariously on banisters—was wildly alive. Afterwards, towards the end, they all started singing.

The hall vibrated with the songs of the Red Army—the song about the cavalry, the air force, the *Katushas,* the partisans. I too vibrated. Wandering through my mind came all those Russian youngsters with whom we had been singing these selfsame songs during two hard, cold concentration camp winters. What had happened to all those lads who, while these tunes struggled against the dark, silent Auschwitz nights, had lain on their bunks dreaming of liberation?

My former companions of Block 66, the Jewish youngsters from Poland, also arranged an artistic evening. It was in Yiddish and the songs were the same as I had already heard previously. Stealing the show, however, were the tableaus, especially the "Dance of the Machines." It showed shadows of working youngsters against the background of a red screen. The shadows toiled in unison, then sang the refrain. "But machines have no hearts, know no pain and understand no jokes."

Those who watched could not help being impressed. It was plain that these youngsters were striving for a future of freedom and security. They would no longer agree to being neglected and kept in ignorance. A new world was in the making, and these lads had broken with the old one.

A friend invited me to come to Block 45, for the farewell party of the Austrians. "It's just going to be a social affair," he said, "without speeches, without pledges, but with plenty of gaiety." I had no idea how to dance, but I went, mainly because I found out that there would be cakes.

It was a room up on the second floor, complete with fiddlers, a jazz band, beer, Chinese lanterns, leather-trousered "mountaineers" and the inevitable Americans. They told jokes, made merry and called it Viennese.

As it grew late, people became still gayer and started to dance. I sipped some beer and sat in a corner seat till I nearly fell asleep; then decided that it was time to go to bed. At that moment, however, I perceived shouts of "Bravo, bravo!" They cleared the floor and onto it stepped two Gypsy girls who had been persuaded to do exhibition dances. I jerked myself up and watched.

These two girls were young and turned and twisted themselves to the strains of dreamy Gypsy music. I felt too fascinated even to move. Probably they were thinking of the same as I was: of the Gypsy people, this peculiar people that knows no home yet ardently loves its family; a people that, however well you know it, would remain a mystery. It was the first time that I had seen Gypsy girls all that near to me. I just stared.

Sunken in my thoughts, I continued to watch them. Suddenly someone crossed the floor towards the stack of beer bottles, and, unavoidably, I looked at him too. It was a boy with far too big a suit on him. How funny, I thought. But soon I seemed to recognize him and I called him. Had I drunk too much? No, he also appeared to know me. He came over to shake my hands. It was Berger, "Little Berger," our favorite Gypsy youngster from the brick-laying school.

He said that he was being taken care of by some of his fellow Austrians who were willing to take him with them to their home town. Just now, however, he admitted that he was drunk.

It was late already and I left. I was still thinking of Little Berger. Would his friends really take care of him? Would he get the future we had always so anxiously wished for him?

*　　*　　*

"May 8th, 1945: Armistice with Germany." The war in Europe was over. Fascism and all it stands for had surrendered.

Someone turned the knob of our radio set to search the ether. It was filled with the peals of victory. There was jubilation everywhere: London's reverberating victory gong, giving the V sign— enthusiastic voices singing the rousing Marseillaise—the solemn, monumental tunes of the Soviet anthem, the chimes of the Kremlin—Berliners rising from the ruins to celebrate.

I turned about on my pillow and contemplated. It was peace. What would we make of it? Soon I would be sixteen. Before long I, too, would have my say.

Then I dozed off, dreaming about the future.

T.G.

APPENDICES

APPENDIX I

"THE SONG OF THE PEAT-BOG SOLDIERS"

Far and wide as the eye can wander
Heath and bog are everywhere.
Not a bird sings out to cheer us,
Oaks are standing gaunt and bare.

Chorus:
>   We are the peat-bog soldiers
>   We're marching with our spades to the bog.

Up and down the guards are pacing,
No one, no one can go through.
Flight would mean a sure death facing;
Guns and barbed wire greet our view.

>   *Chorus*

But for us there is no complaining,
Winter will in time be past;
One day we shall cry rejoicing,
Homeland dear, you're mine at last.

Final chorus:
>   Then will the peat-bog soldiers
>   March no more with the spades to the bog.

APPENDIX II

LOOKING BACK, 1:3,000, AUSCHWITZ, THE CAMP

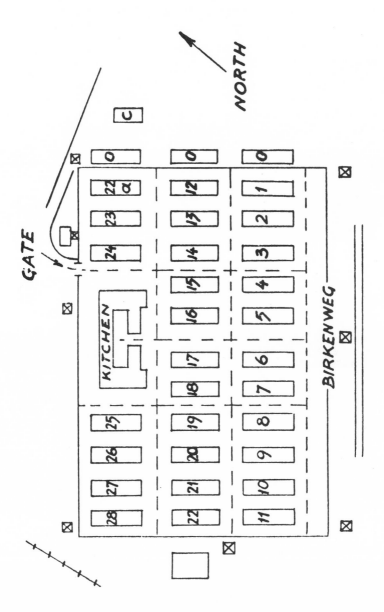

APPENDIX III

LOOKING BACK, 1:20,000, THE WORKING TERRITORY
(Drawn from memory)

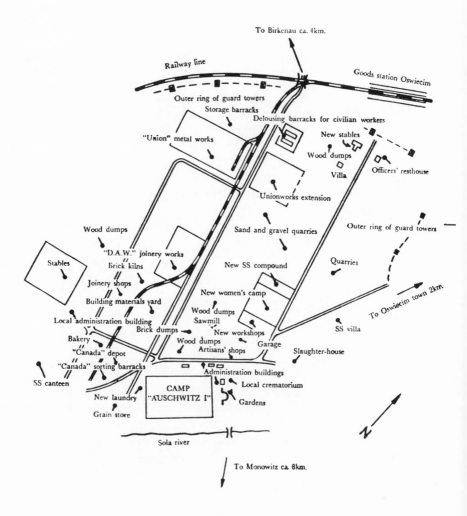

APPENDIX IV

LOOKING BACK, 1:6,000,000, MAP

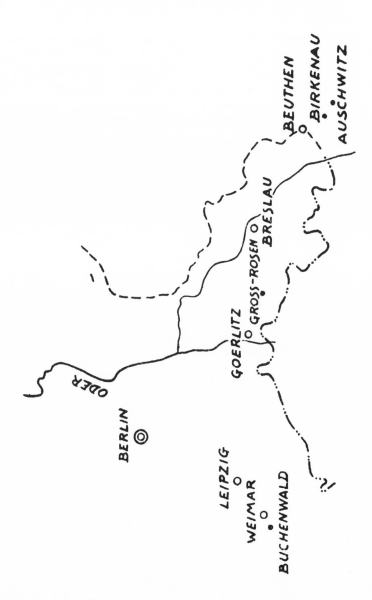

EPILOGUE

What I have reported represents a mere fragment of what happened in the Europe of World War II.

Here is the completed picture, the summary that is recorded in history books—the barbaric total that the youth of generations to come will find hard to believe:

In addition to labor camps there were 1,665 so-called "concentration camps" in Nazi-occupied Europe. Among the better known of these were:

Auschwitz	ca. 3,000,000 dead
Treblinka	ca. 2,000,000 dead
Maidanek	ca. 1,200,000 dead
Mauthausen	123,000 dead
Sachsenhausen	ca. 100,000 dead
Dachau	86,000 dead
Buchenwald	51,000 dead
Bergen Belsen	35,000 dead
Ravensbrueck	23,000 dead
Neuengamme	43,000 dead
Stutthof	ca. 80,000 dead
Flossenburg	73,000 dead
Natzweiler	25,000 dead
Papenburg-Emslager	10,600 dead